ALL ABOUT MORTGAGES

Second Edition

Julie Garton-Good

DEARBORN™

A **Kaplan Professional** Company

This publication is designed to provide accurate and authoritative information in regard to the subject matter covered. It is sold with the understanding that the publisher is not engaged in rendering legal, accounting, or other professional service. If legal advice or other expert assistance is required, the services of a competent professional should be sought.

Acquisitions Editor: Jean Iversen
Managing Editor: Jack Kiburz
Project Editor: Trey Thoelcke
Interior Design: Ophelia Chambliss-Jones
Cover Design: DePinto Studios
Typesetting: Elizabeth Pitts

Library of Congress Cataloging-in-Publication Data

Garton-Good, Julie.
   All about mortgages / Julie Garton-Good. — 2nd ed.
   p.   cm.
   Includes index.
   ISBN 0-7931-3231-2
   1. Real estate business—United States—Finance.   2. Mortgages—
United States.   I. Title.
HD1375.G378   1999
332.7'2'0973—dc21   98-52090
                                                                      CIP

DEDICATION

To my parents, Cliff and Marion Martin, my mother-in-law, Anne Good, my daughter, Crystal, and my wonderful husband, Scott, who have always been there for me.

CONTENTS

PREFACE

Much has changed since I wrote the first edition of *All About Mortgages* in 1994. Lenders now use credit scoring to evaluate borrowers and originate loans using desktop technology. Consumers are now financing their homes via the Internet.

These radical changes require consumers to be even more prepared for the mortgage process—armed with the little-known, insider facts that make the difference between applying for a mortgage and actually obtaining one!

That's why the second edition of *All About Mortgages* is the ultimate real estate finance handbook, providing you with a gold mine of money-saving tips and financing traps, accessible in a time-saving question and answer format.

You'll get a behind-the-scenes look at:

- How to put your best foot forward with the lender
- How to check your credit report, clean up errors, and understand the impact credit scoring has on getting the lender to say yes
- How to negotiate with lenders
- Tips for evaluating loan programs to make sure you don't overpay
- How to use the Internet to obtain mortgage financing

Marginal buyers will discover:

- What to do if the lender says no
- Compensating factors that help buyers qualify for a larger mortgage
- Creative financing using gifted down payments or lease purchases
- How to use a credit card to purchase a first home

And to manage your equity after the closing, you'll learn:

- How to evaluate whether refinancing makes financial sense
- Tips and traps when refinancing over the Internet

- When to and when not to prepay your loan
- Tips for saving your home if your payments fall behind

Let *All About Mortgages* be your financial companion and guide to obtaining a cost-effective mortgage, growing your home's equity, and helping secure your financial future!

Enthusiastically,

Julie Garton-Good, DREI

CHAPTER 1

MORTGAGE MARKET OVERVIEW: PLAYERS AND PROCESS

The mortgage market of a decade ago in no way resembles today's world. Today, lenders evaluate credit using complex credit scoring models, and underwrite and process loans at desktop computers using artificial intelligence. It's merely a matter of time before the entire real estate transaction is paperless and done via electronic signatures!

Yet the more things change, the more they remain the same. Homebuyers are still confused about the requirements, the process, and the roles of the myriad of players involved. This chapter provides an overview of not only how electronic commerce (e-commerce) has expanded the industry and therefore, consumer's options in the mortgage process, but serves as a template to help the consumer understand and more aptly navigate the mortgage loan process.

THE MORTGAGE LENDING PROCESS

Q. *The mortgage loan process seems so complicated. Is there any way the consumer can make it easier?*

The mortgage lending process can seem daunting. I fondly remember a first-time homebuying couple who received word that their loan closing would be delayed due to "a Fannie Mae underwriting glitch." The wife responded, "I don't care who that Fannie Mae woman is, we just want to buy a house!" Had someone taken the time to explain to her that Fannie Mae (FNMA) and other players in the secondary market are vital for recycling lent funds (and in turn pass on greater loan affordability to buyers), she might have been a bit more patient!

To that end, it's important that buyers and sellers alike understand the delicate inner workings of the primary market, the secondary market, and the private mortgage insurer. I refer to this as the *triple challenge.* Understanding it can help clarify the mortgage process.

Q. *Who are the three main players in the mortgage market and how do they work together?*

The players in the triple challenge are (1) the primary lenders, (2) the secondary market, and (3) the private mortgage insurance market. The early years of mortgage lending found local lenders working alone, holding loans originated *in portfolio.* This meant that when ABC Bank made a mortgage to the Brown family, the bank held that loan in its loan portfolio of investments, collecting the monthly payments until the loan was paid in full. This was actually beneficial for the Browns as they developed an ongoing business relationship with the lender. If hard times arose and loan payments fell behind, they had a much better chance of negotiating with their friendly banker to help them over the rough spots than with someone who was unaware of their personal situation and perhaps less empathetic.

Q. *Why did lenders change from the portfolio practice?*

Keeping the loan in portfolio for 30 years was not necessarily in the lender's best interests. As interest rates fluctuated (typically moving upward), it became increasingly evident to many lenders that they should recycle these mortgages in order to receive not only higher interest rates, but also increased loan origination fees. Thus, in the late 1930s the secondary market was born.

The first player in the secondary market was the Federal National Mortgage Association (FNMA), lovingly called Fannie Mae. She was soon followed by a sister, Ginnie Mae, the Government National Mortgage Association (GNMA); and later by a brother, Freddie Mac, the Federal Home Loan Mortgage Corporation (FHLMC). Although each of the siblings serves a particular market segment, the scope of their duties is very similar. They recycle lent funds from primary markets (e.g., banks) in order to return funds to circulation at the local level while creating additional collateral and investment vehicles for the secondary market. For example, ABC Bank's $5 million in mortgage loans written to Ginnie Mae's specifications can be sold to Ginnie with the lender taking a slight reduction on the face value received for the privilege of converting the loans to immediate cash. Ginnie uses these loans, and their monthly payments received, as collateral for issuing GNMA pass-through securities to purchasers. In other words, if the Browns' loan was sold into GNMA in the secondary market, and the Browns subsequently purchased some GNMA pass-through securities, they would actually be purchasing their own flow of cash! (See Figure 1.1.) This approach, although on a much larger scale, has assisted thousands of lenders nationwide in increasing their lending capabilities while increasing their profit margins.

Q. *Was the addition of private mortgage insurance necessary to the secondary market?*

Yes, over time. With more and more loans being sold into the secondary market, Fannie, Ginnie, and Freddie needed to hedge against potential losses on the loans purchased. So private mortgage insurance (PMI) became the third integral part of the triple challenge.

PMI typically insures the top 20 percent of the new loan against the borrower's default. This was exactly the payment assurance needed by the secondary market. General guidelines of private mortgage insurance companies were added to the secondary market's existing list of loan requirements. Local lenders then added these criteria to their buyers' qualifying guidelines.

Q. *If the linking of the three groups was so positive, why have you termed it a challenge?*

Although the melding of primary lenders, secondary markets, and private mortgage insurance players has done much to increase the options and scope of lending in the United States, it still has some shortcomings. The biggest challenge is the one affecting buyers. Tough underwriting guidelines can prove too restrictive for some of today's first-time buyers, forcing them into ill-fitting programs or rejecting them altogether. With the median-priced home exceeding $120,000, median family income well under $50,000, and typical households having to save for nearly two years just to accumulate a down payment, things have to change.

4   All About Mortgages

Figure 1.1   How the GNMA Mortgage-Backed Securities
Program Works

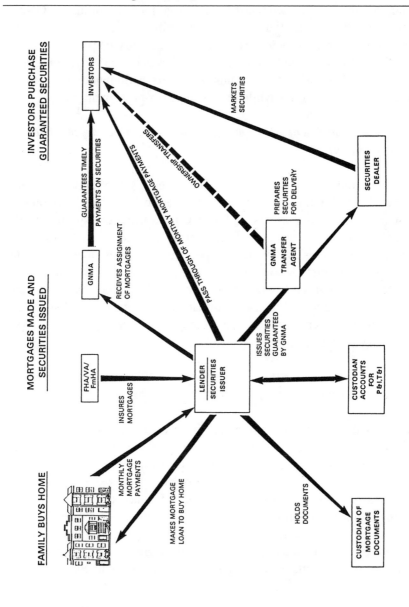

Q. *What is changing to make homebuying a reality for a larger segment of Americans?*

Several things. First, affordable housing programs have expanded. These commonsense programs allow lower down payments, higher qualifying ratios, and even nontraditional employment. (These programs are explored further in later chapters.)

Second, borrowers have become more savvy about real estate. They're negotiating points and fees with lenders and hiring buyer agents to represent their interests. Most of all, they're not easily taking *no* for an answer. If a lender does reject them for a loan, they're uncovering little-known underwriting facts that give them added leverage, troubleshooting glitches on their credit reports, and learning the importance of obtaining preapproval with a mortgage professional before looking for a home.

Last, lenders realize that it's not a perfect world. People get behind on their bills, lose their jobs, and maybe even have to declare bankruptcy. That's why some lenders are bridging the gap between what the secondary market requires and what appears a good and logical business risk by keeping some loans in portfolio. As we'll see in coming chapters, lenders are also creating other leverage vehicles like subprime lending to originate *A–, B, C,* and *D* rated loans to less-than-perfect buyers.

It's truly a whole new world in lending, one that should result in many more of us achieving the American dream of home ownership!

CONSUMER EMPOWERMENT VIA THE WORLD WIDE WEB

Q. *To what degree has online access empowered consumers in the mortgage loan process?*

To an incredible degree. In fact, I suggest that consumers begin their mortgage (and homebuying) hunt electronically! Not only can consumers peruse the vast choices in loan types, lenders, and available properties, but they can do so in anonymity in the comfort of their own homes. (Check out the wide array of Uniform Resource Locators [URLs] found in the Resource Guide section of this book.)

Q. *What's the most time-efficient plan for a homebuyer who wants to check out the Web?*

Here's an approach I've found simple and helpful. If you're a first time homebuyer (or it's been a while since your last purchase), information-gathering sites like www.owners.com; www.homefair.com; ourbroker .com (not a brokerage, but Peter Miller, author and columnist); and, of course, yours truly at frugalhomeowner.com. On your initial trip, don't get bogged down filling in time-consuming forms and micromanaging your visit. Your initial mission is to gather enough information to feel comfortable about homebuying and get a flavor for the online marketplace.

Next, visit several of the interest rate and mortgage sites like www.hsh.com, homeshark.com, eloan.com, quickenmortgage.com and country wide.com. If you're feeling comfortable enough with the process, go ahead and try one of the "how much home can you afford?" calculators you'll see, and check out your credit report online with lenders or by accessing sites like www.equifax.com or one of the other credit reporting agencies.

Q. *Once I've gone that far in the online process, is it wise to go ahead and make a formal application for a mortgage at that time?*

It's your call and should be based to a large extent on what you feel comfortable with. Some buyers feel more comfortable providing the site with their e-mail address, name, and phone number so that a real person can contact them. Others don't mind filling in screens full of information. Much of that information, however, is rarely at your fingertips when you're sitting in front of a computer screen.

Many mortgage sites allow you to send them a streamlined, skeletal application that includes your name, phone number, e-mail address, best time to call, approximate income and debts, and the state in which you wish to buy property. Using the online qualifying calculators and this approach allows you to get an idea of what you can afford, but leaves the detail-gathering to the lender. It also allows you to access quotes from various lenders online, and then have time to check out the companies with the better business bureau. Unlike the old days when you met with the lender at his bank, your virtual lender could be thousands of miles away—never requiring a face-to-face meeting.

Q. *What about Internet safety when transmitting personal and financial information about yourself?*

While most mortgage companies use encrypted transmission to send your personal information (turning it from text to a secure code), some people are still leery of online security. But think about this—information about our credit, medical history, and far more personal buying habits is freely circulating around the planet. So Web security could perhaps be one of our least personal worries!

Seriously, if you have any doubt about the security of the site or the ultimate destination of any information you might submit, either (1) do nothing or (2) use only your e-mail address initially until you can gather further information.

Q. *Can you save money making a mortgage application online?*

Potentially, yes. Lenders tout savings on the interest rate and/or the points, closing fees, or origination fees charged if you apply online. Savings could be as much as $1,500 on a $100,000 loan. The rationale is that the process is more streamlined, requiring less personal contact, which could in turn reduce the lender's cost of business. In addition, buyers applying online are often more savvy and potentially more qualified, so there may be a bit of risk reduction (and thus incentive) for the lender to take the loan.

Q. *What are the cautions when mortgage shopping online?*

Consumers should remember that there's no Web God of Mortgaging that patrols the information, guarantees the source, or even checks to see if the information is current (though most mortgage companies do keep rates current on their sites because it's their stock in trade). It's up to each borrower to double-check the accuracy, timeliness, and availability of the information as it applies to their specific needs.

Q. *What kind of property information can you find online?*

A lot. There are millions of properties listed at sites like www.homeadvisor.com, realtor.com, and in the for-sale-by-owner category of owners.com. You can obtain information about pricing at sites like www.cswonline and experian.com.

THINK LIKE AN APPRAISER TO SELECT A PROPERTY

Q. *Because pricing and appraisals are important in obtaining a mortgage, what's the best way to select a home the lender will approve?*

Most mortgage appraisal guidelines specify that the property be located in a stable neighborhood where values are strong. Even after all these years, the top three criteria of the homebuying process are still location, location, and location. Let's look at four reasons why this is true:

1. Stable property generates a stronger appraisal for the transaction. Because most loans are contingent upon securing a certain loan size based on appraised value, a favorable appraisal can make or break the sale.
2. Private mortgage insurance (and homeowner's insurance, too) is more readily available if the home is in a good neighborhood.
3. The borrower can consider a wider variety of loans if the home and the neighborhood are of good quality.
4. A home in a good neighborhood has a strong potential for appreciation, giving it strong resale value. This factor can also be important to the lender should the loan default.

Q. *If the stability of the neighborhood and the quality of the home are so important, what kinds of things should a prospective homebuyer consider before purchasing?*

An in-depth review of the property and surrounding area would help the borrower evaluate the strength of the purchase. Here are some things to consider:

Looking Around

- *Check the traffic flow.* Make several trips to the property during different days of the week and various times of the day to make sure accessibility is good. If commuting is a concern, make sure traffic flows well to and from the property.
- *Take different routes to access the property.* Make sure there are no unsightly concerns near the property such as wrecking yards, dumpsites, or overgrown vacant lots.

- *Check for noise pollution.* Properties easily accessible to main highway arteries risk higher levels of noise bleeding into the neighborhood. Is the home under an airport flight pattern? Test the noise level from inside and outside the home. Take a stroll up the street to uncover any dog kennels, handyman garages, or day-care centers.
- *Is outside lighting good?* Incidents of crime and traffic accidents increase if neighborhood lighting is poor. Check the home's exterior lighting as well, especially near entrances and garage doors.
- *Analyze the condition of streets, sidewalks and services available.* Is there ample street and sidewalk drainage? How many fire hydrants are there and how close is the nearest fire station? These factors also will affect your homeowner's insurance.

Asking Around

If the opportunity is available, make personal contacts with the neighbors before making an offer. They are often a great source of unbiased information about the neighborhood. Here are some possible questions to ask:

- Is the area generally quiet?
- Where do you shop near the area and why?
- What is the quality of schools?
- Do you think you would have any trouble selling your property? Why or why not?
- Would you buy here again? Why or why not?
- Have you seen much crime or vandalism in the neighborhood? If so, were police and ambulance responses satisfactory?

Checking with several residents can give a well-rounded view of the area, as well as help sidestep any prejudiced remarks.

Checking Around

It's wise to verify material facts before you select a property. If you're working with a real estate agent, he or she can provide much of the following information for you:

- *Check the public records.* Although the title report you receive at closing will reveal items of public record, it's wise to doublecheck for any current or pending assessment to the area, such as for sidewalk repair, or water or sewer line addition.

- *Check the level of crime for the area.* The city police department can provide an overview of the type and volume of crime (if any) in the area. By calling the nonemergency number for the police department and stating the location of the property and the cross streets, the public service officer can provide you with an analysis for the area. Some police departments even do safety checks, coming to the property to offer suggestions for exterior lighting and burglary protection. Online sources like crimecheck.com also can assist your information gathering.
- *Confirm general property values.* Ask real estate agents or appraisers to confirm that property values in the area are stable and have not recently softened. A copy of comparable sales from the Multiple Listing Service, which can be obtained from an agent, should help confirm this. A neighborhood with eroding property values might make the house difficult to sell and could be especially tough if you purchased using a small down payment and needed to sell in a short time. Online resources like cswonline.com and experian.com can help determine market value.
- *Analyze the property itself.* A good way to begin is by asking the seller to provide you with a property disclosure sheet (required by law in more than 30 states), itemizing the contents and condition of the property, including the working order of all heating and cooling units and appliances. Be sure to test the air conditioner in the winter and the heating system in the summer. Turn on all appliances to guarantee their working order, and move throw rugs and other obstructions so you get a complete view of the property.

The buyer may be tempted to jump at purchasing a home based on the gleam of the imported ceramic tile counter tops, the quality of the parquet floor or the lush garden-like backyard. By looking around, asking around, and checking around, the borrower helps ensure the financial investment is a sound one. For a property checklist, see Figure 1.2.

PROTECTING YOURSELF IN THE PURCHASE AGREEMENT

Q. *When a buyer finds a home he or she likes, what kinds of financing contingency clauses should go in the purchase agreement?*

If the purchaser must obtain adequate financing, it's imperative to make the purchase contingent upon receiving suitable financing. If financing

Figure 1.2   Home Inspection Checklist

MECHANICAL SYSTEMS

HEATING

Age, condition, and operation of main
system _____

_____

_____

Thermostat(s) _____

_____

Room-by-room heating _____

_____

COOLING

Age, condition, and operation of main
system _____

_____

Thermostat(s) _____

_____

Room-by-room cooling _____

_____

ELECTRICAL

Adequacy of service _____

_____

Light switches _____

Door bells _____

Exterior lighting _____

PLUMBING

Overall _____

Water heater _____

WASTE (SEWERS OR SEPTIC)

Flush toilets_____

Consult owners on condition_____

_____

Obtain service record _____

APPLIANCES

Range _____

Oven (all controls)_____

_____

Dishwasher (run full cycle)_____

_____

Refrigerator/Freezer _____

_____

Compactor _____

Disposal _____

Washing machine_____

Dryer_____

Other_____

_____

INTERIOR SPACES

WALLS, CEILINGS, AND FLOORS

Overall condition _____

_____

Water stains _____

Cracks_____

Settlement_____

Decay _____

BASEMENT AND CRAWL SPACES

Walls _____

_____

Floor _____

_____

Water penetration _____

_____

KITCHEN

Cabinets _____

Countertop _____

Floor _____

_____

Figure 1.2   Home Inspection Checklist (Continued)

BATHROOMS	EXTERIOR CONDITIONS
Toilets (tank and operation) _____	Roof _____
_____	Floor _____
_____	Windows/Doors _____
Floor (around tub, shower, and toilet)	_____
_____	Steps and stairs _____
_____	_____
Shower (check controls) _____	Decks/Porches _____
_____	_____
Tub (check controls) _____	Pools and accessories _____
_____	_____
Tile _____	Sprinkler _____
GARAGE	Landscaping _____
Doors _____	_____
Floor _____	Drainage _____
Walls _____	_____

cannot be obtained within the parameters spelled out on the purchase agreement or in the time frame specified, the buyer would not have to complete the sale and, barring other conditions, the earnest money deposit would be returned.

The buyer should be specific, stating exactly what maximum size loan (usually a percentage of the sales price) is needed, the type of loan with a maximum rate of interest, term of the loan, and maximum amount of discount points the buyer will pay.

Using this information, a financing contingency might read as follows: "Purchase contingent upon the borrower applying for and receiving a 90 percent FHA [Federal Housing Administration] thirty (30) year fixed-rate loan, with interest not to exceed 8 percent. The buyer will pay up to two (2) discount points to obtain the loan." A real estate agent or real estate attorney can help buyers structure the language to use in the agreement.

THE BASICS OF LOAN DISCLOSURE

Q.   *What does a lender have to tell a borrower about the lending process and the loan?*

A mortgage lender is required to make certain disclosures to a borrower at application or within three days after application. The disclosures describe costs incurred with the loan (closing costs, origination fees, etc.), the effective interest rate being charged, and the possibility that the lender will transfer the servicing rights (payment collection) on the loan (also called selling the loan).

Good Faith Estimate

The Real Estate Settlement Procedures Act (RESPA) requires disclosure of estimated settlement costs to homebuyers based on the parameters of the loan. The Department of Housing and Urban Development (HUD) has a settlement statement that itemizes these costs, including fees to be paid at closing. Fees can vary based on changes in the loan that occur between time of application and closing. In addition, the lender is required to provide the borrower with HUD's *Settlement Cost Guide* booklet describing the homebuying process.

Truth in Lending

The purpose of the federal Truth-in-Lending Law and regulations is to ensure that borrowers are aware of the terms and costs of credit so that they can knowledgeably compare loan programs and lenders. For example, the lender must disclose the annual percentage rate (APR) of the loan, defined as the cost of credit to the borrower expressed as a yearly rate. The finance charge disclosed includes any charge paid directly or indirectly by the borrower and imposed by the lender as a condition of extending credit (including appraisals, credit reports, etc.).

Transfer for Servicing

This document shows the lender's intent regarding servicing of the loan after closing, and tells what percentage of loans they have transferred servicing on in the past.

Lenders also must give adjustable rate mortgage applicants a worst-case scenario of how the monthly payment could adjust over the life of the loan. This requirement is more fully discussed later in this book.

THE LOAN APPLICATION PROCESS

Q. *What does the applicant need to provide to the lender to have a mortgage application considered?*

Following is a checklist of the basics. Additional information needed from the self-employed buyer is discussed in Chapter 2.

Property Information

- [ ] *A copy of the purchase agreement; if a construction loan, a copy of plans and specifications.* The lender also may need information about the purchase and the property in order to complete the loan application. This could include the number of units (e.g., single family or duplex), the year built, and how title will be held.
- [ ] *Legal description of the property.*
- [ ] *A Multiple Listing Service (MLS) information sheet,* if available.

Borrower Information

- [ ] *Social Security numbers for all borrowers and coborrowers.*
- [ ] *A list of the borrowers' home addresses for the past two years.*
- [ ] *The names and addresses of landlords for the past two years,* if the borrower is a renter.
- [ ] *The names and addresses of all employers for last two years.* Borrowers should give the address of the personnel office, because this might be different from the office location. Any employment gaps should be pointed out and explained.

Asset Verification

- [ ] *IRS W-2 forms; personal tax returns from the past two years with schedules.* A buyer needs to demonstrate two years of full-time or part-time employment in the same line of work; however, time spent in technical career training (such as a physician's medical internship or union apprenticeship) could count toward the two-year requirement.
- [ ] *Two most recent paycheck stubs.*
- [ ] *Bank statements for the past three months.*
- [ ] *Checking account numbers and locations.*
- [ ] *Savings account numbers and locations.*
- [ ] *Credit union account numbers and locations.*

☐ *Mutual fund account numbers and locations.*

☐ *IRA and/or 401(k) information.*

☐ *Explanation of any other income the borrower wishes considered toward qualifying,* including the following:

- *Child support.* The buyer needs to show proof of receipt, through a printout from the courts or 12 months of canceled checks. (Payments must have been received for at least 12 months on time and must be scheduled to continue at minimum another 36 months to count as qualifying income, depending on the loan program.)

- *A bonus.* This can be counted if the buyer has received it for the past two years (the lender will average it).

- *Overtime.* Lenders look for a two-year history, and consider the average amount of overtime likely to continue (unless the employer volunteers something to the contrary). If the overtime can't be counted toward qualifying income, it still might be considered as a compensating factor.

- *Social Security and/or disability payments.* The buyer must provide a copy of the award letter and a recent check stub, or a copy of a bank statement if payment is electronically deposited.

- *Pension income.* The buyer should provide a check stub and any forms showing duration of payments.

- *Rental property income.* This information can be provided in income tax returns from the past two years. The buyer should bring leases, if possible. Only 75 percent of rental income is counted, but 100 percent of the expenses are deductions. For example, if rental income is $500 per month and the mortgage is also $500, the lender considers this a net loss each month of $125, because only 75 percent of the income is counted for qualifying.

☐ *Copies of documents and explanations of any other money owed to the borrower,* e.g., receivable contracts.

Debt Verification

☐ *Payment book or monthly billing statement for all debts.* If neither is supplied, the lender needs the name and address of the creditor, account number, monthly payment amount, and the approximate amount owed in order to verify.

☐ *Documentation of current mortgages and home equity loans,* including any recently paid off mortgages. If the buyer is in the process of selling a home, the new lender should receive a copy of the HUD-1 closing statement on that home before closing on the new home.

☐ *If renting old home* (rather than selling upon moving), a copy of a lease (at least one year), signed by the new tenant, prior to the closing of the new home.

☐ *Documentation of car payments.*

☐ *Information about outstanding student loans.*

☐ *Divorce decree or separation agreement* to document alimony or child support due or payable.

☐ *Clarification of divorced person's debts.* For formerly joint debts that the other spouse is now supposed to pay, the buyer may need to prove that he or she isn't paying those bills, unless the debt was refinanced and the buyer's name was taken off the obligation. This may be required even though the divorce decree says it's not your obligation. Proof can include canceled checks from the former spouse to show that he or she is paying that obligation, and on time. Otherwise, the debt may go against the borrower's long-term debt ratios for qualifying. This varies based on the loan program.

☐ *Information about any payments made as a direct withdrawal from a checking account or credit union.*

☐ *A copy of any bankruptcy proceedings,* if applicable, with status and explanation.

☐ *A gift letter or explanation of funds' source for closing costs.*

☐ *If obtaining a Department of Veterans Affairs (VA) loan, original Certificate of Eligibility and DD214.*

☐ *Explanation letter for any late payments, judgments, liens, bankruptcy, or foreclosure.*

☐ *A copy of a Certificate of Resident Alien Status (green card),* if applicable.

☐ *A check for the application fee, credit report, and appraisal,* if applicable.

Q. *What other mortgage loan application questions should the borrower be prepared to answer?*

A section of the uniform residential loan application, called "Information for Government Monitoring Purposes," requests that you state your race, nation of origin, and sex. While it's not mandatory that the applicant answer these questions, if the borrower declines to answer them, the lender is required to complete the questions based on meeting the applicants or by their surnames. This information monitors lenders' compliance with the equal credit opportunity, fair housing, and home mortgage disclosure laws. It also monitors the number and types of minorities being afforded the opportunity to apply for a home loan. Because this information becomes part of a national database to help monitor fair housing laws and reduce discrimination, it's advisable that the applicant answer the questions in this section rather than having the lender guess the answers.

It should go without saying that all information given the lender on the application should be truthful and complete. Penalties for falsifying information are stiff. Intentional and negligent misrepresentations can result in criminal penalties and monetary damages under Title 18 of the United States Code.

Q. *If the lender wants to know information, can't he or she just dig for it?*

First of all, the borrower is expected by law to give all pertinent information to the lender. Moreover, this "find it out yourself" attitude usually catches up with the borrower. By checking credit, verifying assets and employment, and noting facts of public record, there's usually very little that escapes the underwriting process. Up-front and honest is definitely the best policy if the borrower wants the mortgage to be granted.

THE LOAN UNDERWRITING PROCESS

Q. *What happens after the application is taken?*

Several things. The borrower's employment, income, and funds on deposit for the down payment and closing costs are all verified. An appraisal also may be ordered at this time. Depending on the loan type, other documentation may be requested. Figure 1.3 summarizes the process and shows some common causes of delays.

This phase is called *underwriting the loan.* It's perhaps the most difficult part of the loan process because information must be collected and thoroughly analyzed in order to decide whether the loan will be made.

The underwriter, or loan endorser, carefully reviews the borrower's documentation and decides whether he or she would be a sound lending risk. If segments of the borrower's employment, credit, or overall finan-

Figure 1.3   The Loan Underwriting Process

Common Time Delays in New Financing

1. Borrower slow to apply

2. No check to start process

3. Creditors will not respond

4. Creditors respond incorrectly

5. Employers will not respond

6. Employers do not complete verification form properly

7. Explanation needed on late payments

8. Bad credit complicates the file

9. Income is less than reported on application

10. More bills than reported on application

11. Appraisal is lower than sale price

12. Property is unacceptable to lender

13. Inspections and/or repairs

14. File must be restructured due to change

15. Closing documents incorrectly signed

16. Closing requirements not satisfied

17. Lender & underwriter work loads

Financing Sequence

Written Application with Check for Initial Fees

↓

Credit Verification, Employment Verification, Appraisal Ordered

↓

Evaluate: Credit, Employment, Appraisal

↓

Collect Additional Requested Information & Plan Requested Repairs & Inspections

↓

Assemble Completed Loan Package and Submit to Underwriter for Approval

↓

Rejected—Evaluate Problem Areas, Try to Correct & Re-submit for Approval

↓

Approved with Conditions to be Complied with or Satisfied

↓

Lender Prepares Documents and Sends to Escrow Company

↓

Buyers & Sellers Sign Closing Documents at Escrow Company who then Sends Documents Back to Underwriter for Final Approval and Recording

↓

Final Approval and Recording

↓

Loan Funded to Escrow and Funds Disbursed

Adapted with permission of Gary Everett, Steve Scott & Co. REALTORS®, 910 NW Harriman, Bend, OR 97701.

cial picture are vague or appear to be contradictory, the underwriter requests more information. This decision process can take hours or weeks to complete. But as mentioned earlier, much of the process is streamlined today using technology and electronic underwriting and electronic credit scoring to help interpret the buyer's loan qualifications. In the near future, this process may be reduced to a matter of minutes.

The underwriting phase also may include the approval of the borrower and the property for private mortgage insurance, if required on the loan. This insurance protects the lender from the borrower's default, usually on the top 20 percent of the loan, and requires a separate approval based on the private mortgage insurance company's underwriting guidelines.

Underwriting guidelines for major types of loans are discussed later in this book.

Underwriting Roadblocks

Q. *Can a borrower get a loan even if he or she doesn't meet the underwriting guidelines?*

It depends on a lot of factors: the size of the down payment, the borrower's creditworthiness, and whether the lender is selling the loan to the secondary market. Later chapters that discuss the major loan types include information on these and other compensating factors. If a borrower has one or more of these pluses, the loan may be made even though all of the underwriting guidelines aren't met.

Q. *What major roadblocks can come up during the underwriting process?*

Many problems occur with verifying employment, down payments, and income from such sources as child support and alimony. Borrowers sometimes change their financial pictures while the loan is being processed. Whether pro or con, these changes can invalidate the paperwork done up to that point.

It may seem bizarre to mention, but after the borrower applies for the loan, he or she should not change jobs or give notice to quit. If loan processing takes more than a month or so, the lender may reverify everything, including employment.

The same is true with taking on new debt. Just because the application has been taken doesn't mean that the lender won't know if the borrower purchased a new washer and dryer using time payments. A credit inquiry from the appliance dealer will show up on the credit report, and even adding a new small monthly debt may be enough to tip the scales against the loan.

In short, the rule of thumb for borrowers to follow after application and before closing is simply, *don't change a thing!*

Problems also can occur when verifying the borrower's funds, called *verification of deposit.* The lender wants to make sure that the down payment has not been borrowed or gained by illegal means. That means that the lender is likely to verify that the money has been accumulating in an account, usually undisturbed for a minimum of 60 days.

Funds that mysteriously disappear and reappear may send up a red flag, putting the validity of the funds into question and perhaps causing the lender to deny the loan. So if funds have increased or decreased radically (through transfers of accounts to other banks, and so on), the borrower should make sure the lender understands the reasons why.

Any documentation required to verify child support, alimony, and debts incurred in a previous marriage may seem deep and cumbersome, but complying with paperwork requests may make the difference between getting and not getting the loan.

If anything changes, and that includes changes for the better, the buyer should make sure to notify the lender. Salary increases to become effective within 60 days of loan closing may be considered for qualifying, and a larger down payment can make the buyer stronger in the eyes of the lender.

THE LOAN CLOSING

Q. *So, after all the documentation is collected and the underwriter approves the loan, then the closing occurs?*

That's correct. The lender, or an appointed closing officer—such as a title company or attorney—prepares the closing statement, checks the title report, prepares the mortgages and deeds to be recorded, and closes the transaction. Figure 1.4 shows a sample closing statement. It is good to familiarize yourself with these costs, because many could be negotiating points with the seller.

In addition, balances for any outstanding loans are checked and the seller gives his or her permission to pay off that loan.

Figure 1.4   Sample Closing Statement

| SELLER'S STATEMENT | | | BUYER'S STATEMENT | |
DEBIT	CREDIT	ITEM	DEBIT	CREDIT
		Total Purchase Price		
		Binder Deposit		
		First Mortgage		
		Second Mortgage		
		Prorations and Prepayments		
		Rent		
		Interest (first mortgage)		
		Interest (second mortage)		
		Prepayment Penalty		
		Insurance		
		Mortage Insurance		
		Insurance Reserves		
		Taxes (city)		
		Taxes (county)		
		Tax Reserves		
		Expenses		
		Attorney's Fees		
		Escrow Closing Fees		
		Escrow Holding Fees (Long Term)		
		State Tax On Deed		
		Recording Mortgage		
		Recording Deed		
		Title Insurance		
		Brokerage		
		Miscellaneous		
		Total Debits and Credits		
		Balance Due		
		Seller & from Buyer		
		Grand Totals		

Figure 1.4   Sample Closing Statement (Continued)

RECONCILIATION STATEMENT

	RECEIPTS	DISBURSEMENT
Bank Loan (less points/origination fees)	_____	_____
Deposit	_____	_____
Check from Buyer at Closing	_____	_____
Brokerage Fee	_____	_____
Check to Seller at Closing	_____	_____
Seller's Expense	_____	_____
Buyer's Expense	_____	_____
Grand Totals	_____	_____

WHAT TO DO IF THE LENDER SAYS NO

Q. *What can the buyer do if the lender says no?*

As discussed earlier in this chapter, a lender can reject a loan application for myriad reasons. The following are some ways in which a buyer can attempt to piece the sale back together if previous efforts to get the loan approved have failed.

Identify the Source of the Problem

If the problem is borrower-related.   The borrower may ask the lender to reanalyze the borrower's financial situation, based on answers to the following questions:

- *Have any debts been paid off since the application was taken?*
- *Could any assets be converted to cash?*
- *Does any of the buyer's income now fall within the two-year track-record time frame?* Could this income be used to help the buyer qualify for the loan?
- *Would the borrower be willing to forgo this year's vacation to increase the down payment?*
- *Is a raise from the employer scheduled for the near future?* Raises in income that are scheduled to occur within 60 days of closing may be counted as income by the lender.

The borrower may ask to have the loan held in portfolio so that under-writing exceptions can be made. The success of this approach depends on the lender and its programs.

Another approach is to identify the borrower's strengths and ways to showcase them. Be realistic: If a problem is so overwhelming that only time will correct it (such as a recent mortgage foreclosure), getting any loan right now might be impossible.

If all else fails, the borrower may wish to seek a less restrictive loan program or a more lenient lender. (This is usually a last resort. Because precious time and money already have been expended in obtaining the loan, moving the loan may cause duplication of costs.)

If the problem is property-related. Determine strategies for repairing the property. Identify the person who has the most to gain by the sale going through. That person might be willing to pay for repairs. This person may be someone besides the buyer and the seller; for example, the seller's sellers (the people whose house your seller is buying) may need to have the primary sale closed before theirs will close.

Another approach is to determine a creative time frame for completing needed repairs. One option might be to close now and hold funds in escrow. You may be able to escrow two times the amount of the highest bid in order to complete repairs later, for example, in better weather.

You also might consider options other than cash. Perhaps the buyer could use sweat equity in lieu of cash for repairs.

The lender might be more likely to make the loan if the loan-to-value ratio were different, or if you paid a higher rate of interest.

The bottom line is, "It ain't over 'til it's over!"

CONSUMER BOOKLETS TO THE RESCUE

Q. *It seems as though there's a lot to learn about the homebuying process. Are there any consumer booklets you'd recommend?*

The following are some useful homebuying fact booklets, which can be obtained free of charge:

- *Unraveling the Mortgage Loan Mystery*
  Federal National Mortgage Association
  Drawer MM
  3900 Wisconsin Avenue, NW
  Washington, DC 20006

Figure 1.5   Loan Information

Lender: _____   Owner's Name: _____
Lender's Address: _____   Property Address: _____
_____   Loan Number: _____

To Whom It May Concern:

You are hereby directed to furnish _____ and/or
their agent _____ , with the following information
regarding my loan.

_____

_____

Effective Date: _____

Type of Loan

FHA   _____   Original Loan Balance: $_____
VA   _____   Present Loan Balance: $_____
Conv.   _____   Interest Rate: _____
Other   _____   Term: _____

Monthly Payment

Principal and Interest: _____   Assumption Policy: _____
            Taxes: _____   _____
         Insurance: _____   _____
       FHA Premium: _____   _____
      PMI Insurance: _____   Payoff Penalty: _____
      Total Payment: _____   _____

Is this loan in default? If so, please explain: _____
_____
_____

                              Loan Officer: _____
                                     Date: _____

You may wish to request a list of other homebuyer pamphlets available through FNMA.

- *A Consumer's Glossary of Mortgage Terms, Self Test* (for buyers wishing to determine how well they would do in qualifying for a mortgage) and *What Happens After You Apply for a Mortgage?*
  Mortgage Bankers' Association
  1125 15th St., NW
  Washington, DC 20005
- *The Mortgage Money Guide* (comparisons of homebuying options)
  Federal Trade Commission
  Bureau of Consumer Protection
  Pennsylvania Avenue & 6th Street, NW
  Washington, DC 20580

Other publications can be obtained for free or at a nominal cost (to $1.50) through the federal government's Consumer Information Center. To obtain a free catalog, write to the Consumer Information Center, P.O. Box 100, Pueblo, CO, 81002. You can find other booklets (as well as Web site URLs) in the Resource Guide section in this book.

CHAPTER 2

QUALIFYING FOR THE MORTGAGE

In a fast-paced home buying market, buyers need two things in order to be competitive: (1) an awareness of their credit pictures, and (2) preapproval for the mortgage loans they'll need. Without these two components, a buyer's offer may be knocked out of the running by sellers who want to know that they're selling for the highest price to the buyer most likely to follow through on the purchase.

That's why this chapter will focus on how to access and evaluate your credit report (long before meeting with the lender), the powerful role creditworthiness plays in negotiating for and obtaining a mortgage, and the importance of evaluating what you can qualify for before viewing the first house!

And since it's not a perfect world, we'll cover tips for whittling down borrower debt, maximizing available cash, and leverage tips for putting a stronger foot forward with the lender—even if the borrower is self-employed.

CREDITWORTHINESS:
THE BACKBONE OF MORTGAGE LENDING

Q. *Judging from the emphasis placed on verifying the type and amount of borrower debt, it seems lenders are very critical of the buyer's creditworthiness.*

Good credit is important in securing a home loan. In fact, many lenders will tell you that bad credit is one of the major reasons mortgages are denied. In an era of conspicuous consumption when consumers are using more "plastic," lenders are placing much greater emphasis on how well loan applicants manage the credit they have before granting them more. And since the lender must pull a credit report from at least two of the three major credit reporting agencies to compare and evaluate credit, errors and adverse information are more likely to be uncovered. For names, addresses and URLs of these national companies, see Figure 2.1.

A poor credit rating can be the result of a buyer's irresponsibility. More often, however, it arises from unchecked and uncorrected errors on an individual's report.

WHAT THE CREDIT REPORT SHOWS

Q. *If there are three national credit reporting agencies, do they all report the same information?*

Each of the three major credit reporting agencies are independent companies and may or may not report the same information. That's why the lender pulls a merged report, combining information from at least two of the three companies when underwriting the mortgage.

All three reporting agencies report information in five categories:

1. *Identification.* This section includes the borrower's name; address; Social Security number; employer; date of birth; and spouse's name, if applicable.
2. *Credit history.* This section lists all open and paid accounts, the current payment history of each creditor reporting to the bureau, and prior payment history (which includes any late payments). By law, adverse information can remain on the report for seven years; bankruptcies can remain for ten years. These negative postings may arbitrarily not come off automatically and their removal should be monitored by the consumer.
3. *Collection.* This section includes any creditors who have turned over an account to a collection agency.
4. *Public records.* All items of public record affecting financial obligations (such as bankruptcies, liens, judgments, divorce decrees, child support adjudications, and so on) are included in this section.
5. *Inquiries.* This section notes who has checked the consumer's credit as far back as 18 to 24 months. Anyone accessing a consumer's credit without a valid business reason could be in violation of the federal Fair Credit Reporting Act, fined up to $5,000, and imprisoned for one year. (Note: The consumer is awarded the fine!)

Figure 2.1   Credit Reporting Agencies

EQUIFAX
Box 740241
Atlanta, GA 30374
800-685-1111 (8AM-5PM ET)
www.equifax.com
(You can obtain a report using a
major credit card)

EXPERIAN
Box 949
Allen, TX 75013
800-422-4879 (24 hours daily)
www.experian.com

TRANS UNION
Box 390
Springfield, PA 19064-0390
800-888-4213 (24 hours daily)
www.tuc.com

SPECIAL CONSIDERATIONS FOR MARRIED AND DIVORCED PERSONS

Q. *Can a divorced person have a credit report solely in his or her name, apart from the ex-spouse?*

Every person has the right to obtain an individual credit history regardless of marital status. Joint liabilities will appear on both spouses' reports.

Q. *Should a divorced person make special arrangements to ensure that his or her credit rating is not adversely affected by the change in marital status?*

It's especially important to check credit after a divorce, making sure obligations are sorted out, creditors are notified, and the report is listed solely in the consumer's name. Ideally, this should be done before the divorce gavel raps, but usually is not.

Imagine the nightmare created when someone applies for credit after divorce, only to find that the car and corresponding payment awarded to the former spouse is still showing as a joint obligation! Ideally, the former spouse should requalify for that debt and have the posting removed from the other person's credit report. Again, this is not likely to happen. At the very least, a copy of the divorce decree will be requested by the mortgage lender, showing the allocation of assets and liabilities. This could easily add time to the loan qualifying process.

Q. *Could a person who is married to someone with bad credit get a loan in his or her own name?*

A married individual can secure a mortgage in his or her own name provided he or she meets the required income, assets, and creditworthiness guidelines. Again, federal law prohibits discrimination based on marital status; therefore, one spouse's adverse credit cannot be used to deny a loan to the other spouse.

MAJOR AREAS OF CREDIT EVALUATION

Q. *What major credit areas does the lender evaluate before making a loan?*

When it comes to determining an applicant's creditworthiness, a lender examines the three *C*s: Character, Capacity, and Credit.

- *Character* can be evaluated through objective factors such as length of residency at each address, terms of employment, and a report free of financial judgments, liens, and other adverse matters of public record.
- *Capacity* is increasingly important these days, because many consumers carry heavy debts and make many minimum payments on those debts. The lender evaluates the amount of debt compared to income, ways the new obligations may change the debt picture, and the borrower's general economic stability.
- *Credit* is the third measure. The lender evaluates existing credit relationships including bank loans, credit cards, and so on. The lender pays close attention to limits, how the current balances relate to those limits, and how long those accounts have been active. For example, a credit card held by the borrower for less than six months but currently at the maximum could indicate that the borrower could have trouble handling additional debt. A lender making the home loan may require a large down payment to lessen the risk.

CREDIT SCORING—THE CREDITWORTHINESS GAUGE

Q. *Isn't interpreting credit subjective? How can the lender determine if it's being fair?*

Credit interpretation is somewhat subjective. But the introduction of technology and credit scoring has helped take the mystery (and some of the bias) out of evaluating credit.

Credit scoring electronically gives a numerical weighting to various financial factors like income, debts, and job history, and can help predict the likelihood of mortgage default. While there are several credit scoring models, many lenders use the Fair, Isaac & Co. (FICO) score that ranges from 450 to 850—the lower the score, the higher the risk. Borrowers can't view their credit score when obtaining their own report, but credit scoring is done as an added function when the lender pulls a mortgage credit report from the primary credit reporting agencies. At the consumer's request, the lender may be willing to share the credit score with the consumer.

For example, FNMA in the secondary market recommends that lenders obtain credit scores from at least two of the three primary credit reporting bureaus, compare the scores, and then select a representative score to rate the borrower. The lower score would be selected when two scores are obtained; the middle score used if all three reporting bureaus are accessed.

Q. *How does credit scoring work?*

Credit scoring considers a variety of components. For example, errors on a credit report that haven't been removed can cost score points.

Credit scoring also weighs how much available credit the borrower has used. For example, if account balances are 75 percent or more of the credit limit, it can signal high financial leverage and higher risk to the lender. Because the lender compares the amount of debt the borrower carries compared to the amount of income she or he generates, it's important to keep available credit reasonable for the borrower's income level.

Keeping a large number of accounts with zero balances also can lower the credit score because it increases the potential for someone to live beyond his or her means. That's why it's important for the borrower to decide which accounts to keep and close out the rest. In general, the longer the positive credit history, the better the score.

Opening new accounts can lower a score, as can having too many credit inquiries. A score can even be impacted if the borrower transfers a balance to a new lower-interest rate credit card (but the borrower can alert the creditor and the scoring process by making sure the credit reporting bureau posts this to the credit file).

Q. *What is an acceptable credit score and have there been any tests using them?*

Yes, there have been numerous tests to prove their efficacy. FNMA surveyed one million loan records and found that one in eight borrowers with a FICO score below 600 were either severely delinquent or in default. Contrarily, only one in 1300 borrowers with scores above 800 had similar mortgage delinquency problems. From these and other surveys, the benchmark of concern is usually with scores of less than 620.

Most lenders who sell their loans into the secondary market use the following parameters when evaluating scores:

- *Scores greater than 660*—credit risk is generally acceptable. In fact, a high score here can help compensate for other risks in the credit file.
- *Scores between 620 and 659*—comprehensive review to take a closer look at potential risks. Supplemental credit documentation and letters of explanation may be required.
- *Scores below 620*—cautious review required. Borrowers may find themselves locked out of the best loans and terms available. The lender may still be able to make a loan if "compensating factors" can shore up the borrower's picture. But in general, factors like lower ratios, extra cash reserves, and/or a lower loan-to-value ratio on the loan won't compensate for unacceptable credit.

Credit scoring has also caused the lending industry to push towards making loans rated at *A–, B, C,* or *D* to credit-damaged borrowers. Called "customized" or "subprime" lending, we'll cover them later in this chapter as a leverage tool.

Q. *Should a borrower use one of those credit repair companies to improve a low score?*

Absolutely not. They can't do anything that the borrower can't do as well (and it won't cost money, just time). By using the general fix-up tips given in the answers that follow (and then monitoring the report to make sure the correct information is posted), a borrower can improve his or her own credit score, without the aid of companies who profess to rewrite credit history—but can't!

There are excellent articles on credit scoring by two of the secondary market buyers found at www.fanniemae.com and www.freddiemac.com.

WHAT CONSTITUTES "GOOD CREDIT"?

Q. *If credit is so important, how can a borrower work towards "good credit"?*

As seen with the credit scoring model, good credit doesn't have to be perfect, unblemished credit! In general, a borrower is considered to have good credit if his report shows nothing in the past twelve months more detrimental than the following:

- Revolving credit (like credit cards): No more than two payments 30 days past due, and no payments 60 days past due.
- Installment credit (like a car loan): No more than one payment 30 days past due and no payments 60 days or more past due.
- Housing debt (first or second mortgages, rent): No payments past due.

Thorough explanations would need to be provided to the lender for any late payments.

ENSURING THE BEST POSSIBLE CREDIT REPORT

Q. *What errors could consumers expect to find on their credit reports?*

While errors can be found in a variety of forms, frequent mistakes occur in three areas:

1. Misposting due to similar names.
2. Multiple entries of the same credit account or previously closed accounts still showing active.
3. Accounts that are disputed or improperly reported by the creditor.

Q. *When is a person's name likely to be confused for another's in credit reporting, and how can one protect against it?*

If you're a junior or senior—or have a common name like Smith, Brown, or Jones—you are likely to have someone else's credit on your report. While names, addresses, and Social Security numbers are generally used to report credit to the correct name, errors still occur. Upon hearing that someone else's credit was found on his or her report, a homebuyer might remark, "Well, if it's good news, I'll keep it!" The problem is that an additional account, yours or not, could signal extra debt to the lender, which might not be good news for qualifying.

To avoid the name mix-up, it's good to use your full name including spelled-out middle or maiden names (or both) when applying for credit.

Multiple Credit Entries

Q. *Is there anything wrong with multiple entries of the same account showing up on your credit report?*

Yes. The lender may consider that there's a possible monthly minimum repayment on each card (5 percent of the outstanding balance or $10, whichever is greater if the payment is unknown) for the purpose of loan qualifying. In addition, the lender evaluates not just what is owing, but the amount of potential credit available to the borrower.

Closing Out Accounts

Q. *Would it help to qualify by closing out accounts and cutting up credit cards that are no longer in use?*

It may. It's important to go through the process thoroughly. Otherwise, these credit lines may not be canceled and could resurface on credit reports again.

Here's a system I've found to work: Notify the creditor in writing that you wish to close the account. You may want to send the request by certified mail, return receipt requested. That way you know it was received. A credit card, cut up, can be sent along as well. Be sure to take a photocopy of the card pasted to your letter before you send it, just in case you later need verification that you returned it. In the letter, ask the creditor to post the account "closed permanently at customer's request." This clarifies that the account was closed voluntarily and not by the creditor for adverse reasons. Also inform the creditor that the credit report will be checked in 30 days to make sure that the account has been removed. This ensures that the request is handled promptly.

Removing Errors from the Report

Q. *If an error is found on the report, how can it be rectified?*

Some of the greatest credit reporting nightmares come in the form of disputed or improperly reported items. Freeing these errors from your report may be tedious, but it can be accomplished by following these three steps:

1. *File a consumer dispute form* with the reporting bureau, stating that you disagree with the report. By law, they must investigate the complaint in a timely manner (usually in 30 days or less) and report back to the consumer.
2. *Write to the creditor* as well, pointing out the mistake. If the dispute is resolved, have the creditor send letters to all three credit bureaus, asking that they change the information (if they initially received it). By law, the reporting bureau must send a corrected copy of the report to all parties who accessed the report during the time the error appeared.
3. *File an explanation.* If a satisfactory conclusion is not reached with the creditor, the consumer can place an explanation (up to 100 words) on the credit report telling his or her side of the story. This explanation will remain on the report for six months, and the consumer can request the posting be extended for increments of six months.

After correcting an error on a credit report, it's good to request a copy of the corrected report from the credit reporting agency in approximately 30 days to show that the changes were made.

Q. *If there are three major credit reporting networks, do errors have to be corrected with all three?*

Ideally, yes, unless you've obtained a merged report showing information from all of the reporting bureaus. For the best chance at cleaning up an error, submit the change information to all three.

The Credit Appeals Process

Q. *If a problem can't be adequately rectified with a credit agency, is there an appeals process?*

Since credit reporting agencies are monitored under the federal Equal Credit Opportunity Act, a consumer could file a complaint with the Federal Trade Commission, Attn: Correspondence Department, Room 692, Washington, DC 20580. They can be found at www.ftc.gov.

Too Many Credit Inquiries

Q. *Could a buyer have a problem if too many credit inquiries appear on his or her credit report?*

As seen with credit scoring, a mortgage lender might be hesitant to make a loan to someone who had an abundance of credit inquiries in the past six months. This could serve as a red flag that the party was denied credit, is accumulating open lines of credit to borrow against or is leveraging assets prior to declaring bankruptcy. This could also indicate that the borrower is checking the credit report repeatedly in anticipation of an adverse posting. Nevertheless, the lender may want a written explanation as to why the inquiries occurred.

CHECKING SOMEONE ELSE'S CREDIT

Q. *Could just anyone check someone's credit?*

While the law requires that there must be a "valid business reason" to check someone's credit, it does not require that the creditor obtain written authorization from the consumer before the report is accessed. In fact, the consumer may not even be aware that his or her credit has been checked! If the consumer later contested that a valid business reason did not exist to check his or her credit, it would be up to the creditor to prove the validity. A federal fine of $5,000 and up to one year in jail applies if the law is breached.

Q. *Do credit reporting agencies have services that alert the consumer when someone accesses his or her credit?*

Due to the growing importance and interest of creditworthiness, special services such as Experian's Credentials Service alert subscribers when a credit report is requested or when anything adverse is posted to a credit report. In addition, subscribers can receive their own current credit reports by calling a toll-free number and giving a pass code. These services are provided for a small annual fee.

GETTING A MORTGAGE AFTER MARRED CREDIT

Q. *If someone's credit was so bad that the lender suggested the borrower get outside help to untangle it, whom might the lender suggest?*

A nonprofit organization called the Consumer Credit Counseling Service would be a good suggestion. They evaluate income, ability to pay, analyze debt load, and request that the individual surrender his or her monthly income to them, from which they will pay creditors. Their goal is to help reduce debt and make it manageable. The only cost is any voluntary contribution the consumer wishes to make. Locations of centers throughout the United States can be found in the yellow pages of the phone book under "credit."

ESTABLISHING CREDIT

Q. *What's the best way for a person with no credit to establish a credit rating?*

The answer is, very carefully! While amassing large numbers of credit cards may seem to be a great way to establish credit, adding monthly debt to a buyer's long-term debt ratio may hurt loan qualification prospects.

There are several prudent ways to establish credit:

- If a borrower does not believe in credit and pays cash for everything, that practice could be documented to establish creditworthiness. For example, most power companies, utility companies, and small retailers will be glad to verify that the applicant pays in cash and on time when he or she purchases. The more documentation that can be shown to the lender, the better.
- If the buyer is purchasing in several months, the down payment could be put in a bank account and he or she can obtain a loan

against it. By placing this money with a lender as collateral, a loan can be made against the funds and repaid to establish credit. Three to six months is a good minimum time frame to show a credible payment pattern.

- Obtaining a major credit card may make sense if the borrower has room for the monthly payment in his or her long-term debt qualifying ratio and will control spending so as not to run up a huge balance. Consult with a mortgage lender before taking this route.

CHECKING YOUR OWN CREDIT

Q. *How far in advance of loan application should someone check his or her credit?*

Between 60 and 120 days before beginning the house-hunting process is a good time to examine credit. This can alert the buyer to what creditors have reported, allow unused accounts to be closed, and correct any errors that appear in the information.

Q. *How much does it cost to check one's own credit?*

For less than $20, a credit report can be received from one of the three national credit reporting agencies. If someone has been denied credit or employment in the past six months due to adverse credit, the report is free. It's good to access all three reports the first time credit is examined to receive the complete picture. It's a small price to pay for peace of mind.

Q. *Is this the same report the lender will pull at the time of loan application?*

No. An individual receives a consumer credit or in-file report. While it's not as in-depth as the mortgage credit report the lender requires at loan application, it will give you a good overview of what the report contains.

THE CREDIT-CHECKING PROCESS

Q. *How does one locate a credit reporting agency, what information needs to be provided to it, and what will the consumer receive?*

The two-step process is as follows:

1. Call, visit, or e-mail the credit reporting agency. To find a reporting agency, check the yellow pages of your phone directory under

"credit reporting agencies" for the affiliate nearest you, or contact the companies and access their Web addresses listed in Figure 2.1.

2. Provide identification to the reporting agency. This will be a picture ID card if the visit is in person. If the request is made over the phone and the report is to be received by mail, each reporting agency has its own checklist of required information.

3. If applying in person, the consumer can see the report in a matter of minutes. By mail, it may take five to seven working days. Either way, detailed instructions are provided on how to decipher the many symbols and notations on the report.

BE AN INFORMED CONSUMER

With all the knowledge gleaned from your consumer's credit report, you can see why the lender puts such great value on it for making a lending decision. And after the borrower has gathered information, he or she will at least know what everyone else already knew about them!

PREAPPROVAL: KNOWING WHAT YOU CAN AFFORD

Q. *What's the best way for me to figure out what I can afford? Hasn't the procedure recently changed?*

Yes, it has changed. In the past, most buyers began the home search by being prequalified. That meant sharing with a real estate professional (lender, real estate agent, builder) an overview of their income, their debts, and the amount of cash available for their down payment and closing costs. The professional then applied qualifying ratios. For example, if conventional financing was considered, up to 28 percent of the borrower's monthly gross income could go towards housing expense (principal, interest, tax, insurance and any private mortgage insurance premium, and/or homeowner's fees such as monthly condo association charges). And up to 36 percent of the borrower's monthly gross income could be attributed to their housing expense plus any long-term debts (those that couldn't be paid off in ten months or less).

While prequalifying was better than nothing, it didn't take into consideration the impact of credit scoring and verifying funds on deposit, and left both the buyer and the seller with no assurance that financing could be secured.

Preapproval—when you have the assurance that unless something changes in your financial picture, the lender will grant you a mortgage at a certain level—essentially makes you a cash buyer, with the flexibility that represents.

Q.   *What does preapproval require?*

While requirements vary from lender to lender and program to program, lenders require buyers to present verification of income (like the last two pay stubs, or income tax returns if a buyer is self-employed), the last three bank statements, and verification of other assets (like brokerage accounts, etc.).

Using this information combined with the credit report and credit scoring, the lender can then commit to make the borrower a mortgage amount of X, based on a maximum interest rate of Y. Some lenders even present buyers with "preapproval certificates" or credit cards that can be presented to sellers when the offer to purchase is made. Preapproval not only gives the buyer and seller confidence, it's a great marketing tool for the lender!

QUALIFYING RATIOS

Q.   *Lenders talk a lot about qualifying ratios. How do they work? They seem a bit mysterious!*

Don't let the fancy semantics fool you! Ratios are merely percentages. And qualifying ratios simply apply the percentages to the borrower's monthly gross income.

Here's what happens. The lender tallies up the annual gross income, divides it by 12 (to determine monthly gross income), and then multiplies it by the percentage allowed for the borrower's housing debt as well as total long-term debt based on the type of loan the borrower is seeking.

Qualifying Example   See Figure 2.2, grab a pencil, and we'll work through the form together. (Note: This form reflects conventional qualifying guidelines. Check in the appropriate loan chapter for specific ARM, FHA, and VA qualifying forms.)

Step 1   Post the amount of your annual gross income in Column A and then divide it by 12 to determine your monthly gross income. Post that answer in Column B as well.

Figure 2.2   Conventional Quick Qualify

What Can You Afford?

	COLUMN A	COLUMN B
Annual gross income	$ _____	
Divide by number of months:	÷ 12	
Monthly gross income: (Record it in both columns. Perform operations only on figures in the same vertical column.)	= _____	= _____
Lenders will allow 28% of monthly gross income for housing expense.		× 28
Maximum monthly housing expense allowance (column B):		= _____
Many lenders allow 36% of monthly gross income for long-term debt:	× .36	
Long-term monthly expense allowance:	= _____	
Figure out your monthly long-term obligations below, and subtract it from the allowance:	– _____	
child support .... $	_____	
auto loan... +	_____	
credit cards .... +	_____	
other .... +	_____	
other .... +	_____	
total long-term obligations .... =	_____	
Monthly housing expense allowance:	= _____	
Look at the last amount in columns A and B above. Record the smaller amount.	$ _____	
About 20% of the housing expense allowance is for taxes and insurance, leaving 80% for payment of mortgage (principal and interest):	× .80	
Allowable monthly principal and interest (PI) expense:	= _____	
Divide this amount by the appropriate monthly payment factor:	÷ _____	
	= _____	
Multiply by 1,000:	× 1,000	
Affordable mortgage amount (what the lender will lend):	$ _____	

Step 1   Post the amount of your annual gross income in Column A and then divide it by 12 to determine your monthly gross income. Post that answer in Column B as well.

Step 2   The form states that "lenders will allow 28 percent of monthly gross income for housing expense." In Column B, multiply your monthly gross income by 28 percent and post your answer on the line provided. This represents the maximum monthly housing expense (principal, interest, tax, insurance, private mortgage insurance, and/or monthly homeowner's association fees) for which you can qualify.

Step 3   The form states that "many lenders allow 36 percent of monthly gross income for long-term debt." Multiply your gross monthly income by 36 percent and post that answer in Column A. This represents the maximum amount of your monthly income that can go toward your long-term debt, which includes your housing expense plus debts that can't be paid off in ten months (or are recurring).

Step 4   Next comes the fun part. Tally up your long-term obligations (any debt that can't be paid off in ten months or is recurring, such as child support, auto loans, credit cards, etc.) and subtract the total from the previous answer in Column A. This answer will be posted as your "monthly housing expense allowance" in Column A.

Step 5   Look at the last amounts in Columns A and B and "record the smaller amount." (The lender goes with the smaller amount to compensate for the amount of the borrower's debt.)

Step 6   The form considers that you may not yet know exactly what your property taxes and insurance are—so we're estimating that approximately 20 percent of the housing expense allowance will go for taxes, insurance, and any private mortgage insurance, leaving 80 percent for mortgage principal and interest. Multiply your answer from Step 5 by 80 percent to find this amount.

Step 7   Next, look at an amortization table (you can find one located at Figure 2.3). Based on current interest rates in your area, find the monthly payment factor that corresponds to the interest rate and divide it into the last answer you found in Column A. (Example: $900 divided by 6.65, which is the factor for 7 percent interest for a 30-year loan term, gives you 137.825.)

Figure 2.3   Loan Payment Table (Monthly Payment for Each
$1,000 Borrowed)

Interest Rate	15 Years	20 Years	30 Years
4.00%	$ 7.40	$6.06	$4.77
4.50	7.65	6.33	5.07
5.00	7.91	6.60	5.37
5.50	8.17	6.88	5.68
6.00	8.44	7.16	6.00
6.50	8.71	7.46	6.32
7.00	8.99	7.75	6.65
7.50	9.27	8.06	6.99
8.00	9.56	8.36	7.34
8.50	9.85	8.68	7.69
9.00	10.14	9.00	8.05
9.50	10.44	9.32	8.41
10.00	10.75	9.65	8.78

Note: Chart represents principal and interest only.

This table helps you calculate your monthly housing costs (not including property taxes, insurance, and any mortage insurance premium). Each factor represents the principal and interest cost for each $1,000 borrowed. For example, if you're considering a $100,000 30-year mortage at 8 percent, you would multiply 100 × $7.34 = $734 per month principal and interest payment.

Q. *What if you already know what your ratios are? Can you use them to calculate what you can afford?*

Absolutely! All you have to do is back up through the process we just completed. For example, the $137,825 loan required a monthly principal and interest payment of $900. To that amount you'd need to add back the 20 percent you took out for taxes, insurance, and private mortgage insurance (if applicable). So, our maximum PITI (principal, interest, tax, and insurance) payment would be $1,080.

Q. *What amount of monthly income would you need in order to qualify for that payment?*

Using the conventional qualifying ratios, divide $1,080 by 28 percent. This equals $3,857.14. That's the amount of monthly income you'd need to qualify for a $1,080 PITI payment.

Q. *So by using your monthly income and the payment you can afford, you can figure out what your ratio is, correct?*

That's right. Let's say you have $4,200 in monthly income to qualify for that same $1,080 payment. What would your housing ratio be then? To find it, you'd divide the $1,080 payment by the $4,200 monthly income. The answer (and ratio) is 26. This means that with this amount of income, only 26 percent of our monthly income would be going to our PITI payment. That's great! Low ratios are good news because they signal that proportionately only a small amount of your gross monthly income is going for your house payment.

Conversely, a high ratio indicates that you're trying to buy a champagne-budget house on a beer-budget income. The options are to shop for a lower-priced house, find a larger down payment, or find a loan that would give you more leverage (like an FHA loan for higher ratios or an adjustable rate loan with lower interest rates).

Remember that qualifying ratios are merely one test of affordability. That's why it's important to work closely with a good lender who can apply other information (called compensating factors) that may contribute additional positives to your qualifying profile. You can find detailed information about compensating factors by loan type in the chapters that follow.

QUALIFYING THE SELF-EMPLOYED BORROWER

Q. *Is it usually tougher for the self-employed buyer to get a mortgage?*

It depends on the circumstances and the type of loan desired. Because the self-employed buyer's cash flow and profitability is often tough to predict, guaranteeing income can be difficult to prove to the lender. In addition, the so-called low documentation/no documentation (low-doc/no-doc) loans of the 1980s, many of which were made to self-employed borrowers, have shown significantly more defaults than standard documentation loans. Self-employed borrowers, designated as anyone who owns 25 percent or greater interest in the business that employs him or her, are challenged by the mortgage loan process for two reasons:

1. *Income tax write-offs whittle down the self-employed borrower's net income.* While this is favorable come April 15, it's a negative factor in qualifying for a mortgage loan. An applicant currently

making a $1,200 mortgage payment may find it impossible to qualify for even a $600 loan payment on a new loan. Even after the lender adds back some deductions for the purpose of qualifying (such as IRA deposits and depreciation), the applicant may not qualify.

2. *Self-employed applicants must provide extensive documentation to the lender.* This is a mandate from the secondary market because there is greater room for a borrower to embellish verifications if he or she is employer and employee. In addition to the standard items a loan applicant must furnish, the self-employed borrower may be required to provide the following:

- Two years of signed copies of complete income tax returns (with all schedules attached), a balance sheet for the previous two years (audited, or prepared by an accountant or professional tax preparer), and a year-to-date profit and loss statement for the sole proprietor
- If the business is a corporation, S corporation or a partnership, signed copies of the past two years of federal business income tax returns (with all schedules attached), a year-to-date profit and loss statement, and a business credit report

   Because many self-employed entrepreneurs are not the best bookkeepers, pulling these records together may prove tough, if not impossible, for some applicants.

Q. *What "red flag" areas do lenders monitor to make sure the self-employed borrower is revealing his or her entire financial picture?*

Red flags include income and deductions showing only increments of a hundred, for example, $500 or $1,000, on tax returns, a taxpayer in a high tax bracket who prepares his or her own return, and a self-employed borrower who shows no estimated tax payments being paid.

Q. *How is the self-employed person's income calculated to qualify for a loan?*

A rough formula would be as follows: Using income tax returns, add up the applicant's income after expenses (but before taxes) for the past two years. Then calculate the year-to-date income after expenses (but before taxes) for this year. Finally, divide the total of those sums by the number of months involved to get the average monthly income.

Q. *What other requirements must a self-employed person, working on commission, fulfill to qualify?*

For the applicant who works on commission, the lender needs W-2 forms and completed, signed tax returns for the past two years. The income is then averaged over the time period reported.

If the borrower's sole compensation is from commission, a year-to-date income statement will also be required. In general, the lender wants to see the amount of income tending to increase.

Creative Financing for the Self-Employed Borrower

Q. *What other types of loans might a self-employed borrower use?*

Another way the self-employed buyer might qualify would be by using a 75 percent first mortgage, a 10 percent down payment, and having the seller or lender carry 15 percent of the purchase price in second mortgage financing. Called 75/10/15 financing (and discussed in depth in Chapter 9), the borrower may be less scrutinized in taking a 75 percent loan, may sidestep requirements and the cost of private mortgage insurance, and may more readily qualify, since rates and points may be lower.

Q. *What kinds of creative financing could a self-employed borrower try?*

Seller financing is always an option, even though the seller may require the same credit report or other income verification a lender does.

A second suggestion might be to apply for a business loan rather than a mortgage. If a borrower is well established with a lender who understands his or her business workings, the borrower might use a commercial loan to fund the purchase.

While rates can vary, two points over prime is reasonable interest to expect to pay, with most loans being adjustable rather than fixed rate. Loan amortizations may be short-term (10 to 15 years), but the borrower could negotiate a roll-over option with the lender.

A third option would be to take loans against assets, such as certificates of deposit, stock, life insurance, and the like. The benefit is that you keep the asset intact while pulling cash out. We'll investigate a type of mortgage called *pledged asset* in Chapter 9. The leverage techniques section later in this book goes into greater detail on these ideas.

Q. *What tips can you give self-employed borrowers to give them a better chance of getting a mortgage?*

A lender may waive the year-to-date profit and loss statement in the early months of the year, since the year is young and there's not enough history. In addition, a lender who holds others of the borrower's loans may limit some documentation, especially if the lender does not sell the loan to the secondary mortgage market and keeps the loan in portfolio (in-house) instead.

LOW-DOC/NO-DOC LOANS

Q. *Are low- or no-documentation loans available?*

Yes, lenders make so-called low-doc/no-doc loans, usually with a minimum 25 percent to 30 percent down payment.

These types of loans do not require the same level of documentation and verification that a standard qualifying loan does. The abbreviated format for qualifying could include checking the borrower's credit, verifying down payment funds and total assets and doing an appraisal on the property. In fact, some lenders are willing to waive verification of assets entirely if the borrower has a 40 percent or greater down payment.

Depending on the type of low-doc loan, the applicant may be asked to disclose his or her income, but it's not verified by the lender. The lender's rationale is that the large down payment lessens part of the risk of default. In addition, many of these loans are kept in the lender's portfolio, may require high origination fees, and may carry higher interest rates than traditional loans.

SUBPRIME LOANS:
THE ANSWER FOR MARGINAL BUYERS

Q. *I've heard about people with questionable credit who still managed to get a mortgage. How did they do it?*

It's likely in today's lending world of customized credit that even after major credit glitches like bankruptcy and/or foreclosure, a borrower can qualify for some type of mortgage (albeit one with higher interest and/or more points and fees). Instead of the top *A* category loans purchased by the secondary market (that we usually refer to as standard mortgages), a borrower may only be able to qualify for a lower-rated loan; *A–, B, C,* or *D.*

First, some definitions. "Subprime" refers to both the jumbo-sized loans that are outside of the loan limits sold by FNMA and FHLMC. But where mortgage risk is involved, subprime means a category of loans available to borrowers who have had damaged credit on a regular or extensive basis. Problems can fall into three primary areas of credit blemishes: (1) mortgage credit, (2) consumer credit, and (3) public record postings. For example, the latter category would be someone with a foreclosure or a judgment against him or her.

After scoring and grading the borrower's credit, the lender would place the borrower in the appropriate category. For example, an *A–* subprime borrower might be one with a 30-day late mortgage payment in the past twelve months; whereas a *C* subprime buyer might have had a bankruptcy discharged fourteen months ago.

Rates and points vary widely between loan categories. Depending on the loan types and market factors, *B* subprime loans might spread two or more interest rate points above standard fixed-rate 30-year loans, so borrowers are advised to shop diligently before committing to a certain loan program.

Q. *Does the amount of the down payment play a role in the type of loan a subprime borrower can obtain?*

Yes, it does. A rule of thumb is that the greater the amount of equity (e.g, a larger down payment), the weaker the credit can be. So, factoring in the amount of the down payment, it could be possible for a borrower who previously had gone through bankruptcy to be placed in a higher-category subprime mortgage, rather than someone who had been late twice on mortgage payments.

BORROW AGAINST YOUR RETIREMENT PLAN

Q. *Is it true that first-time homebuyers can use monies from their IRA and Keogh plans to make a down payment on a home?*

Yes. As of January 1, 1998, first-time homebuyers (categorized as those who have not owned a home in the previous two years) can withdraw up to $10,000 penalty-free for a down payment and/or closing costs on a home. To be valid, the money must be used to close the home before the 120th day it is withdrawn.

In addition, the borrower could use one or more relatives' IRAs up to the $10,000 maximum.

Buyers who won't be purchasing for a few years are wise to open a Roth IRA. A Roth opened in 1998 will be both penalty-free and tax-free when withdrawing funds as a first-time buyer after five years (2,004).

TAX-FREE GIFTS FROM PARENTS

Q. Is it possible for parents to gift money tax-free to use as a down payment?

Yes. Gifts of up to $10,000 per year, per person can be received without tax consequences. In fact, a couple with two sets of parents respectively could obtain $40,000—ten thousand from each parent! If the couple were to bridge the closing over two calendar years (e.g., closing in January of the new year) the couple could accept $40,000 in December, and another $40,000 in January, for a whopping $80,000 down payment!

Additionally, receiving money from parents can help to whittle down their estate, helping to protect it from the harsh blows of inheritance tax.

TIPS FOR GENERATING EXTRA CASH

Q. What course of action do you suggest for the applicant who finds that he or she does not have enough income and down payment strength to qualify for a loan?

Here are some possible suggestions:

- *Sell an asset,* such as a car, boat, or motorcycle—or have a giant garage sale!
- *Put a lien on an asset.* Borrow against a car, boat, life insurance, stock, certificates of deposit, or other personal property. (Be careful not to create more long-term debt in the process.) The borrower could also create cash by, with permission, putting a lien on a relative's asset. This is best accomplished when the borrower is a co-owner of the asset, such as stocks, bonds, or certificates of deposits.
- *Refinance an asset* such as personal property (either free and clear or with existing debt on it) to free up cash.
- *Receive a gift letter* for the down payment or closing costs from a relative, or perhaps an employer, depending on the type of loan.

- *Barter a service,* use sweat equity as either part of the down payment or closing costs. For example, a roofer may make roof repairs in lieu of using the seller's cash for repairs.
- *Forgo a vacation* and work instead! This could generate extra income. If a bonus is in the borrower's future, now might be a good time to request it. The borrower may even be willing to take a little less for the privilege of receiving the bonus early.
- *Transfer the use of an item.* For example, a buyer could allow a builder to use his or her backhoe in exchange for the builder paying more points on the loan. (This type of transfer would be regulated by the type of loan selected.)
- *Use receivables coming to the buyer.* Notes carried that pay out over time could be assigned to the seller as part of the purchase price.
- *Use a coborrower or cosigner* to help reduce the loan amount for which the borrower needs to qualify.
- *Have the seller or other third party place extra funds with the lender* in a pledged account to add extra collateral to the loan and therefore reduce the lender's risk. This is examined in depth in Chapter 9.

TIPS FOR REDUCING DEBT

Q. ***What could an applicant do to reduce debt in order to qualify for a mortgage?***

The following suggestions might assist the buyer in debt relief:

- *Pay off a debt.* Use cash or another asset to alleviate the debt or sell an asset that has debt against it.
- *Pay down a debt.* Because the secondary market views long-term debt as anything that can't be paid off in ten months, the borrower could pay the debt down below that point. Lenders can choose to be more restrictive on what's considered long-term debt, so check with the lender.
- *Refinance a high-rate loan.*
- *Consolidate your loans.* Doing this may allow the borrower to take several high-rate loans and wrap them into one lower-interest rate loan, and even lower the monthly payments by extending the loan term.

- *Destroy credit cards.* The borrower should ask the lender if and how this might benefit the borrower's ability to qualify.

Before changing a cash or debt position, the borrower should consult the lender to see how what's proposed could help or hurt his or her credit picture.

CHAPTER 3

COMPARISON SHOPPING

Most people spend several months searching for their dream homes and make a very careful—sometimes painstaking—decision. This only makes sense. After all, for most people, the purchase of a home is by far their biggest investment, the lion's share of which is usually the mortgage. Therefore, it also makes sense to be as diligent in shopping for a mortgage. Choosing the right mortgage can save a borrower thousands on a home purchase.

This chapter provides the tools to use in comparing mortgage choices. We start with the broadest of comparisons—might renting be a better option than buying?—and, for those who have the option—is it better to pay cash for the home rather than use mortgage financing?

The mortgage market can be confusing. This chapter will make general comparisons on such issues as points, interest, and lenders. The specifics of loan programs will be discussed later in this book.

RENT OR BUY?

Q. *Before someone considers purchasing a home, shouldn't the individual decide if it's the right economic move for him or her?*

Absolutely. For most people, a home provides not only a physical shelter but also a tax shelter and built-in savings plan. Because mortgage interest and property taxes are tax deductible and equity builds as the real estate appreciates, home ownership usually makes good economic sense.

Some circumstances might make renting a more logical option. For example, if it is likely that the buyer would need to sell the property soon, purchasing might be unwise, because recouping down payment and closing costs is unlikely. Or if the real estate sales market is sluggish with values rapidly declining, renting might be a better bet.

51

Q. *Is there financially a way to calculate whether it makes sense to buy, especially if a buyer would own the house only a short time?*

Yes. Online lending has brought with it rent-versus-buy calculators! One of my favorites can be found at www.homefair.com.

The borrower would supply information about how long the property would be held, the approximate rate of interest charged for a mortgage, borrower's tax bracket, expected appreciation (3 percent is conservative), the monthly amount paid to rent a similar house, and the price of the property considered. The calculator will gauge whether it would pay to purchase at this time using a variety of down payment amounts.

Would-be buyers shouldn't overlook the fact that while the rent versus buy calculations may indicate that purchasing is a sound financial move, when the owner sells he or she will need equity to pay a new set of closing costs and hopefully have enough left over to buy a replacement property.

WHAT'S THE COST OF WAITING TO PURCHASE?

Q. *Besides potentially higher interest rates, are there any other financial impacts to consider if someone waits to buy a home?*

This question is a good one because much of what's lost in waiting to buy can be tallied up in terms of lost appreciation and equity.

Example: Pat Carlisle wants to buy a $100,000 house using a 90 percent loan. If she purchases today at 7.5 percent interest, her monthly payment will be $629.30 per month principal and interest.

If she waits and rates drop one-half percent to 7 percent, would she have won? No. Because based on annual appreciation at even a meager 3 percent, the home Pat wants now costs $103,000, making her 90 percent loan $92,700 and her payments $617.38 principal and interest. She's saved $11.92 per month by waiting to purchase. Or has she?

What about the $3,000 additional cost of the home? Divided by the monthly savings of $11.92, it would take her nearly 21 years to recoup the difference! But that's not all. By waiting to purchase, Pat needed $300 more down payment, and a larger loan could mean more closing costs and would be tougher to qualify for. In addition, the lender's loan underwriting guidelines might have tightened, disqualifying her completely for the loan she needed. And then there's the potential that the type of home she wanted might not be on the market.

We often forget that money is made in real estate with equity buildup and appreciation. These are impacted by length of ownership and compounding. As you can see by Pat's scenario, 3 percent inflation can make a $100,000 home worth $103,000 next year and $106,090 the following year, compounding on and on. And don't forget the tax advantages of ownership.

Pat's lesson is most first-time homebuyers' lesson: All things considered, if you'll stay in the home long enough to recoup your initial down payment and closing costs, waiting to buy may end up costing you money.

PAY CASH OR GET A MORTGAGE?

Q. *Should buyers always take out a loan just to get tax benefits when they purchase a home?*

Certainly not. Buyers must first decide what they want to achieve through home ownership, and then determine what financing options are best for their situations. Following are some of the pros and cons of paying cash versus financing a home.

Benefits of Paying Cash

- *The cash buyer pays no mortgage payments.* This is especially important to some buyers who still have nightmares over the number of homes lost to foreclosure during the Great Depression.
- *The person who buys a property with cash pays no mortgage interest.* Mortgage interest can more than double a property's purchase price if the loan runs full term.
- *The cash buyer doesn't spend money, time, or effort obtaining a loan.* Closing costs are minimized to include minor changes like deed preparation, recording documents, and so on.
- *The buyer who pays in cash doesn't need to obtain the property appraisal* required with most mortgage loans.
- *The cash buyer can take out a loan later,* using the value of the property as collateral.
- *Cash can give the buyer greater purchasing power* in the marketplace, because a cash purchase is free of financing contingencies and finance-related costs.

The Downside of Paying Cash

- *The cash buyer uses precious cash to buy the home,* potentially depleting reserves for other purchases and emergencies. By obtaining a mortgage, the borrower employs the first tenet of real estate leverage: purchase using OPM (other people's money), even if it's the lender's!
- *No mortgage interest* means loss of tax advantages. Also, if consumer loans are needed later to finance other purchases, that interest is not tax deductible like mortgage interest.
- *The cash buyer can't take advantage of tax-deductible closing costs.* With a mortgage, a buyer can finance some fees into the loan to provide greater purchasing leverage. Additionally, discount points paid (even by the seller) are tax deductible for the buyer.
- *The cash buyer who does not obtain an appraisal could be purchasing an overpriced property.* Should the property need to be sold in a short time, it might not bring the full price paid.
- *By taking out a loan later, the buyer becomes both the borrower and the seller* for the purpose of paying costs. These additional fees might include title insurance, discount points, and other closing fees.
- *Mortgages applied for later might be considered refinances* and might not be as liberal as an initial mortgage in interest rates and fees. In addition, this might prohibit the borrower from getting all the cash he or she needs out of the property. The purchaser would also need to anticipate whether he or she could qualify, should a loan be necessary later.

There's nothing to say that a buyer can't find exactly the right financing that gives tax advantages while not being so financially burdensome as to disrupt his or her sleep at night. This will be discussed further in this chapter.

MAKING A FINAL DECISION ON THE LOAN AND THE LENDER

Q. *Before making a final decision on the loan you choose, what should you consider?*

Shopping for a loan is a lot like buying a car—it has to be priced right, comfortable, and be able to last as long as needed! That's why it's increasingly important to shop not only for the actual loan, but for the lender as well.

A good lender will set the stage for a positive win-win loan experience. The loan officer not only will provide all the information the borrower needs to make an informed decision about which loan to choose, but will do everything possible to troubleshoot potential obstacles to bring the transaction to a speedy and successful closing. A lender may provide the information to help the buyer compare loan types, as shown in Figure 3.1.

Some of the best resources for finding the right lender are friends, family members, and coworkers who have recently financed a home. The smart borrower will ask such questions as:

- What lender did you use?
- What kind of loan did you get?
- How long did it take to close? (This might not be the best when evaluating a lender, because other circumstances might delay a closing).
- How have you been treated since the closing? Ask questions about payments, receipt of coupon books, and inquiries about other services.
- Did the lender primarily refinance loans rather than initiate new ones? This could indicate that a new loan might have to wait in the processing line behind large numbers of refinances, which are relatively easier to process. This is particularly impactful during peak refinancing periods when interest rates are low.

As an additional resource, the borrower should ask real estate agents to provide names of lenders they know are reputable. Often this will be based on the types of loans in which lenders specialize, which is great information to have because it can help speed up closing.

Don't overlook the fact that not all lenders make all types of loans. Additionally, a lender may make a certain loan type, but not specialize in it. For example, a lender who does just one or two VA loans a year might not be the best resource for a marginally qualified borrower who needs little-known underwriting leverage to qualify. Borrowers should ask what the percentage of total volume this type of loan constitutes before making a formal application.

Figure 3.1   Financing Options for $105,300

CONVENTIONAL LOAN, 30-YEAR TERM—5 percent down payment

Monthly Payment

P and I	$	657
Property taxes		58
Hazard insurance		50
HO dues/condo fees		
Mortgage insurance		64
Total monthly payment	$	830

Cash Requirements

Down payment	$	5,265
Closing costs		1,946
Prepaids		1,510
Total cash to close		8,721
Cash reserves		1,659
Loan amount		100,035
Financed fees		0
Total Loan Amount		$100,035
Loan to value		95.00%

Note Rate	6.875%	Origination/Discount	1.00%
APR	7.9377%		

CONVENTIONAL LOAN, 30-YEAR TERM—20 percent down payment

Monthly Payment

P and I	$	554
Property taxes		58
Hazard insurance		50
HO dues/condo fees		0
Mortgage insurance		0
Total monthly payment	$	662

Cash Requirements

Down payment	$	21,060
Closing costs		1,738
Prepaids		1,293
Total cash to close		24,091
Cash reserves		1,323
Loan amount		84,240
Financed fees		0
Total Loan Amount		$ 84,240
Loan to value		80.00%

Note Rate	6.875%	Origination/Discount	1.00%
APR	6.9864%		

Figure 3.1   Financing Options for $105,300 (Continued)

FHA LOAN, 30-YEAR TERM

Monthly Payment

P and I	$	693
Property taxes		58
Hazard insurance		50
HO dues/condo fees		0
Mortgage insurance		42
Total monthly payment	$	844

Cash Requirements

Down payment	$	3,388
Closing costs		1,751
Prepaids		1,501
Total cash to close		6,640
Cash reserves		0
Loan amount		101,913
Financed fees		2,293
Total Loan Amount		$104,206
Loan to value		96.78%

Note Rate	7.00%	Origination/Discount	1.00%
APR	7.8296%		

VA LOAN, 30-YEAR TERM

Monthly Payment

P and I	$	715
Property taxes		58
Hazard insurance		50
HO dues/condo fees		0
Mortgage insurance		0
Total monthly payment	$	823

Cash Requirements

Down payment		0
Closing costs		1,739
Prepaids		1,435
Total cash to close		3,174
Cash reserves		0
Loan amount		105,300
Financed fees		2,105
Total Loan Amount		$107,405
Loan to value		100.00%

Note Rate	7.00%	Origination/Discount	1.00%
APR	7.3017%		

These figures are deemed reliable but not guaranteed. This is being provided for informational purposes only and is not a loan commitment.

Reprinted by permission of Shelly Mulberry, Wallick and Volk, P.O. Box 685, 222 E. Eighteenth Street, Cheyenne, WY 82001, 307-771-8364.

Q. *What's the difference between using a mortgage broker and a mortgage banker or other type of lending institution?*

Mortgage brokers, as their name denotes, "broker" mortgages. They locate borrowers who need mortgage money and place them with investors who want to make loans. The mortgage broker receives a fee for making a successful match.

Unlike some other types of lenders, mortgage brokers do not work with their own cash—they merely place borrowers with lenders.

One plus in working with a mortgage broker is that they have access to a variety of investors and a myriad of loan types. They can help marginal borrowers locate financing with investors willing to take more risk.

There's one caution in working with mortgage brokers. They could be receiving additional fees outside of closing (termed "POC"—paid outside of closing) that are not in the borrower's best interest. For example, the broker has the borrower sign a disclosure saying that she endeavors to find the borrower the most cost-effective loan that suits his needs. The borrower also agrees to pay the broker 3 percent of the loan amount as compensation. However, because this particular broker (lacking in ethics) knows additional fees are available (POC) from the mortgage company if she places the borrower at a higher interest rate mortgage than the one he qualified for, the borrower ends up paying more for the loan.

The solution? Look for the words "Premium Yield Adjustment/POC" on your loan settlement statement. That's a trigger that there's more to the story where fees are involved.

Mortgage bankers, on the other hand, not only originate loans but also close the loan using their funds. They make their profit by charging fees and points and also by selling the loan in the secondary market.

Mortgage bankers also profit by servicing loans or selling the servicing rights on loans they originate. Servicing is the process of receiving monthly loan payments and collecting and accounting for the taxes and insurance on mortgages. Many large mortgage banker companies today have separate loan servicing divisions that contribute greatly to corporate profit.

Q. *Can the builder of a home force a borrower to apply for a loan with a certain mortgage?*

No. This is restraint of trade and is illegal. While it's not a bad idea to consider a lender the builder knows and does a high volume of business with because the loan might get special attention, that lender should not be the borrower's sole option.

QUESTIONS TO ASK BEFORE CHOOSING A LOAN

Q. *Once the lender has received information about the borrower and has discussed possible financing programs, what general loan questions should the borrower ask the lender before choosing the best loan?*

The following are some questions a borrower might ask to clarify his or her loan choice:

- *Is the loan assumable?* Many originated today are not, so this might be a bonus, especially if the interest rate is low and you plan to sell in a short time. If it is assumable, under what circumstances, and would the interest rate change? How would that be determined?
- *Can the buyer pay taxes and insurance outside of the loan payments?* This is determined by the type of loan and lender requirements, but is great for the borrower's cash flow!
- *Is there a prepayment penalty on the loan?* In a return to the marketplace, many lenders are using this as a way to recoup profits should a borrower want to refinance or need to sell. The tradeoff for the borrower is a lower-than-market interest rate. If you anticipate refinancing in the short term, you'll want to avoid a loan with a prepayment penalty.
- *Can prepayments be made on the principal?* If so, is there any minimum payment? Some mortgages can only be prepaid in minimums of $100.

INTEREST RATES, LOAN TERMS, AND DOWN PAYMENTS

Q. *Is the interest rate the major consideration when shopping for a loan?*

While one of the first options consumers consider in making an affordable home purchase (and erroneously, often where they stop shopping), the interest rate is certainly not the only factor in mortgage financing. The following is a quick checklist of questions the borrower should ask, followed by an explanation of each.

☐ What are the borrower's financing goals? The borrower should estimate the time he or she will own the property. Short-term owners could use an adjustable rate mortgage (ARM) for short-term savings; elect for a higher interest rate with fewer discount points, which would not be recouped if the property were sold in a short time; or use a loan containing a balloon provision.

Long-term owners could use a 15- or 10-year fixed-rate loan to build equity quickly and sidestep interest over the life of the loan; pay higher points to reduce the interest rate; or use a permanent buydown to reduce the interest rate for the life of the loan.

☐ If and when the borrower does sell, how important will it be to get all equity out immediately? If this is important, the borrower may wish to choose a loan that is assumable and would be market competitive when assumed.

☐ Will anyone else be participating as a co-borrower or cosigner on the loan? The answer to this question may dictate the type of loan available to the borrower, as not all loans allow multiple borrowers.

☐ How much savings does the borrower wish to use as a down payment? Is that including, or in addition to, the closing costs? This can help determine the size and type of loan.

☐ How much of a monthly payment is the borrower prepared to make? The answer to this question should be based not only on what the borrower can afford, but also on the size of the monthly payment he or she is mentally prepared to make.

☐ What are the borrower's current mortgage or rent payments? A lender may hesitate to approve a loan with radically larger payments than a consumer is accustomed to paying without showing a substantial income increase. A severe payment difference may increase financial pressure on the borrower, perhaps enough to cause the loan to default.

☐ Would the borrower mind if the payment amount fluctuated? If so, it's probably not wise to take on an ARM or similar interest-sensitive loan.

15-Year versus 30-Year Loans

Q. *How does one choose between a 15-year and a 30-year loan?*

Many factors go into deciding which loan term best suits a buyer's needs and qualifying abilities. If a borrower qualifies for a 15-year loan, the savings in interest payments is substantial. The monthly principal and interest payment on a 15-year, $100,000 loan at 7 percent is $899, compared to $665 on a 30-year term. Payments on the 15-year loan would total $161,820. The 30-year loan would cost a whopping $239,400— $77,580 more!

Q. *Are there other financial benefits to using a 15-year versus a 30-year loan?*

Interest rates may be lower on the 15-year loan, depending on the lender and the loan program. Because equity builds faster on a 15-year loan, a low down payment may be less of a problem if the borrower has to resell in a short period of time.

Q. *If a 15-year mortgage makes such good financial sense, why doesn't everyone get one?*

First, not everyone can qualify for a 15-year loan. Because of the shorter amortization time, the monthly payment is larger. Going back to the earlier example comparing costs for the 15- versus 30-year loan: To qualify for a 30-year loan's $805 payment, the borrower would have to have $2,875 income per month to meet a lender's 28 percent housing ratio requirements. To qualify for the 15-year loan's $1,015 payment, however, the borrower would need $3,625 income per month, or $750 more than needed for the 30-year loan.

Second, some borrowers enjoy the peace of mind that comes with a lower monthly payment, enjoying the cushion were they to fall on tough financial times. In fact, approximately 80 percent of all loans made are 30-year loans. Borrowers could make prepayments on the 30-year loan to retire it early, if the loan program allowed, but with the 15-year loan they'd be saddled permanently with the higher payment.

The exception to this school of thought is found in homeowners who are refinancing their existing loans. A much larger percentage of those individuals are using 15-year loans, and in some cases, 10-year loans, to reduce their purchasing costs.

Remember that a borrower who is making a higher monthly payment will not have that money available for other investments. This could mean lost financial opportunities.

And finally, not everyone can access a 15-year loan on every mortgage available. Availability can vary based on the lender and the program.

Lenders are usually more than happy to project costs to help buyers decide which loan term best suits their needs and means. Total borrowing costs for different loan terms can be compared by using the chart in Figure 3.2.

Figure 3.2   Comparing Interest Costs by Loan Term

The following table illustrates a $100,000 mortgage at 8½ percent interest as paid to maturity under five different loan terms. Although the payment difference between 30- and 15-year loans is $216, the interest saved over the term of the loan is $99,556!

Terms	Monthly Payment	Months Paid	Total Cost	Interest Cost
30-year	$1,769	360	$276,809	$176,809
20-year	$1,868	240	$208,278	$108,278
15-year	$1,985	180	$177,253	$ 77,253
10-year	$1,240	120	$148,783	$ 48,783

Pros and Cons of Small versus Large Down Payments

Q. *How does a borrower weigh the advantages of making a small versus a large down payment, other than what the lender might require on a certain loan?*

As discussed earlier, it may not be in the short-term buyer's best interest to invest lots of money in the property. Too small of a down payment, however, coupled with low property appreciation, may create a deficit if the owner needs to sell in a very short period of time. If the borrower knows this and is willing to take the risk, he or she should be prepared to make up the shortfall when he or she sells.

A second consideration is that the borrower may want to make a large down payment if it means securing a lower interest rate or sidestepping the costs of fees or PMI. This will be discussed in depth in Chapter 4. A large down payment may even loosen some loan underwriting requirements because the lender's risk is reduced.

DETERMINING LOAN COSTS

Q. *How does the borrower determine which loan program is most cost effective, especially where loan costs and fees are involved?*

Unlike comparing interest rate differences that are fairly obvious and straightforward, comparing loan costs and fees can get complicated. This is because it's not just the loan costs that are being compared, but also the loan program terms.

Fixed Rate versus Adjustable Rate

The lender offers a 90 percent conventional, fixed-rate loan at 8 percent interest that will have total closing costs of $2,500. Costs for a 90 percent ARM at 6 percent interest, however, are $2,900; the loan also can be converted to a fixed-rate loan at any time during the first five years of the loan.

At first glance, it's virtually impossible to tell which is the better buy. The borrower needs to compare financially the two loan programs based on (1) how long he or she anticipates keeping the loan, (2) what the conversion fees might be, and (3) how the rate would adjust if the loan were converted to a fixed rate.

Lenders will prepare comparisons such as these if provided with the necessary information to plug into the scenario. This is the best way for borrowers to make sure they are not being led astray based only on bargain interest rates and low closing costs. A loan comparison worksheet is shown in Figure 3.3.

NO CLOSING COST LOANS

Q. *What are no closing cost loans?*

No closing cost loans, available from lenders for new financing or refinancing, are loans in which the lender pays all closing costs. These nonrecurring closing costs (like title and escrow fees, appraisal, and lender's fees) are one-time fees paid when obtaining the loan, and do not include recurring costs (like interest, property taxes, and insurance) paid in your monthly payment.

Q. *Why would a lender agree to pay a borrower's closing costs?*

As with most financing approaches, there are trade-offs (and benefits to the lender). For example, the lender might offer you a 6.75 percent loan with one-half discount point, a 7 percent loan with zero points, or a 7.25 percent mortgage with no closing costs all for a 30-year fixed-rate mortgage. Your choice could be based on (1) what you can qualify for, (2) what you're trying to achieve financially (i.e., short vs. long-term ownership), (3) the amount of funds you have for closing, and (4) what you're comfortable with paying.

No closing cost loans are good when you're tight on funds for closing or will hold the loan or the property only a short time and don't want to

Figure 3.3 Loan Comparison Worksheet

| | Loan Type | | |
	Conventional	FHA	VA
Sales Price .... $_____		_____	_____ _____
Interest Rate .... $_____		_____	_____ _____
Down Payment .... $_____		_____	_____ _____
Total Loan To Be Amortized .... $_____		_____	_____ _____

Estimated Loan Costs

MIP (Unless FHA Included Above) .... $_____		_____	_____ _____
Loan Origination Fee .... $_____		_____	_____ _____
Assumption Fee .... $_____		_____	_____ _____
Credit Report.. $_____		_____	_____ _____
Appraisal Fee .... $_____		_____	_____ _____
Recording Fee .... $_____		_____	_____ _____
Title (ALTA) Policy (Use Loan Amount) .... $_____		_____	_____ _____
Attorney Fee .... $_____		_____	_____ _____
Escrow Closing Fee .... $_____		_____	_____ _____
Interest Proration .... $_____		_____	_____ _____
Tax Proration .... $_____		_____	_____ _____
Fire and Hazard Insurance 1st year .... $_____		_____	_____ _____
Lender's Application Fee .... $_____		_____	_____ _____
Purchaser's Buydown Points................................ $_____		_____	_____ _____
Long-Term Escrow Set-Up Fee .... $_____		_____	_____ _____
Tax Service Fee .... $_____		_____	_____ _____
Misc., LID, City Code, Reserves......................... $_____		_____	_____ _____
Home Inspection Fee .... $_____		_____	_____ _____
Total Estimated Closing Costs .... $_____		_____	_____ _____

Reserves and Prorates

Property Taxes (Minimum 2 Months) .... $_____		_____	_____ _____
Fire and Hazard Insurance (Minimum 2 Months)$_____		_____	_____ _____
Mortgage Insurance .... $_____		_____	_____ _____
Total Reserves and Prorates .... $_____		_____	_____ _____
Total Cash Outlay... $_____		_____	_____ _____

Estimated Monthly Payment

Principal and Interest... $_____		_____	_____ _____
Tax Reserves .... $_____		_____	_____ _____
Insurance Reserves .... $_____		_____	_____ _____
MIP Insurance (Unless FHA Included Above) ... $_____		_____	_____ _____
Total Estimated Monthly Payment .... $_____		_____	_____ _____

The undersigned hereby acknowledges receipt of a copy of this estimation.

By _____ Signed _____ Date _____

part with closing money you can't recoup. You might also select a no closing cost loan if you want to move quickly to obtain a loan (e.g., when interest rates are falling.) They're especially attractive when refinancing into a lower interest rate. Because there are no upfront costs, your savings are immediate.

If you're a real risk taker, you might consider refinancing your adjustable-rate mortgage every year with a no closing cost loan—keeping your initial teaser (discounted) rate intact! Rates for this type of loan are often 2 percent or more below 30-year fixed-rate mortgages.

CATEGORIES OF CLOSING COSTS

Q. *What are the major categories of loan-related costs?*

Loan-related costs vary depending on the type and size of loan. The following are some general loan-related cost categories that pertain to most buyers:

- *Down payment* (minus any earnest money deposit)
- *Out-of-pocket costs:* fees for appraisal, credit report paid, and any loan application fee at the time of loan application, plus other costs such as home inspection, paid at time of loan application and paid at the time of closing
- *Title insurance:* a one-time fee that varies among states and with the size of the loan
- *Two months' escrow:* two months' impound of property tax, homeowner's insurance, and PMI, if the loan so requires
- *Private mortgage insurance initial premium:* (if not financed into the loan)
- *First year's homeowner's insurance:* a paid receipt showing payment or funds advanced to the lender to pay directly to the insurance company
- *Discount points,* if applicable
- *Prorated loan interest:* interest paid by the day for the closing month, to a maximum of 30 days
- *Two months' cash reserves:* an equivalent of two months of mortgage payments left over in cash as financial padding (required on conventional loans; not given to the lender, just verified to be on hand; can be in savings, a 401(k), IRA, etc. On some home affordability mortgages, this could be reduced to one month of reserves.)

Fees to Negotiate

Q. *What loan fees can be negotiated with the lender?*

As with many things in this world, closing costs and discount points can be negotiated. But it's tougher for the borrower to obtain large concessions unless there are trade-offs with the lender.

For example, the lender may be much more willing to reduce closing fees or require fewer discount points if the borrower is well qualified and is making a substantial down payment. In addition, if a higher interest rate is being charged, it could bring other concessions from the lender.

The lender may be willing to entice a borrower by offering low fees when the company is seeking a larger business market share or introducing a new program. In addition, a lender may give incentives to faithful past customers, or to encourage a new borrower who may bring additional business to the lender.

Low fees, however, can be smoke and mirrors obscuring an overall higher interest rate or other lender benefit. As in the previous question, asking the lender to compare different financing options is the best approach in determining the true cost of borrowing. This can be done in a matter of minutes, using the lender's computer or financial calculator.

Q. *What types of loan costs generally vary widely from lender to lender?*

Fees are as different as the lenders who charge them. The major differences can be found in the following three major categories:

1. *Loan origination fees.* Many companies don't charge this fee, but some do. It's usually considered another point (1 percent of the loan amount) and can make a seemingly great loan package a bad choice. If charged, this is also a fee that may not be explained thoroughly up front.
2. *Separate application fees.* Most companies include the application fee in the out-of-pocket expense quote; others have this as a separate fee (of several hundred dollars), which many not be explained until the borrower applies for the loan. Borrowers should ask about this when calling to check for rates and costs as the amount can vary significantly among lenders.
3. *Miscellaneous fees* (often called "fluff fees" or "garbage fees"). As their name denotes, these are the most extraneous and negotiable of the bunch! They include document prep fees, courier charges, notary fees, administrative fees, document review fees, etc. The

gravest problem here lies in that these fees do not have to be factored into calculating the Annual Percentage Rate (APR) quoted to the borrower. So it's totally possible that a lender quoting a low interest rate is actually making up for it by charging tons of garbage fees! Spend time reviewing the Good Faith estimate provided to you by the lender before committing to a certain loan program.

DISCOUNT POINTS

Q. *What are discount points and how are they used?*

One point is equal to 1 percent of the loan amount. Points are used to increase the lender's financial yield on the loan. For example, if the lender has the choice between making a loan at 8 percent and one at 8.5 percent interest, it's pretty obvious which one he or she would choose.

Points bridge the gap between interest rates, allowing the lender to make the loan at a lower interest rate. While the value of points can vary, depending on financial markets, most lenders consider that it takes roughly four to six points to lower the interest rate by 1 percent. This can be illustrated through the following example:

> Example: If a lender quotes that it will take two points (2 percent) to lower a 7 percent interest rate to 6.5 percent on an $80,000 loan, that's $80,000 × 2 percent, or $1,600 payable in cash at closing to bridge the financial gap in interest by one-half percent.

Most loan types allow the seller and buyer to negotiate payment of points in the purchase agreement. See chapters on specific loan types for further clarification.

Determining How Many Points to Pay

Q. *If the lender gives the borrower the option of how many points to pay for a certain rate of interest, what's the best way to decide?*

The prime factor to consider is the time the borrower will own the property and keep the loan. The following is a formula to help determine the "dollars and sense": Calculate the difference in the monthly payment amounts and the difference in the cost of the points. Divide the amount paid in points by the amount saved by the lower monthly payment to obtain a "break-even" mark for holding the property. Here is an example.

Mr. Fredericks is getting a $90,000 mortgage for thirty years. The lender tells him that there are two choices: He can pay 7.5 percent interest with zero points for a payment of $629.30 per month, or obtain a 7 percent loan with two points for a payment of $598.78 per month.

The mortgage payment difference is $30.52. The difference in points is $1,800. So to calculate the break-even point he would take the expense ($1,800) and divide it by the monthly payment savings ($30.52). We find that it would take Mr. Fredericks nearly 57 months to break even. Obviously, if he won't keep the house or the loan that long, it doesn't make financial sense to pay the extra points to obtain the lower interest rate.

Keep in mind that this example is a relatively simplistic analysis, and doesn't take into consideration time-value of money (including the lost financial opportunity of not investing the money), tax ramifications, or the long-term savings of the lower interest rate.

Q. *Can a borrower negotiate points with a lender?*

Possibly. Lenders determine points primarily based on the price they have to pay for funds, the type of loan involved, and other lender competition in the marketplace. If the lender does decide to charge fewer points, one or more of the following offsetting factors could be in the picture:

- *Is the borrower willing to pay a premium rate of interest?* Remember, points bridge the gap in the lender's financial yield on the loan, so this shortfall may need to be recouped somewhere.
- *How strong is the borrower?* If the lender could risk losing the applicant by not being competitive enough on the points, there may be a concession.

Remember, points are merely one piece of the borrowing puzzle. No amount of discount point concessions is worth dealing with a slow loan processor or unscrupulous lender.

Q. *Are points tax deductible on mortgage loans?*

For the purpose of acquiring residential real estate, discount points are tax deductible in the year paid. The IRS specifies that in order for points to be deducted, they must not exceed points generally charged in the area.

In March of 1994, the IRS surprised everyone when it changed its policy to reflect who could deduct points on mortgages (retroactive to January 1, 1991). The ruling allows buyers to deduct points on mortgages— even if paid by sellers. Previously, points were deductible only if the buyer paid them at closing.

The change comes after the IRS decided that the buyer really pays the points, even if the seller helps share the expense. The rationale was that the seller typically increases the sales price to include the points.

Points paid in refinancing are handled differently. Owners who refinance must deduct points over the life of the loan, not all at once.

For example, if a borrower paid $3,600 worth of points when refinancing to obtain a 30-year loan with a lower interest rate, he or she could deduct only $10 for each of the next 360 months, or $120 per year. For this reason it may help to minimize points paid to refinance a loan.

USING BUYDOWNS

Q. *How does someone buy down an interest rate?*

Buydowns are prepaid interest used to reduce the interest rate on a loan temporarily or permanently. The buyer or other party pays this money at closing, allowing him or her to qualify at the lower interest rate and reduce the monthly payment.

Buydowns can bring the interest rate down for a short period (called a temporary buydown), or permanently lower the interest rate for the life of the loan. One of the more familiar approaches is the 3-2-1 buydown, where the interest rate is 3 percent lower than the note rate of the loan for the first year, 2 percent lower during the second year of the loan, and 1 percent lower during the third year of the loan, after which it stays at the note rate—the interest the borrower agreed to pay—for the life of the loan.

Q. *If buydowns are used, does the borrower qualify at the buydown rate?*

Because this varies among programs, please refer to individual loan types in the chapters that follow.

DETERMINING LOCK-INS

Q. *When would it make sense for the borrower to lock in the interest rate?*

With fluctuating interest rates, this has turned out to be the real estate $64,000 question. Locking in an interest rate means that if interest rates rise during a specific time frame (usually 45 to 60 days), the rate quoted will remain the same. Again, this depends on a variety of factors. The following are answers to the basic questions one might ask to decide whether it is advantageous to lock in an interest rate:

- *If the borrower doesn't lock in and the rate increases, could he or she still qualify for the loan?* Logic dictates that if a bump in the rate will disqualify the borrower, locking in is not only prudent, it's advised!
- *How long is the lock-in and how far away is the closing?* A 45-day lock will be useless if closing is projected for 60 days.
- *Is there a fee for locking in?* When is it paid? Is it refundable? This often applies to fees for extended rate lock-ins that extend an interest rate guarantee to 60, 80, or 110 days. It's therefore wise for the borrower to know what's being paid, when it's paid, and under what circumstances, if any, it can be refunded.
- *If rates drop, would the rate-lock float downward?* Many lenders use this provision in order to stay competitive when interest rates drop. During times of falling interest rates, loan shoppers should make sure they have this float-down provision.
- *How long will the borrower keep the loan?* Should he or she pay more points up front to get the lower interest rate, or less points and go with a higher interest rate? (Isn't it amazing how many decisions are based on how long someone will keep the loan and the property?) Again, the standard answer: Short-term ownership favors less points paid at closing and higher interest rates. Long-term ownership favors more points paid at closing to receive lower interest rates.

The borrower can check several sources before deciding to lock in the interest rate:

- *What have been the lender's interest rate trends on that particular type of loan and what is projected?*

- *Check financial indicators:* the federal discount rate—the rate at which banks borrow money from the Federal Reserve; actions of the Federal Reserve Board (which tightens or loosens monies in circulation); and especially the ten-year treasury note market, which has a big impact on determining short-term interest rates. These can be monitored through local papers such as the in-depth coverage in *The Wall Street Journal,* found online at www.wsj.com. Also check online resources such as www.interest.com and www.hsh.com.
- *Remember the role international events play in interest rates.* As the U.S. shifts to a global economy, international crises play an even bigger part in the volatility of U.S. interest rates. In fact, many lenders advise that if negative world news is brewing, it probably makes sense to lock in the rate.

CHAPTER 4

CONVENTIONAL LOANS

This chapter explains single-family conventional loan programs. Information is from lenders' programs in many states with a variety of economic climates and real estate markets, and from current secondary market guidelines. Check with individual area lenders to apply information in this chapter to loan programs currently available.

A *conventional loan* is any mortgage that is neither insured nor guaranteed by the government. It stands to reason, then, that conventional loans were the first traditional loans made by local lenders. Loans were held in the lender's investment portfolio until they were paid in full or, heaven forbid, foreclosed upon. While this enabled the borrower to build a business rapport with the lender, it was usually not in the lender's best financial interests. When rates fluctuated, particularly upward, the lender received below-market interest on the loan, while not being able to recycle the funds to lend other borrowers.

It's fair to say that the advent of the secondary market in the late 1930s was most welcome! Now lenders could sell their loan packages to the secondary market, recycling lent funds (for a slight discount off the loans' interest), bringing funds back home to create new loans.

Today, although some lenders still keep loans in portfolio, most sell their loans to the secondary market.

In this chapter, we'll investigate the advantages and disadvantages of conventional lending and uncover little-known facts regarding underwriting that can help the borrower get the loan.

PROS AND CONS

Q. *What are the advantages to the borrower of a conventional loan?*

The advantages are:

- The interest rate is set for the life of the loan. This prevents escalating interest and payments.
- Lenders may be willing to keep the loan in their own lending portfolio, thus allowing more underwriting flexibility.
- Lenders may negotiate or eliminate certain loan fees.
- Lenders may allow comortgagors.
- A lender may allow collateral other than or in addition to the real property being mortgaged.
- A lender may be willing to finance personal property with the real estate loan; e.g., appliances and/or furniture. Such "package loans" may be made when a newly constructed property is sold furnished by the builder.
- Appraisals need to meet only the lender's guidelines (if the loan is held in portfolio) or the secondary market's (if applicable), instead of the strict appraisal standards of FHA and VA.
- If PMI is required, its premiums are usually less expensive than with ARM programs or FHA mortgage insurance.
- For a borrower who may have difficulty obtaining PMI, the lender may self-insure the loan, increasing the interest rate to compensate for any potential loss.
- The lender can fund a portion of the closing costs in exchange for a higher interest rate. (We'll cover "premium pricing" later in this chapter.)

Home affordability programs allow buyers to purchase with as little as 3 percent down. Under some programs, the down payment can be borrowed on the buyer's credit card!

Q. *What are the disadvantages to the borrower of the conventional fixed-rate loan?*

The disadvantages are:

- The interest rate is set for the life of the loan. If interest rates fall, the purchaser's rate does not.
- Interest rates are set by each lender and can exceed those of FHA and VA.

- Origination fees and other loan costs are determined by each lender and can therefore be higher than similar programs.
- Because mortgage documents for fixed-rate loans can vary depending on state and lender, a lender could specify certain clauses to be included in a mortgage document. These include the alienation (or due-on-sale) clause, prepayment penalty, and acceleration clause.
- Most loans with greater than an 80 percent loan-to-value ratio will require the borrower to purchase PMI.
- Conventional loans may require larger down payments than those of government programs.
- Some lenders may require nonrefundable application and processing fees at the time of loan application.
- Lenders may not allow some creative financing options for the buyer.

Q. *Who makes the rules regarding what a lender can and can't do in conventional mortgage lending?*

It depends. A lender who wants to sell loans into the secondary mortgage market has one set of rules. If those borrowers require PMI, there's another set of rules. In addition, local lenders' boards of directors might be more restrictive still.

Because a majority of all conventional loans are sold to the secondary market, those guidelines often apply and become the benchmark for conventional mortgages.

PROFILE OF A CONVENTIONAL-LOAN BORROWER

Q. *Is there a standard profile of a borrower who could best benefit by using a conventional fixed-rate loan?*

In general, conventional-loan buyers

- have at least a 3 to 5 percent down payment, or are making the purchase with a gift of 20 percent or more from a third party.
- have money for closing costs, and reserves.
- have good to excellent credit.
- can qualify for loans using standard ratios and market-rate interest.
- don't usually need a lot of special loan underwriting considerations.

- desire a fixed-rate mortgage (for financial or emotional stability).
- have fairly light debts in proportion to their income.
- might ask the lender to keep the loan in portfolio (particularly if they have been a long-time customer, or are using a large down payment).
- can wait the standard 30 to 45 days it takes to close the loan.
- may have jobs where income increases are either rare or nonexistent.
- have room in their qualifying and loan payments for PMI insurance.

If this profile fits you, maybe there's a conventional loan in your future!

SECONDARY MARKET GUIDELINES

Q. *If a borrower's loan was sold to FNMA or FHLMC in the secondary market, what kind of qualifying ratios would be required?*

FNMA and FHLMC Loan Underwriting Guidelines for Fixed-Rate Loans

Qualifying ratios are based on the type of loan program and its underwriting guidelines.

Qualifying ratios. For owner-occupied, single-family residences (excluding Affordable Housing programs), and for second home and investor loans, PITI can't exceed 28 percent of the borrower's gross monthly income; and PITI plus long-term debt (any debt that extends ten months or more) can't exceed 36 percent of the borrower's gross monthly income. This ratio is expressed as a 28 percent housing ratio/36 percent total long-term debt ratio.

Loan-to-value ratios. The maximum loan-to-value ratio is 95 percent on single-family residences (excluding Affordable Housing programs), 80 percent on second homes, and 70 percent on investor loans (FNMA is fixed-rate only; FHLMC negotiates investor loans on a case-by-case basis.)

Affordable Housing Programs

Qualifying ratios   FNMA Affordable Housing programs

Fannie Mae Community Homebuyer Program:
    33 percent housing ratio; 38 percent total long-term debt ratio
97 percent loans: 25-year mortgage:
    33 percent housing ratio; 36 percent total long-term debt ratio;
97 percent loans: 30-year mortgage:
    28 percent housing ratio; 36 percent total long-term debt ratio
Start-Up Mortgage^{SM}:
    33 percent housing ratio; 36 percent total long-term debt ratio
Loan-to-value ratios for FNMA Affordable Housing programs:
    97 percent for all except a Start-Up Mortgage^{SM} which is 95
    percent

Qualifying ratios   FHLMC Affordable Housing programs (including Freddie Mac Affordable Gold 5, Affordable Gold 3/2, and Affordable Gold 97)

No maximum monthly housing expense to income ratio.
Debt to income ratio is 40 percent; higher with compensating factors.

Loan-to-value ratios for all FHLMC Affordable Housing programs: 97 percent
On owner-occupied and second-home purchases with subordinate financing (a second mortgage), the first mortgage cannot represent more than 75 percent of the lesser of the sales price or appraised value. This requirement also applies to owner-occupied refinances.
Maximum loan-to-value ratio based on size of primary residence is:

Number of Units	Loan-to-Value Ratio
1	95 percent
2	90 percent
3	85 percent
4	80 percent

A qualifying sheet for conventional loans to help assist in calculating loan payments is at Figure 4.1.
Adjustable-rate mortgage qualifying ratios are shown in Chapter 6.

Figure 4.1   Conventional Loan Qualification Form

Sales Price   (1)_____
   Less Loan Amount (2)_____ Equals Required Down Payment $_____

Estimated Closing Costs *Plus* Estimated Prepaid Escrow   +_____
   Total Closing Cost $_____
Less Cash on Deposit   −_____
Required Cash To Close $_____

   (2) _____ Divided by (1) _____ Equals LTV _____%

Gross Income (Mortgagor)_____ and (Comortgagor)_____ = $_____ (A)

Proposed Housing Expense

      Principal and Interest $_____

      Other Financing   _____

      Hazard Insurance   _____

      Taxes   _____

      Mortgage Insurance   _____

      Homeowner Association Fees   _____

      Other:_____   _____

Total Housing Payment   _____ (B)

Total Obligations (Beyond Ten Months)   _____ (C)

Total Housing Payment (B), *Plus* Monthly Obligations (C) = _____ (D)

   (B) _____ Divided by (A) _____ = _____ %   Housing Ratio

   (D) _____ Divided by (A) _____ = _____ %   Total Debt Ratio

Guidelines for Condominiums and Townhouse Purchases

Q. *What about loans for condominiums and townhouses? Are they under-written the same way as detached housing?*

Lenders will generally lend up to 95 percent loan-to-value ratio for fixed-rate loans on owner-occupied condos and townhouses, but only up to 90 percent when an adjustable rate is used. Condos and townhouses as second-home purchases usually require a 20 percent down payment.

There are no specified minimum square footage restrictions in the secondary market because lending is based solely on the unit's marketability. The development project must be FNMA or FHLMC accepted or have lender warranties. In addition, the project cannot have heavier investor concentration (nonowner-occupied units) than a certain percentage of the total—usually approximately 40 percent for established projects and 30 percent for new developments.

What Counts as Long-Term Debt?

Q. *You mentioned that the secondary market considers long-term debt to be any debt that can't be paid off in ten months. Could the lender choose to be more restrictive?*

Yes, if the lender found the borrower marginally qualified or determined that payments were a substantial percentage of gross income and could affect the repayment of the loan. An example would be a marginally qualified buyer, making a small down payment, who has a $450 car payment with five payments remaining.

The lender could also choose to be more restrictive if defaults in the area are high. A cautious lender could allocate a minimum payment of 5 percent of the outstanding balance, or a minimum of $10 per month, to revolving debts for the purpose of calculating long-term debt. Short-term obligations or others that don't have set monthly payments may be considered to have at least the interest due monthly.

Contributions Help the Buyer Qualify

Q. *What contributions does the secondary market allow the seller to make?*

A contribution, also called a financing concession, is the payment of a cost that is typically paid by the buyer, but instead is paid by the seller or a third party.

Such items can include transfer taxes, cost of title insurance policies and surveys, recording fees, tax stamps, attorneys' fees and any seller-paid buy down or seller-paid financing costs.

Seller contributions that can be made over and above the following limits are those that occurred when market interest rates shifted and the seller used points to buy down the interest rate. Lender-paid buydowns and lender-funded transaction costs do not have to be counted against what the seller can contribute to the buyer.

If contributions exceed the following limits, any excess will be subtracted from the sales price before the loan amount is calculated:

Maximum Contributions for Owner-Occupied Property
3 percent of the property value on a 95 percent loan
6 percent of the property value on a 90 percent loan

Secondary Market Maximum Second-Home Contribution Limits
6 percent of property value on an 80 percent loan

Because the Government National Mortgage Association (GNMA) deals with government-insured and guaranteed loans, we'll cover these underwriting guidelines in Chapters 7 and 8.

Guidelines for the Property

Q. *We've talked so far about borrower qualifications. What are the standard property guidelines for the secondary market?*

Although properties are approved on a case-by-case basis, properties must generally meet the following guidelines:

- The property should be in an area with properties of comparable value and quality.
- Streets must be dedicated and properly maintained.
- Land value cannot be excessive compared to the improvements on the property.

An estimate of value from an appraiser is used to substantiate all loans sold to the secondary market.

PREMIUM PRICING: LENDER CONTRIBUTIONS

Q. *A lender can contribute to the buyer's closing costs and that contribution can be in addition to what the seller contributes. Do lenders do this very much?*

When the lender contributes to payment of the buyer's costs, it's called *premium pricing.* That is a subtle indication that it's not really a gift! The borrower pays less out of pocket to purchase the property, but the lender usually recoups any contributions by charging a higher interest rate on the loan.

For example, the Batemans find themselves $500 short on closing costs for their home purchase. If the lender picks up the $500 shortfall, it adds a premium (e.g., an additional one-eighth percent to the interest rate) to recoup the contribution.

The good news? Premium pricing helps cash-poor buyers purchase a home. The bad news? Calculated over the life of the loan, that $500 expands into thousands of dollars in additional interest! Premium pricing makes sense if (1) It's the only way a buyer can qualify for a loan and is initially willing to pay more to do so; and/or (2) The buyer will keep the loan for only a short time.

Q. *Where can buyers find lenders open to premium pricing?*

Almost anywhere, especially when lenders want to expand their existing market shares or if one is "the new lender on the block" wanting to garner market attention.

USING COMPENSATING FACTORS WHEN RATIOS DON'T FIT

Q. *If a borrower's ratios exceed the standard guidelines, could he or she ever qualify for a loan?*

Possibly. While secondary market qualifying guidelines set the standard for granting loans, there can be exceptions to the rules. Examples might include a borrower with a history of handling a higher-than-average rent payment—especially if other long-term debt is relatively low, or a borrower who consistently saves a high percentage of his or her annual income. Situations such as these are what the secondary market terms "compensating factors."

Fully documented compensating factors can be used to approve conventional fixed-rate loans with loan-to-value ratios of 90 percent or less when borrowers:

- make a large down payment.
- purchase a property that qualifies as "energy efficient." This can add 2 percent to both the housing and long-term debt ratios to equal 30 percent and 38 percent, respectively.
- demonstrate the ability to devote a greater portion of their incomes to housing expenses (especially if they've paid rent equal to or exceeding the payment they want to qualify for).
- show a consistent pattern of saving, maintain a good credit history, or have a debt-free position.
- demonstrate a potential for increased earnings because of education or job training.
- have short-term income (Social Security income, child support, and so on) that traditionally is not counted in qualifying because it would not continue three years or more beyond the date of the mortgage application.
- purchase a home due to corporate relocation of the primary wage-earner and the secondary wage-earner (with a previous work history) is expected to find employment (called a trailing spouse).
- have substantial net worth.

Fully documented compensating factors can be used with 90 percent or greater loan-to-value ratios if, in addition to meeting one or more of the criteria listed earlier, borrowers meet one of the following conditions:

- Have financial reserves that can be used to carry the mortgage debt, part of which must be in the form of liquid assets equal to at least two months of PITI payments.
- Demonstrate that they are able to carry a substantial housing payment, new housing expenses don't exceed their old expenses, and they have a good prior mortgage payment record and acceptable credit.
- Have a total long-term debt ratio of 30 percent or less, excellent payment histories on prior mortgages or rent, and acceptable credit.

Having one or more of these compensating factors can serve as strong leverage for the borrower who needs a little extra *oomph* in qualifying for a loan.

LITTLE-KNOWN FACTS ABOUT UNDERWRITING

Q. *Are there ever any differentiations between what local lenders allow and what the secondary market will accept?*

There certainly are. In fact, if the borrower knows what to ask for, some of the following little-known facts can help put loans together:

- The lender will allow qualifying ratios to be exceeded by 2 percent on the housing and long-term debt ratio if a purchaser is buying an energy-efficient house.
- The secondary market will allow the seller to take the borrower's existing property or an asset other than real estate in trade as part of the down payment on the property, as long as the borrower has made a 5 percent cash down payment on the new loan.
- The seller can give the purchaser credit toward the down payment for a portion of previous rent payments made under a rental purchase agreement. The minimum original term of the rental must be 12 months, and only those rents that exceeded the market rent, as determined by an appraiser, can be counted. For example, if market rent is $800, but the purchaser actually paid $900, the monthly credit toward purchase would be $100.
- A borrower can pool his or her funds with funds received as a gift from a relative who lives with him or her in order to come up with the minimum 5 percent cash down payment. But the giver of the funds does not have to qualify, nor does he or she take title. Both parties must reside in the new residence. In addition to these funds, the borrower could receive an additional down payment gift from a relative or a gift or grant from a church, municipality, or nonprofit organization.
- When the loan-to-value ratio for a mortgage is 80 percent or less, the full down payment may come from a gift from a relative or a gift or grant from a church, municipality, or nonprofit organization. This means that one of these parties would make the entire 20 percent down payment and the borrower would not have to make any other down payment from his or her own funds.

Q. *How can a prospective borrower take advantage of all these great underwriting exceptions and little-known facts?*

If a lender doesn't qualify the borrower, or claims that borrower resources are marginal for the loan size, the borrower could use this information to negotiate additional purchasing leverage. It can't hurt!

Q. *Does the secondary market have any maximum loan limits for loans it purchases?*

Yes. These are recalculated every year to reflect increases in purchase prices. Single-family one-unit dwellings have maximum loan limits for 1999 of $240,000, with multiple unit financing available up to $461,350 for four-family properties. The borrower should check with the lender to determine the current maximum loan amount available for the property he or she wishes to purchase.

Loans in excess of these secondary market loan ceilings can still be made by a lender. These are called "jumbo loans" and are sold separately to investors rather than through the usual secondary market channels.

Because these loans are not the standard size, the borrower may have to pay a higher interest and other lender incentives, such as additional points.

Q. *Does the secondary market limit making loans based on the amount of properties held by an owner?*

Yes, with clarification. The secondary market will allow a borrower to have any number of properties with financing on them as long as the property currently being purchased will be a principal residence.

The borrower can have no more than four properties currently financed if the new property being purchased is a second home or investment property.

These guidelines apply to all properties held by the borrower, not just those purchased by the secondary market, but do not apply to properties that are free and clear with no outstanding financing.

BORROWERS WITH BANKRUPTCY OR FORECLOSURE HISTORIES

Q. *Can someone who has previously declared bankruptcy apply for a loan to be sold to the secondary market?*

A bankruptcy must have been discharged fully and the borrower must have reestablished good credit. Usually, a two-year period between discharge of the bankruptcy and the mortgage application is required; but an exception may be made after one year if the lender is able to document that extraordinary circumstances caused the bankruptcy (such as extended illness not covered by health insurance).

Q. *Can borrowers who have had previous foreclosures get conventional loans?*

The secondary market usually won't purchase loans of borrowers who have had mortgage foreclosures within the last three years. As with bankruptcies, however, an exception might be made if extenuating circumstances show that a foreclosure was beyond a borrower's control. These circumstances might include a serious, long-term illness, death of a family's principal wage earner, or loss of employment due to industry reduction. The borrower must have established good credit and show an ability to manage his or her financial affairs.

TYPES OF QUALIFYING INCOME AND VERIFICATION

Q. *What kind of income will conventional lenders accept and how is it verified?*

In general, the lender wants to determine the probability and stability of the borrower's income sources. This means verifying two years' history for all income, full-time or part-time.

The secondary market verifies income in one of two ways. The lender may request that the employer fill in and return via regular mail "verification of employment" forms, or the lender could use a streamlined verification method which allows the lender to contact the employer's personnel office by phone, fax, or other electronic medium to verify employment and income.

If a borrower is employed by a relative or family-owned business, federal income tax returns must be provided to the lender.

The following is a checklist of additional income sources that might be considered:

☐ Part-time income can be counted, provided it has been uninterrupted for the past two years and is anticipated to continue; seasonal work is acceptable and the borrower requires reasonable assurance that he or she will be hired back for the next season.

☐ Overtime and bonus income that has occurred for the past two years and which will probably continue can be counted. (If the employer doesn't say that the overtime will end, it can be considered to continue.) The lender will average the past two years of such income; if this income is more than 25 percent of borrower's total income, income tax returns must be provided.

☐ Raises guaranteed to occur within 60 days of loan closing may be included for the purpose of qualifying.

Other income sources could include:

☐ Retirement income
☐ Military income
☐ Veteran's benefits
☐ Social Security income
☐ Alimony
☐ Child support
☐ Notes receivable
☐ Interest and dividend income
☐ Employer subsidized mortgage payments
☐ Trust income
☐ Unemployment benefits
☐ Rental income
☐ Auto allowances and expense account payments

VERIFYING THE BORROWER'S DOWN PAYMENT

Q. *Does the lender have to verify that the borrower has the down payment?*

Yes. The lender can use methods similar to those previously mentioned for verifying employment: sending out a "verification of deposit" form to be signed by the depository institution where the funds are held, or have the borrower provide the last three bank statements to verify the funds.

In addition to the down payment, the lender needs to verify that the required cash reserves are available in an account (usually equal to two months of mortgage payments) after closing monies are paid out.

USING GIFTED FUNDS AS LEVERAGE

Q. *It's great that a borrower can use down payment funds given by a relative or institution, but what kind of documentation has to be shown to the lender?*

A gift from a relative must be evidenced by a letter signed by the donor. It must specify the dollar amount of the gift and the date the funds were transferred; list the donor's name, address, phone number, and relationship to the borrower; and include the donor's signed statement that no repayment is expected.

The lender must verify that the funds are in the donor's account or have been transferred to the borrower's account. This could mean obtaining a copy of the donor's withdrawal slip and the borrower's deposit slip, or a copy of the donor's canceled check.

If funds haven't been transferred prior to settlement, the donor can give the closing agent a certified check for the amount of the gift. Because funds borrowed by a donor as a gift to a buyer might later put strain on the buyer to repay the amount, some lenders will want to check the donor's account history to determine the original source of the gift (for example, to ensure that the donor has been accumulating it in a savings account). The donor should be advised that this investigation could occur so that he or she won't be personally offended if it does.

If a gift or grant comes from a church, municipality, or nonprofit organization, it must be evidenced by a copy of an award, gift letter, or the legal agreement that specifies the grant or gift's terms and conditions. In addition, the lender must include a copy of the documents showing the transfer of the funds.

CITIZENSHIP IS NOT A REQUIREMENT

Q. *Does a borrower have to be a U.S. citizen to qualify for a loan to be sold to the secondary market?*

No, mortgages can be made to resident aliens. A lawful, permanent U.S. resident can qualify under the same terms and conditions as a U.S. citizen. He or she must prove residency with an Alien Registration Card or a green card.

Mortgages can be made to nonpermanent resident aliens as well, as long as the borrower occupies the property as a primary residence and the loan-to-value ratio does not exceed 75 percent.

REFINANCING WITH CONVENTIONAL LOANS

Q. *What kinds of refinancing guidelines does the secondary market use?*

Guidelines for Changing Loan Interest Rate or Term

- Loan-to-value ratio on owner-occupied properties can't exceed 95 percent.
- When subordinate financing (a second mortgage) is less than one year old, FNMA will not allow it to be paid off from the proceeds of a "no cashout" refinance.
- Junior liens (second mortgages) obtained through FHLMC must have had at least one year of payments from the origination date of the mortgage in order to be refinanced. If not, it is considered as a cashout and all applicable guidelines apply.
- Loan-to-value ratios on investment property and second homes cannot exceed 70 percent.
- Loan-to-value ratios on owner-occupied properties cannot exceed 75 percent. This option is not available on second homes or investor properties.

Guidelines for Pulling Equity (Cash) Out

Q. *Does an owner who refinances have to requalify with the lender, just as with a new loan?*

A streamlined refinance procedure is available to the borrower who doesn't have to requalify based on ratios. This option is available only if the new loan will be placed with the same lender, the loan will remain a conventional loan, and the borrower's income has not declined. In addition, the borrower's mortgage payment record has to be satisfactory for the past 12 months and the new mortgage payment can't exceed the old payment by more than 15 percent.

CLOSING COSTS

Q. *Does the secondary market require that the borrower pay certain closing costs?*

The secondary market requires that the borrower pay the following pre-paid settlement costs:

- Interest charges and real estate taxes for any period after the settlement date
- Hazard insurance premiums
- Impounds for PMI, unless it is financed as part of the mortgage amount

Other costs may be paid by the buyer or seller, based on what they've negotiated. As discussed previously, however, costs paid for the buyer by the seller would be considered contribution amounts and maximum limits would apply before being subtracted from the appraised value of the property, prior to calculating the maximum loan available.

Exceptions to contributions are third parties who are not participants in the sale, including the buyer's relatives or an employer. There are no restrictions as to the amounts they can pay, but the funds might need to be tracked as gifted monies. The borrower should check with the lender regarding specific examples of nonparticipant funds that could be used. Buyer and seller cost estimate sheets follow at Figure 4.2 and 4.3.

Q. *Besides 20-year and 30-year amortization schedules, what other types of conventional loan programs will the secondary market accept?*

Besides the 30 types of ARM that the secondary market will purchase, some of which we'll discuss in the next chapter, lenders can originate a myriad of programs.

Programs vary from somewhat common construction-permanent financing to infrequently used leasehold estate loans, and everything in between. There are loans for cooperative housing, energy improvement, rehabilitation of properties, and loans for manufactured housing.

Biweekly, growing equity, and balloon mortgage programs give borrowers differing degrees of leverage to help them purchase; these concepts will be discussed in depth in Chapter 10.

Figure 4.2   Buyer Cost Estimate Sheet

Buyer_____

Property Address_____

　Sale Price .... $_____
　1st Mortgage Balance To Be Assumed .... $_____
　2nd Mortgage or Contract To Be Assumed .... $_____
　Contract .... $_____
　Down Payment .... $_____

Estimated Loan Costs:
　Service Charge/Origination Fee .... $_____
　Assumption Fee .... $_____
　Credit Report .... $_____
　Appraisal Fee.. $_____
　Recording Fees... $_____
　ATA Policy (Title Insurance)............................... $_____
　Escrow Fee .... $_____
　Escrow Preparation Fee .... $_____
　Interest Proration.. $_____
　Tax Preparation Fee .... $_____
　Fire Insurance .... $_____
　Home Inspection Fee .... $_____
　Discount Points (If Applicable) .... $_____
　Initial Mortgage Insurance Premium* .... $_____
　Total Estimated Closing Costs .... $_____

Reserves and Prorates:
　Property Taxes .... $_____
　Fire Insurance .... $_____
　Mortgage Insurance† .... $_____
　Total Reserves and Prorates .... $_____
　Total Estimated Cash Outlay............................... $_____

Type of Loan _____ for _____ years
Rate of Interest _____ % (Approximately)
Principal, Interest .... $_____
Taxes Reserves .... $_____
Insurance Reserves .... $_____
Total Monthly Payment....................................... $_____

The undersigned purchaser hereby acknowledges receipt of a copy of this estimate and it is hereby understood that it is an *estimate only.*

Buyer _____

Buyer _____   Date _____

*VA loans do not incur this cost. For FHA loans, use FHA one-time premium (if not financed).
† FHA and VA loans do not incur this cost.

Figure 4.3   Seller Cost Estimate Sheet

Prepared for: _____ Address: _____

Prepared by: _____ Estimated Closing Date:_____

Selling Price .... $_____

Approximate Indebtedness
    First Loan .... @_____% $_____
    Second Loan .... @_____% $_____
    Other .... @_____% $_____

Gross Equity .... $_____

Seller's Estimated Costs:
    Brokerage Fee .... $_____
    Title Insurance Policy (Sales Price) .... $_____
    Long-Term Escrow Set-Up Fee .... $_____
    Escrow Closing Fee .... $_____
    Mortgage Discount .... $_____
    Contract Preparation .... $_____
    Attorney Fees .... $_____
    Appraisal Fee .... $_____
    Interest to Closing .... $_____
    Property Tax Proration .... $_____
    Payoff Penalty .... $_____
    Recording Fees .... $_____
    Reconveyance Fee .... $_____
    Required Repairs .... $_____
    City Inspection .... $_____
    Local Improvement Districts (LIDs) Assessment .... $_____
    Misc. .... $_____
    _____ .... $_____

If Income Property:
    Prorated Rents .... $_____
    Security or Cleaning Deposits .... $_____

Less Total Estimated Costs .... $_____

Subtotal .... $_____

Estimated Credits
    Reserve Account .... $_____
    _____ .... $_____

Plus Total Credits .... $_____
Estimated Seller's Proceeds .... $_____
Less Loan Carried by Seller .... $_____
Estimated Net Cash Proceeds .... $_____

Seller _____   Date _____

Both FNMA and FHLMC in the secondary market have a variety of home affordability programs. The following is an overview of some of the loan programs available.

AFFORDABLE HOUSING PROGRAMS

Affordable housing programs were created by the federal government's Community Redevelopment Act to provide affordable housing to a larger sector of Americans.

As seen previously, qualifying ratios are easier, cash reserves to close are less, and compensating factors can be used (such as a history of paying high rent). In addition, Mortgage Credit Certificate tax credits may be used with some programs to whittle down the PITI and allow buyers to qualify for more home.

Depending on the affordable housing program, buyers receive education on aspects of home affordability including energy efficiency and home maintenance. Most programs cap the price of the home as well as the maximum income allowable to qualify.

Both FNMA and FHLMC in the secondary market have a variety of home affordability programs. Following is an overview of some of the loan programs available.

Community Homebuyer Programs

These loans were the pioneers of the affordable housing movement. Designed to assist low- and moderate-income first-time homebuyers, this 3 to 5 percent low down payment mortgage allows debt ratios of 33 percent and 38 percent. No cash reserves are required, and homebuyer education is required (but can be waived under certain circumstances).

3/2 Option Programs

These programs allow the borrower to use only 3 percent down payment from their own funds, with the remaining coming from a family member gift, or a grant or unsecured loan from a nonprofit organization or government agency. Ratios of up to 33 percent and 38 percent are allowed and there are no cash reserves required to close the loan. Homebuyer education is required prior to closing the loan.

97 Percent Mortgages

Geared to the first-time buyer who can financially handle the monthly payment but hasn't accumulated the down payment, these programs allow the buyer to borrow the down payment—even on a credit card! Borrowers can choose either 25-year mortgages with qualifying ratios of 33 percent and 36 percent, or 30-year loans requiring ratios of 28 percent and 36 percent. Only one month of PITI reserves is required for closing.

Start-Up Mortgage^{SM}

This is a 30-year fixed rate graduated-payment mortgage featuring interest-only payments during the first year. After the first year, the monthly payment (but not the interest rate) increases 2 percent each year until the loan becomes fully amortizing. At that point, the monthly payment is fixed for the balance of the term. Debt-to-income ratios are 33 percent and 36 percent and only one month's reserves is required at closing. Borrowers must use 5 percent of their own cash as the minimum down payment.

OTHER CONVENTIONAL-MORTGAGE PROGRAMS

Pledged-Asset Mortgage

These programs allow home buyers to borrow up to 100 percent of the sale price (or appraised value, if less) of a home when they pledge a stable financial asset (typically certificates of deposit). Assets can come from the borrower or a family member and can range from a minimum 10 percent pledge from the borrower to a maximum 30 percent pledge from a family member. The borrower is required to make a down payment of between 3 and 5 percent (depending on the loan program chosen).

Two-Step Mortgage®

This program combines the benefits of shorter term pricing with the stability of longer term financing and is great for borrowers who move frequently. As the name implies, the Two-Step is an adjustable rate mortgage for five or seven years (depending on the plan you choose). Then it adjusts one time to a fixed rate not to exceed currently a 6 percent increase. A 10 percent down payment is required, and temporary buydowns are permitted to lower the initial interest rate.

Balloon Mortgages

Balloons are short-term mortgages that have some features of a fixed-rate mortgage. First, they provide level monthly payments that amortize over a stated period of time (i.e., 30 years), but provide for a balloon payment that is due at the end of an earlier specified term (e.g., five, seven, ten, or fifteen years). Depending on the program chosen, at the end of the balloon term (e.g., five years), the borrower can convert the loan into a fully amortizing market-rate loan (e.g., for 25 years) in either fixed-rate or adjustable rate formats.

Because balloon mortgages are considered short-term mortgages, interest rates are generally lower than traditional 30-year fixed mortgages.

Online Programs

Don't forget to browse large online mortgage sites like www.quicken mortgage.com, homeshark.com, and countrywide.com for a wide array of current conventional-mortgage programs.

CHAPTER 5

PRIVATE MORTGAGE INSURANCE ON CONVENTIONAL LOANS

Lender guidelines and the rules of the secondary market restrict the ability of lenders to make high loan-to-value mortgages without some guarantee against borrower default. Private mortgage insurance allows lenders to increase their loan-to-value ratios and still sell their mortgages in the secondary market. If it approves the loan, the PMI company will issue a commitment to insure the lender. With this guarantee, the lender can increase the loan amount to as much as 97 percent of the property value. The borrower pays the PMI premium and gets the benefit of a smaller down payment.

The biggest challenge for most first-time homebuyers is raising the money for the down payment. Private mortgage insurance is therefore one key to affordable housing, making the dream of home ownership possible for many.

This chapter explains the cost of PMI and how it impacts the mortgage. The focus is on how PMI companies work with lenders of conventional loans. (Federal Housing Administration has its own insurance program, which is covered in Chapter 8. VA loans, also described in Chapter 8, are guaranteed.)

THE BASICS OF PRIVATE MORTGAGE INSURANCE

Q. *Is there any way a lender would make a loan to a buyer who might be considered a marginal risk?*

The lender might require that the buyer purchase PMI to indemnify the lender for any loss caused by default during the early years of the loan. Typically, any loan-to-value ratio greater than 80 percent (particularly if the loan is to be sold in the secondary market) will require the purchaser to include PMI as a requirement of securing the loan. Private mortgage insurance originated in the 1950s with the first large carrier, Mortgage Guaranty Insurance Corporation (MGIC), referred to as *magic*. For this reason, early PMI methods were deemed to *magically* assist in getting lender approval on an otherwise unacceptable loan package. Today, however, there are eight PMI insurance underwriting companies in the United States. (See Figure 5.1 for addresses and phone numbers.)

Q. *How does PMI work?*

PMI companies write insurance protecting approximately the top 20 percent of the mortgage against default, depending on the lender's and investor's requirements, the loan-to-value ratio, and the particular loan program involved. (For a claim illustration, see Figure 5.2.) Should a default occur, the lender sells the property to liquidate the debt, and is reimbursed by the PMI company for any remaining amount up to the policy value.

Q. *Could obtaining private mortgage insurance help me qualify for a larger loan?*

Yes. Let's say that you're a family with $42,000 annual gross income and monthly revolving debts of $800 (car payment and credit cards) and have $10,000 for a down payment and closing costs on a mortgage at 7 percent interest. Without private mortgage insurance, the maximum price you can afford is $44,600. But with private mortgage insurance covering the lender's risk, you can buy a house worth $62,300. PMI has afforded you 39 percent more house. Check out the calculators at www.pmigroup.com to see how much more house PMI will allow you to buy.

Q. *What does PMI cost?*

Costs vary from insurer to insurer, as well as from plan to plan. For example, a highly leveraged adjustable rate mortgage would require the borrower to pay a higher premium to obtain coverage. Buyers with 5 percent down payment can expect to pay a premium of approximately .78 percent times the annual loan amount ($92.67 monthly for a $150,000 purchase price). But the PMI premium would drop to around .52 percent times the annual loan amount (or $58.50 monthly) if a 10 percent down payment was made on the loan.

Figure 5.1 Private Mortgage Insurance Companies

Amerin Guaranty Corporation
303 East Wacker Drive, Suite 900
Chicago, IL 60601
800-257-7643
Fax: 312-540-0564

PMI Mortgage Insurance Company
601 Montgomery Street
San Francisco, CA 94111
800-288-1970
Fax: 415-291-6175

Commonwealth Mortgage Assurance
  Company
1601 Market St.
Philadelphia, PA 19103-2197
800-523-1988
Fax: 215-496-0346

Republic Mortgage Insurance
  Company
P.O. Box 2514
Winston-Salem, NC 27102-9954
800-999-7642
Fax: 919-661-0049

G.E. Capital Mortgage Insurance
  Corporation
P.O. Box 177800
Raleigh, NC 27615
800-334-9270
Fax: 919-846-4260

Triad Guaranty Insurance
  Corporation
P.O. Box 25623
Winston-Salem, NC 27114
800-451-4872
Fax: 919-723-0343

Mortgage Guaranty Insurance
  Corporation
P.O. Box 488
MGIC Plaza
Milwaukee, WI 53201
800-558-9900
Fax: 414-347-6802

United Guaranty Corporation
P.O. Box 21567
Greensboro, NC 27420
800-334-8966
Fax: 919-230-1946

Q. *How is private mortgage insurance paid?*

PMI fees can be paid in several ways, depending on the PMI company used. Borrowers can choose to pay the first-year premium at closing; then an annual renewal premium is collected monthly as part of the house payment. Or the borrower can choose to pay no premium at closing, but add on a slightly higher premium monthly to the principal, interest, tax, and insurance payment. Buyers who want to sidestep paying PMI at closing but not increase their monthly house payment can finance a lump-sum PMI premium into their loan. With this type of payment plan, should the PMI be canceled before the loan term expires (through refinancing, paying off the loan, or removal by the loan servicer), the buyers may obtain a rebate of the premium.

Figure 5.2   PMI Claim Illustration

Original purchase price	$100,000
Original loan (10 percent down)	90,000
Principal balance due	88,915
Accumulated interest	
(excluding any penalty interest or late charges)	7,850
Subtotal	$ 96,765
Attorneys' fees	$ 2,420
Property taxes	1,140
Hazard insurance (premiums advanced)	710
Property maintenance (preservation expenses)	350
Disbursement and foreclosure cost	525
Subtotal	$101,910
Less escrow balances and rent received	240
Total claim	$100,670

Generally after a lender has instituted foreclosure and acquired evidence of marketable title to the property, a claim can be submitted. On receiving the claim, the insurer will decide whether to pay the entire claim and take title to the property or pay the coverage amount stated in the policy. The insurer will typically take title only in those cases when acquisition and sale by the insurer is likely to reduce the insurer's loss. When the insurer does take title, the lender will receive the full amount of the claim.

On receiving this claim, the insurer will attempt to determine the likely resale price. The expenses resulting from a sale would include the real estate agent's commission and other settlement costs, which on average would run at about 10 to 15 percent of the sale price. The insurer obtains this and other information in order to decide what option to take. From the lender's perspective, if the policy was written with 25 percent coverage, the claim payment option made by the insurer would have been $25,168, which means the lender could sell the property for approximately $80,000 and not suffer loss.

Q. *How does the buyer apply for PMI?*

Although the buyer typically bears the cost of PMI, the lender is the PMI company's client, and shops for the PMI on behalf of the borrower. Many lenders deal with only a few PMI companies because they know the guidelines for those insurers. This can be a problem when one of the lender's prime companies turns down a loan because the borrower doesn't fit its risk parameters. An unenterprising lender might follow suit and deny approval on the loan application without consulting even a second PMI company. Pandemonium results: the buyer is upset, wondering what's wrong with him or her; the lender is apologetic while responding that the borrower didn't meet the underwriting guidelines.

Let's look at it from the lender's point of view. He or she desires the very best quality as well as an assurance that the PMI company will stand behind its loan guarantee commitment. And today, when tough times abound for many types of insurance companies, lenders are putting an even higher priority on the strength and credibility of the PMI companies with which they do business. In fact, hundreds of thousands of dollars in PMI claims could be uncollectible should a PMI company declare bankruptcy.

The lender has an increasingly difficult task to be fair to the borrower while shopping for the most effective method to soften liability. Sometimes, it may appear that a lender has no justification for doing what he or she does—but look deeper, it's undoubtedly there.

Q. *What can the buyer or agent do if PMI is denied by one insurer?*

If PMI is denied by one insurer, consider the following possibilities:

- The borrower can ask the lender to submit the application to another (or several other) PMI insurers. A list of those licensed to do business in the borrower's state can be obtained from the lender or the state's insurance commission. Note, however, that the first question asked by the subsequent PMI company may be, "Has this party ever been denied insurance?" It's difficult to tell just how much impact the answer to this question has on consideration of the application. If the lender refuses to shop for another insurer, the borrower may not only be teaming up with the wrong PMI company, but the lender also may leave much to be desired.
- The borrower can ask the lender to hold the loan in portfolio and not require PMI (primarily a strong requirement of the secondary market). The buyer might entice the lender to keep the loan by transferring accounts held with other lenders or by increasing the note rate (a form of self-insurance for the lender).
- The borrower can explore ways to decrease the loan-to-value ratio so that PMI will not be required by the secondary market.

For example, a gift letter donor could be located for the down payment, leaving the borrower's funds to be used as an additional amount down; or the borrower could team up with a relative or friend to create leverage as coborrowers. A lender might be willing to make the borrower a 10 percent second mortgage in tandem with an 80 percent first mortgage, using a 10 percent down payment from the buyer (called piggyback financing). The borrower benefits by not paying PMI. However, the second mortgage creates a second lien on the property with payments often at a higher interest rate than that on the first mortgage. And of course, the borrower must financially qualify to repay both loans.

Additionally, the buyer might ask that a seller carry back part of the financing (structured much in the same way as piggyback financing). The lender will want to see a copy of the security document for the seller financing so that its impact can be considered in the loan underwriting of the first mortgage, especially regarding large monthly payments or balloon payments.

Q. *How would financing the entire PMI premium into the loan differ from using a second mortgage in a piggyback situation with an 80 percent first mortgage, 10 percent down payment, and a 10 percent second mortgage?*

$150,000 purchase price; first mortgage at 7 percent; second mortgage at 9 percent; financed PMI premium at 2.35 percent.

	80-10-10	Financed PMI
Monthly payments	$ 919.05	$ 919.27
Total payments (5 years)	55,143.00	$55,156.00
Tax deduction at 28 percent	13,395.00	13,173.00
PMI refund (in 60th month)	0	1,270.00
Total cost over 5 years	$41,848.00	$40,713.00

Financing the premium would cost the borrower less than taking on the second mortgage. Here's why. Let's assume that the home's purchase price is $150,000. The first mortgage rate is 7 percent; the rate of the second mortgage is 9 percent. The financed premium costs the borrowers just $.22 more per month. When they sell in five years, they can obtain a PMI refund of $1,270. The bottom line is that by financing the PMI, the buyer saves $1,135 over financing with the two-mortgage approach. Great articles about the benefits of private mortgage insurance can be found online at www.mgic.com.

PMI APPROVAL GUIDELINES

Q. *Does PMI insure only first mortgages?*

No. Some PMI insurers will take on second mortgage risks. Be prepared, however, to pay some heftier premiums for second mortgage insurance.

Q. *How could a buyer best be apprised of the PMI guidelines and regulations?*

The best buyer is an informed buyer. Even though removal guidelines may change somewhat with a particular PMI company and the secondary market during the life of a loan (if the mortgage is originated prior to July 29, 1999), if the borrower knows the general guidelines up front, decisions can be made *before* taking on a potentially adversarial situation. The borrower should ask the lender the following questions simultaneous to applying for PMI insurance:

1. How many companies' programs will be shopped?
2. How does the selected policy compare overall to others in the marketplace, evaluating the following criteria:
   - Rates
   - Size of policy (particular loan-to-value ratio insured)
   - The lender's current guidelines for removing PMI insurance (such as percentage of equity needed in property or other determinant)
   - Ways current guidelines could be expected to change (such as this particular company's history of changes, whether there are any guaranties against changes, and who makes the final decision for removing the PMI requirement (e.g., a board of directors)
   - Documents from the lender outlining the procedure for requesting removal of PMI

Q. *What can the borrower expect the PMI company to look for in approving him or her for PMI insurance?*

PMI companies look at many of the same questions posed by the lender, plus the following questions. Giving the "wrong" answer to these has proven to increase the risk factors of default on the loan. Here are some "red flag" questions from PMI insurers:

- Are payment increases scheduled in the loan, and if so, is it feasible that the borrower can meet them?

- Does the loan have a discounted "teaser" rate, such as on some ARMs?
- Are there any temporary buydowns that may mean increased interest and payments later on?
- Is the loan-to-value ratio high (for the type of loan used, as well as for the marketplace)?
- To what financial degree is the seller contributing? (Most PMI companies allow up to 3 percent of the sales price for a loan with a loan-to-value ratio over 90 percent, and 6 percent when the loan-to-value ratio is less than 90 percent and under. Although the appraiser is expected to adjust for seller contributions, the amounts specified are the maximum amounts allowable by most PMI insurers.)
- How much cash does the borrower have on hand? (PMI companies are putting much more emphasis on reserves as a cushion against delinquent payments.)
- Is the economy of the area sound? (Insurers are often wary of single-industry situations.)
- Is there an oversupply of housing in the area? (This might indicate declining market values.)
- How stable is the borrower's employment?
- Is the borrower a professional or unskilled laborer? (While this may appear to be a form of discrimination, blue-collar workers statistically have higher levels of loan defaults.)
- Is the borrower using a gift letter to fund any part of the purchase?

Q. *What part does the property play in receiving PMI approval?*

Cautious of the impact weak properties have in contributing to defaults, PMI companies are increasing their scrutinization of properties. The following questions address some appraisal "hot buttons":

- How is the neighborhood rated? (Unexplained or unacceptable appraisal explanations of fair and poor neighborhoods indicate factors that may weaken the borrower's commitment to the property. This may negatively affect the insurability of the loan.)
- Who appraised the property? (Most PMI companies reserve the right to declare appraisers and appraisals unacceptable.)
- How does the property compare to others in the area? (If a property is valued at 90 percent or more of the highest property value in the neighborhood, it is considered to be a high-risk property. It typi-

cally may have overimprovements and thus a longer marketing time in case of foreclosure.)

- Is the property physically sound and in good repair? (A low rating in this category may cause the property to be uninsurable.)
- What are the comparable properties used in the appraisal, and where are they located? (Typically, PMI companies will allow no more than one of the three required comparables to be supplied by the lender or developer from its own files unless justified by the appraiser. In addition, except for rural locations, at least two of the three required comparables must be located within one mile of the appraised property, or the difference in location must be fully explained. This one-mile range normally encompasses the neighborhood of the property.)
- Was there a sales concession? (This might be personal property, such as a car or boat, that is included by the seller to consummate the transaction. The value of the item will be deducted from the sale price and appraised value by the PMI company if it has not been deducted by the appraiser.)

Q. *So PMI has its own set of qualifying guidelines, one for the borrower and one for the property?*

Yes. If the borrower or the property doesn't fit in one PMI company's guidelines, the lender should take a proactive position to, if possible, find one that accepts the risk.

While qualifying for PMI may seem to be an extra hoop for the borrower to jump through, the application and paperwork is handled entirely by the lender. And considering the number of borrowers who couldn't purchase at all because they lack a 20 percent down payment, the minimal effort and cost that PMI insurance adds doesn't seem like a very great price to pay.

REMOVING PMI FROM A MORTGAGE

Q. *Can PMI ever be removed?*

Potentially. For loans originated after July 29, 1999, federal law requires the lender to remove the private mortgage insurance once the borrower has 22 percent equity and payments are current on the loan.

This law, enforced by the Department of Housing and Urban Development (HUD), also requires that lenders inform consumers of this at the time of loan commitment and on an annual basis.

Consumers have the option to petition the lender at any point in time to request that PMI be removed. Done on a case-by-case basis, most lenders require that the borrower provide the lender with a fee appraisal showing at least 20 percent equity in the property (through appreciation and/or principal reduction), the payments must have been made on time, and that the property's value has remained stable.

One word of caution. If you petition the lender/loan servicer to remove PMI using a fee appraisal as documentation, be sure the appraiser you use is one approved by the lender. It has the right to accept (or not) the appraiser to evaluate the property. If the appraiser is not lender approved, you could end up paying for another appraisal to meet the lender's guidelines.

The federal law governing PMI allows exceptions on loans originated as community homebuyer and other highly leveraged loans such as FHA where mortgage insurance is required to remain for the life of the loan.

CHAPTER 6

THE ADJUSTABLE-RATE MORTGAGE (ARM)

The adjustable-rate mortgage (ARM) products of the early 1980s gave ARMs an initial "black eye" in the financial marketplace. Many of these early loans were actually RRMs (renegotiable rate mortgages), meaning that on an anniversary date, the mortgagor would have to renegotiate with the mortgagee. This was no easy task because inflation and interest rates were skyrocketing. Many consumers couldn't qualify for the higher loan rates, sometimes forcing them to sell the property or face foreclosure.

The ARMs of today are much better products, with caps (maximum limits set on mortgage adjustments) and strong secondary market underwriting guidelines, as well as mandatory rate disclosure regulations for lenders. Additionally, the secondary market is increasingly paring down the number of programs that could lend themselves to negative amortization (a payment shortfall insufficient to cover interest due on the loan that's added back onto the principal loan balance). Like any mortgage loan program, ARMs best serve buyers with particular needs to be satisfied and problems to be solved. After we examine how ARM products work, we'll be able to determine which buyers and situations are best suited for this type of loan.

PROS AND CONS

Q. *What are the advantages of ARMs?*

The advantages are:

- Lower interest rates than for fixed rate mortgages allow the buyer to qualify more easily for the loan or leverage into a more expensive property than he or she could otherwise afford.

- Rates adjust based on increases and decreases in the particular index used, which is a gauge of inflation in the economy. (Indexes, or indices, are discussed later in this chapter.) This creates an equitable situation for lender and borrower alike because the lender's costs are covered, while the borrower's wage increases cover the rise in payment amounts.
- Various indexes are available on which to base the ARM.
- Various adjustment periods are available to the borrower, e.g., six months, one year, three years, five years, or ten years.
- Some ARMs can be converted to fixed-rate mortgages during a specific time frame in the loan.
- Initial lower-than-market teaser rates may drastically reduce the borrower's monthly payment in the first year of the loan.
- Many lenders keep ARMs in portfolio, allowing the buyer to request special concessions of the lender, such as no PMI or no reserve account for taxes and insurance.
- ARMS are more frequently assumable than are other types of mortgages.
- Adjustable-rate mortgages are good to use in times of low inflation as well as for short-term ownership.

Q. *What are the disadvantages of ARMs?*

The disadvantages are:

- There are no interest rate guarantees because indexes fluctuate with the economy.
- The buyer's financial situation may change after the loan is cast, making payment increases financially prohibitive for the borrower.
- The buyer may overleverage, using an unrealistically low initial teaser rate to get into the loan without being able to make the later, higher, payments.
- The loan may contain a negative amortization clause, allowing any shortfall of interest not paid monthly to be added back on to the principal balance. (This could cause a resale nightmare should the buyer have to move while the loan is showing negative amortization. It may also create an unsalable property, with the loan balance exceeding the market value.)
- The buyer may not fully understand ARMs and not be aware that the lender's program is using an unfavorable index as a base.

- The lender may be charging an unusually high margin, the lender's cost of doing business plus profit, which is added to the index to create the interest rate. This margin is set at loan origination and remains constant for the life of the loan.
- Convertible ARMs may have high interest rates or margins as a bonus to the lender. If the buyer chooses not to convert to a fixed-rate mortgage, this premium may defeat any cost savings with the ARM or perhaps make the program less cost-effective than a fixed-rate program might have been.
- Convertible ARMs have conversion fees for changing the interest to a fixed rate; the new fixed rate is not determined by the cost of the lender's current fixed-rate program. It is usually based on the note rate for that particular investor (e.g., FNMA securities) plus an additional ⅝ percent interest.

BASICS OF ADJUSTABLE-RATE MORTGAGES

Q. *What's the best way to learn how ARMs work?*

To understand an ARM, you must have a working knowledge of its components. Those components are:

- Index: A financial indicator that rises and falls, based primarily on economic fluctuations. It is usually an indicator of inflation and is therefore the basis of all future interest adjustments on the loan. Mortgage lenders currently use a variety of indexes.
- Margin: A lender's loan cost plus profit. The margin is added to the index to determine the interest rate because the index is the cost of funds and the margin is the lender's cost of doing business plus profit.
- Initial interest: The rate during the initial period of the loan, which is sometimes lower than the note rate. This initial interest may be a teaser rate, an unusually low rate used to entice buyers and allow them to more readily qualify for the loan.
- Note rate: The actual interest rate charged for a particular loan program.
- Adjustment period: The interval at which the interest is scheduled to change during the life of the loan (e.g., annually).
- Interest rate caps: Limit placed on the up-and-down movement of the interest rate, specified per period adjustment and lifetime

adjustment, (e.g., a cap of 2 and 6 means 2 percent interest increase maximum per adjustment with a 6 percent interest increase maximum over the life of the loan).

- Negative amortization: Occurs when a payment is insufficient to cover the interest on a loan. The shortfall amount is added back onto the principal balance.
- Convertibility: The option to change from an ARM to a fixed-rate loan. A conversion fee may be charged.
- Carryover: Interest rate increases in excess of the amount allowed by the caps that can be applied at later interest rate adjustments (a component that most newer ARMS are deleting).

Q. *How are rates set for ARMs?*

Rates are comprised of two components: the index and the margin. The index is an indicator of inflation and can come from a variety of sources. The margin is the cost of doing business for the lender, including profit, and is added on to the index to make the interest rate. This formula is used to determine each interest rate adjustment.

Q. *What are teaser (discount) rates? Are they a good idea?*

A teaser rate is an unrealistically low introductory rate, less than what the current index plus margin would total. Lenders may offer these to introduce a new program to the marketplace or to boost business. The benefit to the buyer is the lower initial interest and payments (although some lenders qualify the buyer at the fully indexed—post-introductory—rate). The danger is that when the payments do adjust, their increase may cause "payment shock" to the borrower who may fall behind or default on the loan. The borrower should go into this type of payment schedule with eyes wide open. Particularly if loan qualification is marginal, the borrower must realize how the full-rate mortgage payments will fit in the family budget.

INDEXES

Q. *What indexes does a lender use for ARMs?*

Although lenders can choose from a wide variety, it is not always possible for the consumer to request that a certain index be used with the loan program desired. The lender offers types of loans that the secondary market has agreed to purchase, which includes a predetermined index.

But a consumer could research various ARMs offered by several lenders to determine which programs contain the best combination of indexes and program benefits. The informed buyer should be aware of the most common indexes:

Treasury Securities Index

- *One-year treasury securities index:* This index is widely used in ARMs. It's best to use when rates are high and likely to go down. The initial rate is usually 2 percent or more below the fixed rate. It can adjust quite rapidly, causing quickly changing interest costs. Buyers using this index would be well served to have strong caps.
- *Three-year treasury securities index:* This is best to use when rates are stable or expected to rise. This index sometimes has sizable gaps between its initial interest rate and that of fixed-rate loans. Over time, however, the gap may decrease, causing a loss of incentive for using an ARM.
- *Five-year and ten-year treasury securities indexes:* These offer good stability due to long periods between rate adjustments. A disadvantage is that many times the initial gap between the index and the fixed rate is slight. These are best to use when rates are expected to increase.

For current treasury securities index rates, contact a local lender, *The Wall Street Journal,* or *USA Today,* or request *H.15* (a weekly newsletter) from Publications Services, Mail Stop 138, Board of Governors, Federal Reserve System, Washington, DC 20551. Online resources like www.hsh.com and interest.com provide up-to-the minute quotes.

The Federal National Mortgage Association also has a 24-hour hotline, 202-752-6799, for current index quotes.

Treasury Bills Index

The six-month T-bill is the most volatile of these indexes. This index is best to use when interest rates are very high and rate decreases appear inevitable. The initial rate is usually 2 percent or more below the fixed rate. However, it increases and decreases quickly, so it can be termed "fast."

National Mortgage (NACR) Interest Rate Index

This index is based on the average monthly contract rate charged by all lenders on mortgage loans for previously occupied homes. It's good to use this index at the low point in its cycle. It adjusts very slowly and is therefore preferential to buyers. In addition to averaging fixed-rate loan interest rates, other ARM indexes are also averaged and added into this index, allowing it to stay low. Unlike most other indexes, the contract interest rate index typically carries no additional margin.

Eleventh District Cost of Funds Index

The 11th district refers to the 11th District of the Federal Reserve Bank, headquartered in San Francisco, California. This index is generally one of the slowest to adjust, which makes it favorable from the borrower's point of view. Once rates increase, however, they also are slow to decline. That's why you might term this index *slow*—slow to rise, slow to decline. It's particularly good to use on the upswing of inflation (when rates are rising), rather than when rates are predicted to fall. Be sure to ask the lender, however, how often interest rates can change. If adjustments are as often as monthly, negative amortization might occur, depending on the terms of the loan.

London Interbank Offered Rate (LIBOR)

The London Interbank Offered Rate (LIBOR) is an extremely competitive index designed to protect against wide swings in interest payments based on steady adjustments. Given its international acceptance, LIBOR helps garner worldwide attraction to secondary market investments.

DISCLOSURE PROVIDED BY LENDERS

Q. *How does the lender help the prospective borrower understand the choices available in ARMs?*

The lender provides a great deal of information about ARMs.

The lender must give the borrower written disclosure about ARMs either at the time a loan application form is provided or before the consumer pays a nonrefundable fee, whichever comes first.

The lender must make educational material available to the consumer. Many lenders use the *Consumer Handbook on Adjustable-Rate Mortgages,* published jointly by the Federal Reserve and the FHLBB. A copy of this handbook can be found online at www.hsh.com.

Additionally, lenders must provide ARM buyers with a loan program disclosure for each adjustable rate program they're considering. The disclosure information must reveal that the interest rate or loan term can change, identify the index used and the source of information for that index, and explain how the index adjusts and when. A statement must be included advising the consumer to ask about the current margin, interest rate, and discount points.

One last piece of information ARM buyers will review will be the historical example for each index illustrating how payments on a $10,000 loan would have changed historically. Obviously because your loan will be in multiples of $10,000, make sure you apply the correct numbers when considering adjustments.

Q. *What are the requirements for notifying the consumer about ARM interest rate changes during the life of the loan?*

During the term of the outstanding ARM loan, notice must be given to the borrower of an adjusted payment amount, interest rate, index rate, and loan balance. This notification must be made once every year there is a rate adjustment, regardless of whether there is a payment change. The notice must be mailed not less than 45 days before the new payment amount is due. Further, the disclosure must indicate the extent to which any increase in the interest rate has *not* been fully implemented (e.g., the index rate plus margin would exceed the cap). The notice also must state the payment required to fully amortize the loan if it is different from that being charged.

MARGINS

Q. *If a consumer shopped for the most stable and reasonable index, would that loan result in the lowest interest rate?*

Not necessarily. The index could be a dream, while the loan's margin could be a nightmare! Even though searching for the best index is important, shopping for the lowest margin can make thousands of dollars' worth of difference over the life of a loan.

Q. *Who sets an ARM's margin, and how does it affect the interest rate?*

As stated previously, the lender determines the margin because it is the combination of his or her costs of making the loan, plus profit. The margin is set at the time of loan application and remains constant for the life of the loan. The index rate *plus* the margin combine to make the note or accrual rate, also called the fully indexed rate. So even if the index is favorable, a high margin could counteract any expected interest savings.

Refer to the comparative example in Figure 6.1. In this example, the one-year treasury index is 3.75 percent. This index, added to the lender's margin of 2.75 percent, would make a note or accrual rate of 6.5 percent. (This note rate isn't necessarily the first-year rate charged by the lender, however, because it may have offered a lower or teaser rate to attract borrowers.) In the example, the lender gave the borrower the 6.5 percent initial interest rate—which is effective until the first interest rate adjustment—resulting in a monthly payment of $632.08.

When it's time for the annual review of the interest rate on the loan, the borrower finds that the index has increased 2 percent, to 5.75 percent. After adding the margin of 2.75 percent to the index, the interest rate escalates to 8.5 percent, and the payment jumps to $766.83.

While the index may wax and wane, the margin remains fixed for the life of the loan. So, all other points being equal, the loan with the higher margin will end up costing the buyer more.

Q. *Is there ever a time when it would benefit the buyer to take a program with a higher margin?*

Perhaps, if that program had other redeeming characteristics such as low caps, a good index or a convertibility option to change the ARM into a fixed-rate mortgage. The benefits to the borrower should financially outweigh the higher margin.

Q. *What percent could you expect to be charged for a margin?*

Lenders quote margins anywhere from 1 to 4 percent.

Q. *Do all ARMs have margins?*

No. ARMs using the NMCR index mentioned previously do not use a margin in addition to the index. However, this index is typically .75 percent, or more, higher than other indexes.

Figure 6.1   Mortgage Comparison—Adjustable Rate versus
                   Fixed Rate

	Fixed Rate Mortgage	Adjustable Rate Mortgage
Mortgage Amount	100,000	100,000
Interest Rate	9%	6.5%
Year 1	9%	8.5%
Year 2	9%	10.5%
Year 3		
Year 4		
Year 5		
Loan Term	30 years	30 years
Adjustment Period	N/A	1 year
Maximum Cap Per Period	N/A	2%
Lifetime Cap	N/A	6%

	Fixed	Adjustable	Cumulative Savings Adjustable Mortgage Over Fixed
1. Interest Rate, Year One	9%	6.5%	
2. Monthly Payment x 12	9,655	7,585	
3. Total Payments Made, End of Year One (#2, above)	9,655	7,585	2,070
4. Interest Rate, Year Two	9%	8.5%	
5. Monthly Payment x 12	9,655	9,193	
6. Total Cumulative Payments, End of Year Two (lines 3 + 5)	19,310	16,778	2,532
7. Interest Rate, Year Three	9%	10.5%	
8. Monthly Payment x 12	9,655	10,879	
9. Total Cumulative Payments, End of Year Three (lines 6 + 8)	28,965	27,657	1,308

Q. *What factors would cause a lender to charge different margins on various programs?*

Some programs might allow an ARM to be converted into a fixed-rate mortgage while other programs might charge higher margins for the privilege of using a more stable index. Or a lender might have a loan program that makes other concessions that it needs to cover in the form of a higher ongoing charge (margin). Some lenders may be willing to negotiate slightly on margins if they could be shown trade-offs such as higher initial interest or loan origination fees, or the ability to do additional business with the borrower.

INTEREST AND PAYMENT CAPS

Q. *What would prevent the fully indexed rate from hitting astronomical heights?*

Caps. Caps are limits, specified per loan adjustment period (called adjustment caps) as well as for the life of the loan (called lifetime caps), that prevent interest rates from going through the ceiling. Just as they protect the upward movement, so too do they prevent the rate from falling to levels where the loan is no longer cost-effective for the lender.

Q. *Besides knowing what they are, what does a borrower need to know about caps?*

It's important to know what they apply to—the introductory rate or the note rate? And, particularly if you're using a teaser rate, do the rate caps apply to the first adjustment?

Q. *Is it possible to find an ARM program that has no caps?*

Perhaps on an old loan you might be assuming, but not on a new loan. The Competitive Equality Banking Act of December 1987 prohibits lenders from originating programs without lifetime caps. Instead of a program having an interest adjustment cap, it might have a payment cap (e.g., 7.5 percent increase in payment per adjustment).

Q. *Where do most lenders set caps?*

The range swings are as wide as 1 to 3 percent for adjustment period caps, and from approximately 3 to 6 percent for lifetime caps. Some loans, however, may have flat rates stated for lifetime caps in lieu of interval amounts (e.g., the rate cannot drop below 8 percent or exceed 14 percent during the life of the loan).

Q. *How do payment caps work?*

Just like the rate cap, a payment cap limits the amount a monthly payment can increase per adjustment period. A normal range of payment caps is anywhere between 5 to 12 percent, with 7.5 percent being the most common. This is because it takes a payment change of approximately 7.5 percent to offset 1 percent of interest increase in a loan. It's also possible to have rate caps and payment caps in the same loan.

Q. *What kinds of questions should borrowers ask themselves before getting into an ARM with a payment cap?*

First of all, do they anticipate that their incomes will increase to cover the additional monthly payments? They should also ask themselves how much they could afford to have the loan increase—in other words, what is their financial threshold?

Next, they should ask whether the loan has a maximum amount of negative amortization allowed. This is important so that leverage can be controlled, particularly any in excess of the property value. Within this should be the question of whether the property's value will increase enough to offset any negative amortization.

Finally, but perhaps most important, borrowers should measure the gap between the interest rate and the payment cap. The greater the difference, the greater the risk of potential negative amortization.

Obviously, payment caps, just as ARMs, need to be evaluated based on the desires and capabilities of the individual borrower.

NEGATIVE AMORTIZATION, CARRYOVER, AND ADJUSTMENT PERIODS

Q. *Why would anyone want a loan with negative amortization in it?*

If handled prudently, negative amortization doesn't have to be a time bomb. For example, if the property is appreciating and the borrowers are not able to increase monthly payments over time to make up for the interest shortfall, it may not have any adverse effects. Remember, too, negative amortization is a form of leverage. Used wisely, it's good business; used haphazardly, it's a keg of dynamite.

Q. *Obviously, most lenders aren't crazy about negative amortization. How do they handle it?*

Lenders deal with negative amortization in several ways. They limit the amount that can accrue on a loan, usually to a ceiling of 125 percent of the original loan balance. If the lender deems it necessary, it can ask to increase the monthly payments, extend the loan's term, or ask that the borrower make a cash payment to reduce the balance.

Most lenders today are lessening negative amortization up front by requesting larger down payments, particularly in programs where this problem of deferred interest is liable to occur. In addition, many are not marketing ARMs containing negative amortization.

Q. *How does carryover differ from negative amortization?*

Carryover is excess interest that can't be charged during an adjustment period because the caps prevent it. Unlike negative amortization, carryover is not added on to the principal. The amount of the carryover is noted on the loan and is applied by the lender at a subsequent adjustment period. For example, if the interest rate could jump a maximum 2 percent cap from 6 percent to 8 percent, but the total rate change would have been from 3 percent to 9 percent, the extra 1 percent could be applied at a future adjustment. Carryover deals with the interest rate change, whereas negative amortization deals with the principal balance and the payment amount. Most newer ARMS avoid the carryover component.

Q. *Can the borrower choose the adjustment periods for his or her loan?*

It depends. Not all loans offer a choice of adjustment periods. This is based not only on the lender's decision, but also on the index used. For example, the three-year treasury note index program will have the interest and the payment adjustment period at the same time—every three years.

Borrowers should gauge the adjustment period to probable increases in income, if possible. A young doctor setting up practice and purchasing her first home might be wise to go with a three-year or longer adjustment period to allow time for getting the heavy start-up costs of the business out of the way, and for stabilizing income before any hefty payment increases take place.

Q. *How much impact would rate trends have on the adjustment period chosen?*

Quite a lot. If rates appear to be edging upward, a borrower would not want a program that adjusts monthly. To sidestep negative amortization, the borrower would not want a program where the rate adjusted monthly while the payment adjusted annually. With rising rates, the longer the adjustment period, the better. However, lenders may charge higher rates on longer-adjusting programs, so this should be a consideration. Most lenders prefer the one-year adjustment term and will usually reflect this preference in their rates and fees.

If rates appear to be falling, a quicker adjustment period may help to bring down the rate. Remember, too, as discussed previously, the particular index chosen has an impact on how rapidly the changes occur.

CONVERTIBILITY OPTIONS

Q. *Wouldn't it be best for the borrower to choose an ARM that could be converted to a fixed rate, in case interest rates went wild?*

Although the convertibility option has gotten a lot of press since appearing in ARM programs, it is not for everyone. The convertibility option allows the borrower to convert the rate from adjustable status to a fixed rate, but not without a cost. Loan options are like items in a cafeteria line—the more you chose, the more you pay. The same is true of ARM options. The cost will be reflected in a higher lender's margin, a higher interest rate, or steeper origination fees.

A borrower who chooses the convertibility option in a loan and fails to use it is tacking on useless costs that may make the ARM less cost-effective than a fixed-rate program. The conversion option can be the cherry pie in the cafeteria line—eat the pie and the customer is glad to have paid the price—leave the pie on the table, and the customer has wasted money.

Q.   *When would a convertibility option in an ARM benefit a borrower?*

Conversion options make sense in several circumstances. First, when interest rates are high but the borrower feels that they will go down. A borrower can benefit initially by the adjustable rate being lower than a fixed rate; and, when rates do fall, he or she can lock into a reasonable fixed-rate program without requalifying or paying the costs of refinancing.

Second, convertibility options make sense when an ARM is chosen for its attractive initial rates, but the borrower feels that rates in general are edging up. This may apply to a borrower who needs the initial qualifying leverage of the lower rate, but may be leery of being locked long-term into an adjustable rate program. It's not just the cost of the convertibility option that is being weighed, but also the overall cost of the ARM loan package (including origination fees, margins, and the particular index), compared to the costs of the fixed-rate package.

How long one expects to hold the mortgage also affects the desirability of convertibility options. Obviously, if a borrower chooses the ARM for short-term ownership, he or she may not benefit from exercising a convertibility option to cover the extra cost of the option. On the other hand, if ARM programs are not the norm in a market area, having the convertibility option available to a new purchaser assuming a loan may be an enticement. (Note: Once conversion options are exercised to change the loan to a fixed rate, most loans are no longer assumable).

Q.   *How long does a borrower have in which to exercise the conversion option?*

The conversion option period varies from loan to loan. The most common period is between months 13 and 60. Most loans state a maximum time during which the conversion may place. If not exercised, the option is lost.

In addition, the conversion option may be void if the loan is assumed. This will usually be stated on an addendum rider to the ARM. It's critical that the borrower realize this before misrepresenting to a new assumptor that a loan is convertible.

Q. *Can a borrower predict what the new fixed rate will be when he or she exercises the convertibility option?*

It depends. A few lenders may quote a predetermined rate, but most will wait to compute the new rate until the option is taken. Contrary to popular belief, when an ARM is converted to a fixed-rate mortgage, most borrowers do not receive the lender's current 30-year interest rate for fixed-rate loans. Adjustable-rate mortgages sold into the secondary market base the new rate on the 30-day commitment price of the index plus an additional percentage (e.g., ⅝). These commitment rates are typically higher than what you would expect to pay if you initially chose a fixed-rate loan. So this rate, coupled with an additional five-eighths percent, may lessen the attractiveness of the conversion to a fixed-rate loan, and of the convertibility option in general.

Q. *When should we ask what the cost of converting the loan from ARM to a fixed-rate mortgage will be?*

This is one question the borrower should ask up front before closing the ARM. There should be no reason why a definitive answer regarding conversion fees can't be given at that time. In the past several years, these costs have become much more tempered. In fact, most fees to convert the adjustable rate to a fixed rate range from $100 to $250, although loans held in portfolio might have substantially different fees.

ASSUMPTION OPTIONS

Q. *Is assuming an ARM possible?*

Although it depends on the loan, many adjustable rate loans are assumable at the lender's current rate and terms. Exceptions to assumability could be programs that have convertibility options. Once converted to fixed rates, they are no longer assumable.

Other adjustables that are not assumable include the two-step program and the Stable Mortgage^{SM} (which will be reviewed later in this chapter).

The borrower should ask to see a copy of the current assumption guidelines prior to loan origination.

Q. *Is it true that some lenders require the new assumptor of an ARM to be even more qualified than the original purchaser?*

This is very often true. Before releasing the original obligor, the lender wants to be guaranteed that the new assumptor is as qualified, if not more so, than the original borrower. Part of the rationale here is that the interest rate may have been adjusted substantially higher, creating even more of a risk for the lender. While the loan disclosure statement may state that the loan is assumable, it generally does not state the specific conditions for the assumption. The terms and conditions specified in the deed of trust, mortgage, addendum rider, or note will give more in-depth assumption specifics.

Q. *I'm sure you can guess the next question—what are typical assumption fees on ARM loans?*

The answer to this question may sound familiar: They vary! New buyers should always check assumption fees with the lender before agreeing to assume a loan.

OTHER RISKS

Q. *Do ARMs contain prepayment penalties if the loan is paid in full prior to the due date?*

Not usually, but it would most likely occur if a loan had a low teaser rate to entice borrowers into a program. If rates did rise, causing borrowers to refinance into a competing lender's program, the first lender would stand to lose a sizable amount of money—thus the prepayment penalty. However, were the borrower to refinance with the same lender, the penalty might be waived. This is yet another point that should be negotiated in the early stages of choosing a lender and a loan program.

Private Mortgage Insurance

Q. *Doesn't PMI shield the lender from risk with ARMs?*

Yes, to a degree. Even though PMI is typically used to insure the lender from the borrower's default on approximately the top 20 percent of the loan, lenders have recently required borrowers under some ARM programs to insure lesser loan-to-value ratios.

Private mortgage insurance for ARMs can come at considerable cost. The PMI premium rates for ARMs can be as much as 25 percent higher than for fixed-rate loans. For some borrowers, this may mean that what they have saved by using the ARM has been partially eroded by increased PMI costs. Be sure to consider this increased cost when comparing adjustable programs to those of fixed-rate programs.

Q. *Can a borrower shop around to get the ARM buyer's PMI rates down?*

It certainly wouldn't hurt. But keep in mind that many times a PMI insurer will have lower rates for a certain program because its risk is minimized in some way, such as through tougher qualifying criteria for the buyer. Because many ARM buyers are already fairly leveraged, this is often the straw that breaks the camel's back. The borrower wouldn't want to put a high priority on securing lower PMI rates just to find that he or she has not qualified for the loan according to the PMI company's underwriting guidelines.

Remember this option: Ask that the lender keep the adjustable rate loan in portfolio, because ARMs tend to be the most profitable loans for lenders. In this way, the lender may choose to waive PMI insurance or to self-insure.

THE QUALIFYING PROCESS

Q. *In general, isn't it easier to qualify for an ARM?*

Because interest rates for ARMs tend to be lower than for fixed-rate loans, this is typically true. Many lenders, however, work within the secondary market guidelines that require a borrower to be qualified at the first adjustment period rate if the loan has 2 percent annual adjustment caps, a term longer than 15 years, and a loan-to-value ratio above 70 percent. The rationale is that equity in a higher-leveraged loan tends to build slowly, increasing the lender's up-front risk on the loan. The Federal Home Loan Mortgage Corporation uses an even more detailed approach to qualifying ARM borrowers, based on loan-to-value ratios and buydowns.

Q. *What loan-to-value ratios can a borrower get on an ARM and what are the qualifying ratios?*

Traditionally, a borrower can get up to a 90 percent loan-to-value loan with qualifying ratios of 28 percent housing debt and up to 36 percent long-term debt.

If the interest rate on the loan is temporarily reduced by buying down the interest rate, the long-term debt ratio for qualifying will be 33 percent.

As with all qualifying ratios, lenders could allow these ratios to be exceeded if fully documented with compensating factors. For example, a borrower who has a history of above-average income growth or a recent college graduate who has obtained professional employment with high growth potential might be allowed to exceed traditional ratios. For more information, see the qualification sheet found at Figure 6.2.

PROGRAM TYPES

Q. *How many different types of ARMs are there?*

Because ARMs are designed to fit borrowers' financial situations, more ARMs exist than can be enumerated here.

The following are some of the most common combinations of terms, caps, and options a borrower might find. The first number in the cap is the maximum amount of interest rate adjustment per period, and the second number is the cap on how high the interest could go over the life of the loan.

- One-year treasury securities index, with caps of 2 and 5 percent with or without convertibility option to fixed rate
- 3-1, 5-1, 7-1, and 10-1 ARMs, fixed rate for the first respective number of years, then adjusts annually thereafter with a cap of 2 percent per adjustment
- Cost of funds index, 6-month adjustments; caps of 1 and 6 percent, has a convertibility option

Q. *How does the two-step mortgage work?*

It may help to think of the two-step mortgage as a 30-year fixed-rate loan with one rate adjustment during its life. Tied to the ten-year U.S. Treasury index, the two-step has a fixed interest rate for the first five or seven

Figure 6.2   ARM Qualification Sheet

Sales Price   (1)_____
     Less Loan Amount (2)_____ Equals Required Down Payment $_____

Estimated Closing Costs *Plus* Estimated Prepaid Escrow   +_____
     Total Closing Cost $_____
Less Cash on Deposit   −_____
Required Cash To Close $_____

     (2) _____ Divided by (1) _____ Equals LTV _____%

Gross Income (Mortgagor)_____ and (Comortgagor)_____ = $_____ (A)

Proposed Housing Expense

     Principal and Interest $_____

     Other Financing   _____

     Hazard Insurance   _____

     Taxes   _____

     Mortgage Insurance   _____

     Homeowner Association Fees   _____

     Other:_____   _____

Total Housing Payment   _____ (B)

Total Obligations (Beyond Ten Months)   _____ (C)

Total Housing Payment (B), *Plus* Monthly Obligations (C) = _____ (D)

     (B) _____ Divided by (A) _____ = _____ %   Housing Ratio

     (D) _____ Divided by (A) _____ = _____ %   Total Debt Ratio

years, depending on the program chosen. After that, the interest rate adjusts once to a new fixed rate, where it remains for the life of the loan.

Because the initial scheduled payment is lower, the two-step can help a borrower qualify for a larger loan than might have been allowed for a 30-year fixed loan. It's also good for short-term ownership.

Q. *What is the Stable mortgage?*

The Stable mortgage is an ARM tied to the treasury securities index, with caps of 2 and 6, and which adjusts annually. The unique feature of the Stable mortgage is that it blends some of the features of the ARM with those of the fixed-rate loan. Thus, it's more stable than the standard ARM.

Here's how it works. The margin for a Stable loan is higher than with other adjustable loans, requiring that only 50 percent of the index be added to adjust the interest rate per period. The result is less volatility in payments than with a traditional ARM. But the trade-off is that the borrower would have a higher initial interest rate than with a standard ARM program.

Q. *Is the Federal Housing Administration's ARM a good program?*

Yes, it is. First, it has 1 percent annual and 5 percent lifetime caps. These are becoming more and more rare in the marketplace, so it's good to find them within an affordable program. Second, the program allows no negative amortization. Many times with low caps, negative amortization defeats the other cost-effective qualities of a program. That's not a concern with the FHA ARM. And third, and perhaps most important, the qualifying and down payment requirements are the same as those under the standard FHA 203.b. loan program.

If there is a shortcoming to the program, it may be in the index used. It's based on the one-year treasury bills index. This index tends to adjust fairly quickly in times of rising inflation, although the caps of this program will prevent runaway interest.

The FHA ARM qualifies the borrower at the initial rate plus 1 percent and even allows coborrowers on the loan who will not reside on the property. Therefore, it's particularly good for first-time purchasers, which is exactly why FHA loans were created.

CALCULATION ERRORS

Q. *Do errors ever occur in adjusting rates?*

Yes, they do. In fact, surveys estimate that between 20 and 30 percent of all adjustable-rate mortgages contain calculation errors. It's up to each borrower to monitor adjustments on his or her individual loan and query the lender if it appears an error has been made.

Each loan has its own set of variables, including the date the loan is to be recalculated, the index to use, and how the interest is to be rounded off. An error in one or all of these areas could change the interest rate charged.

That's why it's wise for the borrower to check his or her loan documents to determine when adjustments are calculated and then check the particular index used on that date. This can be found in *The Wall Street Journal, USA Today,* and most major newspapers. If the borrower checks index information on the renewal/adjustment date and compares that information to what the lender sent when notifying of an upcoming adjustment, the borrower can help guard against errors. If the information is different, the current loan servicer (where payments are mailed) should be contacted. Most lenders have a review process in place to field and answer borrower inquiries.

Warning signs that a borrower may need to review the ARM include loans with frequent adjustment periods using complicated formulas, loans written prior to 1986 (when guidelines were very loose), or any loan that has recently been sold to another investor.

A comprehensive online tutorial for checking the accuracy of your adjustable-rate loan can be found at www.hsh.com or www.homefair.com.

DETERMINE ARM SAVINGS

Q. *When is the best time to use an ARM?*

As seen in this chapter, interest rate differentials alone are not enough to justify using an ARM over a fixed-rate loan. The deciding factor should be determined by analyzing the savings between loan programs. As a very broad rule of thumb, if the borrower can save at least 2½ percent in interest by using an ARM, and will hold the property for less than four years, it may pay to go with the ARM. Obviously, the smaller the gap between the fixed and adjustable rates, the less attractive adjustable rates become. Consider the following example:

Joe Singh knows he is going to be transferred in two years. He can get an ARM today of 6 percent (with caps of 1 and 5) instead of a conventional fixed-rate loan of 8.5 percent. The ARM might be cost effective for him, given his circumstances, because his monthly payments will be lower, and the maximum the interest rate adjusts can't exceed 1 percent per year for a maximum of 8 percent (.5 percent lower than the conventional loan rate).

Remember, however, there are a lot of variables to compare in selecting a loan, including the up-front costs of borrowing on each loan considered.

The smaller the gap between rates, the less attractive adjustable rates become.

QUESTIONS TO ASK BEFORE TAKING OUT AN ARM

Q. *What questions about the loan should the consumer be able to answer before taking on an ARM?*

- What is the history of the particular index used by the lender? (Ask to see historical documentation.)
- Where do economists think interest rates are currently headed? If up, your interest savings may not be as great as you thought. If down, you may have an even bigger win than anticipated. (Be sure to compare the answer to this question to our previous discussion about index selection.)
- What are the terms of the loan? When does the ARM payment adjust? How will the new rate be figured? What is the maximum to which the payment could rise, and the minimum to which it could fall?
- What is the lender's margin? (Because this remains constant for the life of the loan, it has as much, if not more, impact on where the rate adjusts to as does the index.)
- Is there a convertibility option? If so, what does it really cost? (Take into consideration any higher interest rate on the loan as well as conversion fees.) Remember to ask how the fixed rate will be determined at the time of conversion. To answer these questions, the borrower should obtain a completed copy of the ARM loan disclosure statement. A borrower who has difficulty weighing the options should seek the expertise of a financial adviser.

- How long will the property be held? Remember, ARMs are usually most advantageous with short-term ownership (approximately less than four years during times of rising inflation).
- Will the ARM chosen be attractive as an assumable loan when the property is sold? Is there anything in the loan that would hinder the loan's transferability? What are current assumption fees, as well as policies and procedures for assuming this type of loan?
- What are the up-front costs of the loan? Do they offset any potential interest savings? Is there any creative way to finance these into the loan to eliminate out-of-pocket cash at closing? If so, how will that affect the monthly payment and any future resale value?
- Is the lender willing to hold the loan in portfolio? If so, how might that benefit the buyer?

Q. *Which loan provides the best adjustable rate program?*

That's like asking how long someone's legs need to be (long enough to reach the ground). If a particular ARM program suits a buyer's needs, then that's the best loan. Ask the following questions to determine which type of ARM best suits the borrower's needs:

- What are the borrower's goals in buying this property? If rapid equity buildup is desired, the borrower should stay away from any product allowing negative amortization; if the goal is a first home purchase on tight qualification, perhaps a low introductory rate or rate adjustments that occur every three or five years should be used. The index and margin will also be important.
- How long do the borrowers plan on owning the property? Short-term owners should consider a loan with good assumability, a slow-moving upward index, low up-front loan origination fees, low down payment, and no negative amortization.

  Long-term property owners may be wise to avoid ARMs completely. If an ARM is selected, however, these buyers should select one with a good convertibility option with low conversion fees. Index and margin are very important to long-term owners, who also could use more leverage going in (including negative amortization) because they have more time to recover equity.
- How important will it be to get equity out immediately upon selling the property? Purchasers who will need all the equity and who are selling via an assumption should select a program that is readily assumable at a good market rate and should save the conversion option intact.

- Who else will participate in the purchase? If there is only one purchaser, then virtually all ARM programs are available. Many ARM programs sold into the secondary market may not allow coborrowers. Among those that do, each has its own strict guidelines. Check each investor (FNMA, GNMA, and FHLMC) for its own underwriting requirements.
- How much savings does the borrower wish to use as a down payment? If the borrower wishes to make only a small down payment, high-rate PMI insurance will be required, as will squeaky-clean credit, strong income base, and cash reserves of at least two or three months. This type of purchaser will have limited negotiating power with the lender, due to extreme leverage.

   The borrower who is prepared to make a large down payment will have an easier time qualifying, and a portfolio approach will be more likely; he or she will be in a stronger negotiating position for lower margins and origination fees, and may request to pay taxes and insurance outside of the monthly payment.
- How much of a monthly payment is the borrower prepared to make? Consider affordability and desirability issues. For most ARMs, the housing ratio (depending on which investor buys the loan) must use an approximate maximum of 28 percent of gross income. The total debt ratio, including all debts of ten months or more plus PITI payment, cannot exceed 36 percent of gross income.
- Would the borrower mind fluctuating payment amounts? If the answer is "yes," the borrower is not suited for any type of ARM. If the answer is "no," the borrower could choose his or her financially and emotionally preferred frequency of payment adjustment (e.g., every year, three years, five years, or ten years) and choose the type of loan to match.
- If necessary, what of the borrower's current assets, including personal and real property, could be mortgaged or liened or sold to raise extra collateral cash? If the borrower's debts are low, he or she could borrow against an asset, but repayment may be considered in long-term debt ratio. In addition, an asset can be converted to cash to use as additional down payment to negotiate a loan with a lower margin or lower cap.
- What are the borrower's short-term and long-term liabilities? Balances are needed to determine this, as well as repayment schedules. If the borrower has lots of credit accounts and small liabilities, he or she may not be able to qualify for a high loan-to-value ARM, or may

have to pay off and close some accounts to qualify. If the borrower has few debts, but is short on down payment or cash reserves, he or she should consider obtaining a gift letter or borrowing from a low-interest source, such as life insurance or a credit union.

Figure 6.3 includes a mortgage checklist from the Federal Reserve Bank that is helpful in choosing the best ARM program to fit a buyer's needs.

PROFILE OF AN ARM PURCHASER

Q. *What are the characteristics of the typical ARM purchaser?*

Each buyer's qualification and profile are unique. If you have one or more of the following characteristics, ARM financing may be best for you. You

- can expect with some certainty that your income will increase.
- desire a home that is slightly out of your financial reach.
- desire short-term ownership.
- cannot qualify at market rates and need a lower initial interest rate.
- wish to buy property when conventional fixed-rates are high or when rates are expected to decline.
- wish to take advantage of an ARM's conversion option.
- don't need the security—emotional or financial—of a fixed-rate mortgage.
- want the loan to adjust based on inflation and economic swings.
- need a better loan assumability feature than available with fixed-rate mortgages.
- want to shop for an index and adjustment period that best coincides with your needs in purchasing the property.

One last note: Many borrowers forget about using ARMs when interest rates for conventional fixed-rate loans are low. By offering borrowers extra purchasing power tailored to their individual financial situations, coupled with loan assumability when the property is sold, ARMs give added benefits fixed rates don't offer. Borrowers should not overlook them when shopping for an affordable loan.

Figure 6.3   ARM Checklist

	Mortgage A	Mortgage B
Ask your lender to help fill out this checklist.		
Mortgage Amount	$	$

Basic Features for Comparison

Fixed Rate Annual Percentage Rate
(This is the cost of your credit as a yearly rate,
which includes both interest and other charges.) _____ _____

ARM Annual Percentage Rate	_____	_____
Adjustment Period	_____	_____
Index Used and Current Rate	_____	_____
Margin	_____	_____
Initial Payment Without Discount	_____	_____
Initial Payment With Discount (If Any)	_____	_____
How long will discount last?	_____	_____
Interest Rate Caps: Periodic	_____	_____
Overall	_____	_____
Payment Caps	_____	_____
Negative Amorization	_____	_____
Convertibility or Prepayment Privilege	_____	_____
Initial Fees and Charges	_____	_____

Monthly Payment Amounts

What will my monthly payment be after
12 months if the index rate:

stays the same?	_____	_____
goes up 2 percent?	_____	_____
goes down 2 percent?	_____	_____

What will my monthly payment be after
three years if the index rate:

stays the same?	_____	_____
goes up 2 percent per year?	_____	_____
goes down 2 percent per year?	_____	_____

Take into account any caps on your mortgage
and remember it may run 30 years.

CHAPTER 7

FEDERAL HOUSING ADMINISTRATION LOANS

This chapter contains basic information about FHA single-family mortgages. Because this information was gleaned from standard FHA guidelines, practices could vary slightly in certain states and cities.

The FHA was established in 1934 under the National Housing Act. It is part of the federal Department of Housing and Urban Development (HUD). Its birth paved the way to mortgage affordability for many Americans who had previously been locked out of home ownership due to a combination of high interest rates and short-term loans, making payments costly. Programs of the FHA expanded loan terms to 30 years at interest rates typically below those of conventional loans.

FHA was also instrumental in determining the first set of construction and appraisal standards for inspecting property prior to loan approval. Many of the quality and safety standards that the housing industry uses today are by-products of early FHA guidelines.

Before 1983, FHA retained the right to control rate ceiling maximums on FHA loans. It's interesting to note, however, that though interest rates are no longer capped, FHA loan rates have remained generally lower than conventional rates. This is the result of supply and demand, default protection to the lender, and discount points, because:

- Low down payments on FHA loans, as well as fairly liberal underwriting guidelines, make FHA loans attractive, thus creating demand.
- The lender is insured against borrower default for the life of the loan, the lender can offset the lower interest received for the security of loan repayment in case of default.
- Discount points charged by the lender help sweeten the pot financially, increasing the desired yield to the lender.

LEVELS OF FEDERAL HOUSING ADMINISTRATION LOANS

While FHA national loan underwriting guidelines establish basic guidelines for loan administration, regional FHA offices and local lenders can choose to be more restrictive.

For example, if loan defaults in a local lender's market have been edging up, that lender might choose to be more cautious about taking risks.

That's why it's important for the borrower to shop not only for the type of FHA loan, but for the lender who will make it. In general, lenders who do a high volume of FHA loans will be aware of little-known exceptions and underwriting allowances that make the loan possible.

PROS AND CONS

Q. *What are the advantages of using FHA financing?*

The following are among the many advantages FHA loans afford borrowers:

- There is a low down payment requirement. On the standard Section 203(b) homeowner's program, the down payment is 3 percent, up to the maximum loan amount allowable in the particular region.
- The entire down payment can be gifted or borrowed from a relative.
- Unlike conventional loans, there are no reserve requirements of two months' PITI payments at closing.
- Loan rates are typically lower than for market-rate conventional fixed-rate loans.
- A seller or other third party is allowed to participate in paying the buyer's closing costs.
- Loans originated prior to December 1, 1986, are simply assumable, meaning that the purchaser does not need to formally qualify. Other FHA loans are assumable with qualifying.
- Loans are assumed at the note rate under which they were originated, with the exception of FHA ARMs, which are assumed at the loan's current rate of interest.
- FHA loans have no prepayment penalty when the loan is retired (if FHA is given a 30-day notice to prepay).
- Because a new FHA loan pays off existing encumbrances, the seller receives all of his or her equity, less costs of sale.

- Qualifying guidelines assist the average buyer in the marketplace; some underwriting guidelines are less restrictive than those of conventional fixed-rate loans.
- The lender is insured against loss for the life of the FHA loan.
- It is possible to place subsequent mortgages after an FHA first mortgage. New financing could even be placed around an FHA mortgage originated before December 1, 1986.
- A second mortgage can be initiated simultaneous with a new FHA first mortgage.

Q. *What are the disadvantages of using an FHA loan?*

- Loans originated after December 1, 1986, are no longer assumable without qualifying.
- On loans originated before December 1, 1986, purchasers who do not receive a release of liability when selling may be secondarily liable should the loan default.
- Buyers and sellers may object to paying discount points or other closing costs attributed to FHA financing.
- Because a seller may be requested to pay fairly heavy costs to assist a buyer, the seller may want to sell only if full price is received.
- A mortgage insurance premium (MIP) is required up front, or can be financed into the loan, and an annual renewal premium is charged, payable in the monthly payment.
- A 1 percent loan origination fee is charged on FHA loans.
- Appraisal guidelines for FHA loans may be more stringent than those of conventional mortgage appraisals.
- Loan processing for FHA loans may take longer than for conventional loans.
- Generally, borrowers are allowed only one FHA loan at a time.

THE BASICS

Q. *What is the basic FHA loan called?*

The primary single-family program is the Section 203(b) loan, which provides financing for a one- to four-family owner-occupied dwelling. This includes a condo, Planned Unit Development (PUD), and new construction financing, all of which must be on the FHA's approved list. Loans are available in rural and urban areas and have loan terms for 15 to 30 years.

Q. *Are FHA loans only for low-income buyers?*

That's a common misconception. Although there have been some FHA-subsidized programs to assist low-income families, FHA's mission is to insure lenders on housing loans made to borrowers who do not meet the necessary down payment requirements or other conditions of conventional mortgages. With FHA loans, borrowers still need to meet monthly income guidelines sufficient to support housing obligations. Because the loans are insured by HUD, however, the lender is protected against the borrower's default and can offer more liberal terms and competitive interest than a buyer might otherwise be able to obtain.

Q. *Who is the typical FHA buyer?*

Although each buyer's qualification and profile will be unique, the following are some general characteristics. The FHA borrower:

- is only moderately qualified and needs a qualifying interest rate lower than required for a market-rate conventional loan.
- needs leverage in qualifying, with lower down payment or gifted funds.
- is working with a seller or other third party to pay part or all of the closing costs and prepaids.
- requires a loan that is assumable.
- desires an insured loan (with possibly some of the mortgage insurance eventually rebated) if the loan is paid off early.
- wants to place a second mortgage initially behind the FHA first mortgage, or later during ownership of the property.
- is interested in leveraged programs of ARMs, GPMs, or GEMs.

Q. *What are the general buyer qualifications for FHA loans?*

Borrowers need to have a satisfactory credit record; the down payment required (or gifted funds available for the down payment); cash needed to close; and steady, verified income to make the monthly payments without difficulty.

Citizenship Is Not Mandatory

Q. *Is U.S. citizenship mandatory for obtaining an FHA loan?*

While the borrower must reside on the property, U.S. citizenship is not a requirement for obtaining an FHA loan. Under the Equal Credit Opportunity Act, lawful permanent residents of the United States are entitled to the same credit benefits as any American citizen and may not be discriminated against due to national origin. Permanent and nonpermanent resident alien borrowers must show an established employment history and evidence employment will continue.

Borrowers Restricted to One FHA Loan at a Time

Q. *Why are FHA buyers restricted to one loan at a time?*

Several years ago, FHA experimented with allowing borrowers to have multiple, simultaneous FHA loans if the first loan did not have a high loan-to-value ratio. If the borrowers wanted to purchase again with an FHA loan, they could pay down the balance on the first home to 75 percent loan-to-appraised value.

Foreclosures ensued, so now borrowers are allowed only one FHA loan at a time. Exceptions to this rule include the borrower who relocates from another area and can only qualify by using an FHA loan, or whose family size has increased so that the present home no longer meets his or her needs.

QUALIFICATION GUIDELINES

Maximum Mortgage Limits and Loan-to-Value Ratios

Q. *Are there national guidelines that dictate what size FHA loan a borrower can obtain? Have these changed from past guidelines?*

Yes. Effective December 21, 1998, FHA: (1) Specifies geographic areas within states as either high closing cost or low closing cost areas. (2) Increases loan limits for high cost areas from 75 percent to 87 percent of the conventional loan maximum (designated as $240,000 for 1999 as determined annually by the secondary market) or up to a maximum ceiling of 95 percent of the median house price for the area, whichever amount is less. Additionally, Alaska, Guam, Hawaii, and the Virgin Islands are allowed maximum loan amounts up to 150 percent of the conventional loan limit. (3) Increases low-cost area loan limits to 48 percent of the maximum conventional loan amount. (4) Changes how FHA minimum down payments are calculated, requiring that the borrower have a minimum cash investment of 3 percent into the property (which may include closing costs). The new formula allows the maximum mortgage amount to be based on a fixed percentage of the property's sales price (or appraised value, if less).

Q. *Weren't borrowers able to finance a big portion of their closing costs previously with an FHA loan?*

Yes. Previously, borrowers were allowed to finance a certain amount of predetermined closing costs into the loan (based on the purchase price and the geographic area of the property). Called *allowable closing costs,* this amount was placed on top of the purchase price (or appraised value, whichever was less) before the maximum loan amount was calculated. That number became the *acquisition cost* and was used as the benchmark for calculating the maximum loan amount. As you'll see by the calculations in the questions that follow, the acquisition cost now includes only those closing costs that are the financial responsibility of the borrower (exclusive of prepaid amounts like property taxes and insurance).

By increasing the maximum loan limits overall (to make FHA more competitive with conventional loans), HUD feels that it benefits most buyers, allowing them to qualify for more loan. It also keeps uniform the formula for determining the maximum allowable loan, independent of closing costs that can vary from area to area, and changes in closing dates.

Q. *How is the FHA (203)b maximum mortgage amount calculated?*

The borrower first must determine if he or she is in a low closing cost or high closing cost area. This information can be obtained by contacting a real estate agent or the lender, or by visiting HUD on the Web at www. hud.gov/fha/sfh/sfhhicos.html and accessing the table for your appropriate state and region. A state roster can be found at Figure 7.1. Using that information, apply the following formulas.

Maximum loan-to-value percentages for low closing costs states are:

- 98.75 percent for properties with values/sales prices equal to or less than $50,000
- 97.65 percent for properties with values/sales prices in excess of $50,000 up to $125,000
- 97.15 percent for properties with values/sales prices in excess of $125,000

Figure 7.1   States and Territories with Low and High Average
Closing Costs

Alabama	high	Montana	high
Alaska	high	Nebraska	high
Arizona	low	Nevada	low
Arkansas	high	New Hampshire	high
California	low	New Jersey	high
Colorado	low	New Mexico	low
Connecticut	high	New York	high
Delaware	high	North Carolina	high
District of Columbia	high	North Dakota	high
Florida	high	Ohio	high
Georgia	high	Oklahoma	high
Guam	low	Oregon	low
Hawaii	high	Pennsylvania	high
Idaho	low	Puerto Rico	high
Illinois	low	Rhode Island	high
Indiana	low	South Carolina	high
Iowa	high	South Dakota	high
Kansas	high	Tennessee	high
Kentucky	high	Texas	high
Louisiana	high	U.S. Virgin Islands	low
Maine	high	Utah	low
Maryland	high	Vermont	high
Massachusetts	high	Virginia	high
Michigan	high	Washington	low
Minnesota	high	West Virginia	high
Mississippi	high	Wisconsin	low
Missouri	high	Wyoming	low

Maximum loan-to-value percentages for high closing costs states are:

- 98.75 percent for properties with values/sales prices equal to or less than $50,000
- 97.75 percent for properties with values/sales prices in excess of $50,000

Let's use the following scenarios to see how FHA maximum mortgages are calculated. You may want to follow along using the Mortgage Credit Analysis Worksheet found at Figure 7.2. Later you can use this worksheet to pencil in your own qualifying information.

Figure 7.2   Mortgage Credit Analysis Worksheet

Mortgage Credit Analysis Worksheet Purchase Money Mortgages

U.S. Department of Housing and Urban Development
Office of Housing
Federal Housing Commissioner

OMB Approval No. 2502–0059 (exp. 7/31/2000)

See back of page for Public Burden and Sensitive Information statements

All numbered entries in $ except where noted.

Case number	Section of the Housing Act	Check one
		☐ Existing Construction ☐ Proposed Construction

1a. Borrower's name	2a. Social Security Number

1b. Co–Borrower's name	2b. Social Security Number

3a. Mortgage without Upfront MIP	3b. Total UFMIP	3c. Mortgage with UFMIP	4. Appraised Value (without CC)	5. a. Total Closing Costs (CC) _____
				b. Less Paid by Seller _____
				c. Equals Borrower's CC _____

6. Current housing expenses	7. Term of loan years	8. Interest rate %	9. Adj. buy-down interest rate %	

10. **Statutory Investment Requirements**	
a. Contract Sales Price	
b. Borrower-Paid Closing Costs (from 5c)	
c. Unadjusted Acquisition (10a + 10b)	
d. Statutory Investment Requirement (10a x 0.03)	
11. **Maximum Mortgage Calculation**	
a. Lesser of Sales Price (10a) or Value (from 4)	
b. Required Adjustments (+/-)	
c. Mortgage Basis (11a + 11b)	
d. Mort Amt. (11c x LTV Factor % or Less)	
12. **Cash Investment Requirements**	
a. Minimum Down Payment (10c-11d)	
(This amount must equal or exceed 10d)	
b. Prepaid Expenses	
c. Discount Points	
d. Repairs/Improvements (Non-Financeable)	
e. Upfront MIP Paid in Cash	
f. Non-Realty and Other Items	
g. Total Cash to Close (Sum of 12a thru 12f)	
h. Amount Paid (Earnest Money, etc.)	
I. Amount of Gift Funds [Source _____]	
j. Assets Available	
k. 2nd Mort (if applicable) [Source _____]	
l. Cash Reserves (Sum 12h thru 12k, minus 12g)	

13. **Monthly Effective Income**	
a. Borrower's base pay	
b. Borrower's other earnings (explain)	
c. Co-borrower's base pay	
d. Co-borrower's other earnings (explain)	
e. Net income from real estate	
f. Gross monthly income	

Remarks (attach additional paper if needed)

14. **Debts & Obligations**	Monthly Payment	Unpaid Balance
a. Total installment debt		
b. Child support, etc.		
c. Other		
d. Total monthly payments		
15. **Future monthly payments**		
a. Principal & interest – 1st mortgage		
b. Monthly MIP		
c. Homeowners Association Fee		
d. Ground rent		
e. Principal & interest – 2nd mortgage		
f. Hazard insurance		
g. Taxes & special assessments		
h. Total mortgage payment		
i. Recurring expenses (from 14d)		
j. Total fixed payment		

16. **Ratios**		
a. Loan–to–value (11d divided by 11a)	.	%
b. Mortgage Payment–to–income (15h divided by 13f)	.	%
c. Total fixed payment–to–income (15j divided by 13f)	.	%

17. **Borrower rating** (enter "A" for acceptable or "R" for reject)	
a. Credit characteristics	
b. Adequacy of effective income	
c. Stability of effective income	
d. Adequacy of available assets	

18. Borrower's CAIVRS Number	Co–borrower's CAIVRS Number
LDP/GSA (page no. & date)	LDP/GSA (page no. & date)

Attachment A Information
A1. Contract Sales Price of Property (line 10a above)

A2. 6% of line A1

A3. Total Seller Contribution

A4. Excess Contribution

17. **Final application decision** ☐ Approve ☐ Reject	18. Examiner's signature & date X X	19. Underwriter's signature & date	CHUMS ID Number

Previous editions are obsolete

form **HUD-92900–PUR** (10/98)
ref. Handbook 4155.1

Scenario 1: Buyer Responsible for Closing Costs

Q. *How would the maximum mortgage amount be calculated on a $100,000 property sale (and appraisal) if the buyer is paying $1,000 in closing costs in a high closing cost area?*

First, calculate the maximum mortgage ($100,000 × 97.75 percent = $97,750). The borrower needs at least 3 percent ($3,000) cash into the purchase (excluding prepaid expenses like taxes and insurance).

The borrower's acquisition cost is $101,000 ($100,000 plus $1,000 of closing costs that are his or her responsibility). $101,000 less the maximum mortgage of $97,750 requires a cash down payment of $3,250. Because this represents at least 3 percent of the sales/appraised price, no further calculation is necessary.

Scenario 2: Seller Pays the Closing Costs; Buyer Receives Premium Pricing

Q. *What if the property sold and appraised for $100,000; but the seller was paying part of the closing costs, and the balance was paid by the lender increasing the interest rate (called **premium pricing**).*

Oops—you didn't tell us if it was a high or low closing cost area! (Let's use high cost.) The maximum mortgage calculation ($100,000 × 97.75 percent) equals $97,750. Because this loan amount represents less than a 3 percent cash down payment ($2,250), the maximum mortgage must be reduced to $97,000 to ensure that there's a minimum of $3,000 down (exclusive of prepaid expenses). The required investment must be from the borrower's own funds, a bona fide gift, a loan from a family member, or from a government agency. It may not come from an increase in the interest rate of the loan (premium pricing) or from sources like the seller, builder, or real estate agent.

Scenario 3: Buyer Responsible for Closing Costs; Seller Contributes a Decorating Allowance

Q. *What about a property (in a high closing cost area) that sells for $100,000, appraises for $103,250, with the buyer paying $2,000 in closing costs, and the seller contributes a decorating allowance of $1,000?*

Decorating allowances and other inducements to purchase, as well as sales concessions exceeding 6 percent, must be subtracted from the lesser of the sale price or value before calculating the maximum mortgage amount. So first we subtract the decorating allowance from the sales price

($100,000 – $1,000 = $99,000) and then multiply that amount by 97.75 percent. This results in a maximum mortgage of $96,773. In this case, the decorating allowance penalized the borrower, requiring him to make a larger down payment.

Q. *Can the 3 percent borrower cash requirement consist of discount points or prepaid amounts?*

No. The 3 percent must be exclusive of both discount points and any prepaid amounts.

GIFTS

Q. *Could the borrower use gifts for the down payment on an FHA loan?*

Yes. Gifts for down payments can come from a relative of the borrower, the borrower's employer or labor union, a charitable organization, a governmental agency, or a close friend with a clearly defined interest in the borrower. Parties to the transaction (real estate agents, a builder, etc.) are not allowed to gift down payments to buyers without the donated amount being first subtracted from the sales price (before the maximum allowable loan is figured).

In 1997, bridal registry accounts were initiated by FHA to allow friends and relatives to contribute to an account for down payment and closing costs.

Here's how it works. Prospective home buyers contact lenders who originate FHA loans to set up individual federally insured depository accounts in the parties' names. Funds may be deposited by friends and relatives directly into the account, or given by cash or check to the party(ies) for deposit.

Depending on how they wish to market the homeowner bridal registry program, lenders can provide information about the program directly to friends and relatives of the potential home buyer(s) using FHA's promotional brochure, or one designed by the lender. In addition, lenders can provide "gift cards" with the gift-giver's name for the purpose of documenting the gift. Not only will the program help buyers obtain a down payment, the monies will be tracked and accounted for using FHA guidelines, ready as part of the loan documentation when the buyers are ready to apply for the loan.

The funds remain under the control of the individuals for whom they're deposited. The funds can be withdrawn at any time and aren't required to be used to purchase a home. (What a neat way to help pay the wedding expenses!) In addition, engaged couples don't have to be married before they use the monies to close on a home loan.

BORROWING THE DOWN PAYMENT

Q. *Can a buyer borrow the down payment for an FHA loan?*

Yes. Buyers can borrow the down payment secured against assets like stocks, bonds, automobiles, and real estate (other than the property being purchased).

In addition, loans could be secured against deposited funds like life insurance policies and loans against 401(k)s. If repayment of the loan against the asset can be obtained by converting the asset to cash, the repayment for the purpose of loan qualification would not be required.

CLOSING COSTS

Q. *How could a seller financially assist a buyer?*

The seller can pay discount points, buydowns, and other financial supplements (called *financing concessions*) for the borrower up to a maximum of 6 percent of the sales price. Past that point, deductions will be made dollar for dollar from the sales price before the maximum loan amount is figured.

Any charge considered to be a seller-paid closing cost for the buyer will be subtracted likewise from the sale price as well as being contributed to the 6 percent ceiling.

NO CASH RESERVES REQUIRED

Q. *Does the borrower need two months of reserve PITI payment in cash as with other loans?*

There is no reserve requirement set by FHA on single-family, one-unit dwellings. The lender could impose reserves of three months' PITI on multifamily occupied dwellings, such as two-unit to four-unit properties.

QUALIFYING INCOME

Q. *What are the qualifying income criteria for standard FHA loans?*

It's a common misconception that buyers who do not fit within the exact qualifying ratios will not receive FHA loans. Although the following ratios are guidelines, they are not absolutes. The loan underwriter will carefully weigh each individual situation before making a lending decision.

Housing ratio   The following monthly expenses should not exceed 29 percent of the borrower's monthly gross income: PITI (including MIP); any homeowner association or condo fees; and any local improvement district or improvement assessments.

Total debt ratio   The following monthly expenses should not exceed 41 percent of the borrower's monthly gross income: total mortgage payment, auto payments, installment charges, loans, child support, alimony, or other obligations to run more than ten months. You can refer to the worksheet found at Figure 7.2.

Compensating Factors

Q. *What exceptions could the lender make on these ratios?*

Strong consideration to exceed the ratios could be given an applicant who uses a large down payment and has substantial cash reserves after closing, a history of light use of credit, excellent job history, and no other large debt payments such as a car loan.

Also considered as compensating factors would be the borrower's track record of managing a large house payment, a new house payment that will increase only slightly, or compensation or income not reflected in qualifying, but which could directly assist repayment of the mortgage. Changing circumstances, such as child support with only two years of payments left to pay, may also be considered. If a home is being purchased due to job relocation and the trailing spouse is expected to return to work, that could count as a compensating factor.

In addition, a property that meets energy efficiency guidelines can allow the borrower's ratios to be increased by 2 percent on both the housing and total debt ratios.

Q. *On which of the two ratios—housing or long-term debt—is the lender usually the more flexible?*

Lenders are usually more flexible on housing ratio. The rationale is that if the borrower's long-term debt ratio is 41 percent or less, the borrower could perhaps handle a larger house payment.

Documenting Income

Q. *What kind of income qualifications must the borrower prove to qualify for an FHA loan?*

As with all mortgages, the borrower must prove stability of income. While FHA does not mandate a minimum length of time a borrower must have held a position, the lender must verify the most recent two full years of employment. If part of this history included school or military time, the borrower must provide evidence supporting this, such as college transcripts or discharge papers. Allowances for seasonal employment—such as are typical in the building trades, etc.—may be made.

Changing jobs need not be viewed as negative if the changes were in the same line of work, advanced the borrower's position, and were accompanied by income increases.

Q. *Are pay increases counted in qualifying income?*

Pay increases, such as performance raises, bonuses, and cost-of-living adjustments, can be included as income if they will begin within 60 days of loan closing and can be verified by the employer.

Q. *Will overtime and bonus income count toward FHA qualifying?*

Overtime and bonus income may be used to qualify if the borrower has received it for the past two years and will in all likelihood continue to do so. The lender will use an average figure based on the past two-year history.

Q. *Does part-time income count?*

HUD recognizes that many low-income and moderate-income families rely on part-time and seasonal income. So FHA lenders may include part-time and seasonal income in qualifying if the borrower has worked the job uninterrupted for the past two years and appears likely to continue. Seasonal employment is viewed the same way, focusing on the rehire for the next season. Other situations that do not meet the two-year history can be seen only as compensating factors by the lender.

Q. *How does the lender verify commission income?*

Commission income is averaged over the previous two years, and the borrower must provide his or her last two years' tax returns along with a recent pay stub to verify it. A borrower showing income decreases from year to year will need to show significant compensating factors to receive loan approval.

Q. *Do retirement and Social Security benefits count as income?*

Yes, but it needs to be verified from the source (usually the former employer or Social Security Administration) or through federal tax returns. If any benefits expire within approximately five years, it will be considered only as a compensating factor.

Q. *How is alimony or child support verified?*

Alimony and child support must be projected to continue for at least the first three years of the mortgage. The borrower must provide a copy of the divorce decree and evidence that payments have been made for the past 12 months.

Self-Employed Borrowers

Q. *Are self-employed borrowers qualified for FHA in the same tedious way they are for conventional loans?*

More or less; but FHA may make an exception for self-employed borrowers who have been employed less than two years, but more than one year. The self-employed borrower may qualify for an FHA loan if he or she has at least two years' previous employment in the same line of work or a combination of one year employment and one year formal training.

DETERMINING DEBT FOR LOAN QUALIFYING

Q. *How does the lender view debt for FHA loan qualifying?*

The borrower's liabilities included in the long-term debt ratio for qualifying include installment loans, revolving charge accounts, real estate loans, alimony, child support, and all other continuing obligations. The basic guideline is that any debt that extends ten months or more must be considered in the qualifying ratios. Debts lasting less than ten months need not be counted unless they substantially affect the borrower's ability to repay the mortgage in the early months of the loan. An example of a debt that might be counted would be a substantial car payment with four payments remaining.

Q. *Does child care count as a borrower debt?*

No, it no longer counts as a borrower debt.

Q. *Are cosigned loans counted as debt for qualifying?*

If the individual applying is a cosigner on a car loan, student loan, or any other obligation including a mortgage, the lender requires verification that the primary obligor has been making payments on a regular basis and has no history of delinquent payments on the loan over the past 12 months.

Q. *What are the other special guidelines that relate to debt for an FHA loan?*

If a borrower has a debt projected to begin within 12 months of mortgage closing, such as student loan repayment, the lender must include the anticipated monthly obligation in the underwriting analysis. Similarly, balloon notes that come due within one year of loan closing must be considered as debt.

ALTERNATIVE DOCUMENTATION

Q. *Is quick processing available with FHA, similar to TimeSaver on conventional loans?*

Lenders can use the alternative documentation method, which expedites processing. The borrower is required to provide the following to use this method:

- Bank statements for the most recent three months
- W-2 forms for the past two years
- Pay stubs covering the most recent 30-day period, with the borrower's name and Social Security number

The lender will verify employment by phoning the employer prior to closing, confirming the buyer's position and salary range.

If all of these cannot be obtained, standard processing is required.

BANKRUPT BORROWERS

Q. *Can borrowers who have previously declared bankruptcy purchase a home using an FHA loan?*

Yes. In fact, FHA's evaluation of previous bankrupt borrowers is one of the most liberal in the mortgage lending industry. A lender may allow a bankrupt borrower to secure a mortgage loan if the bankruptcy has been discharged for at least one year and credit has been satisfactorily reestablished, and it appears that the problems surrounding the bankruptcy are unlikely to recur.

Borrowers who have filed bankruptcy under Chapter 13 must be one year into the payout and have trustee approval to add the debt.

In either case, borrowers must provide detailed letters of explanation and supporting documentation to the lender.

PROPERTY GUIDELINES

Q. *What kinds of property certifications need to be done to secure an FHA loan?*

FHA will require termite inspections if applicable, testing of wells for bacteria and chemical analysis, and other property certifications based on the borrower's geographic area.

Q. *Are there any safeguards that govern the condition of property insured by FHA?*

In 1998, HUD launched a Homebuyer Protection Plan designed to reinvent FHA's home appraisal process and create a new level of consumer confidence in the homebuying process.

Under the plan, homes purchased with FHA-insured mortgages:

- Require a more thorough basic survey of the physical condition of the home to uncover potential problems.
- Require appraisers, for the first time, to disclose property defects to potential buyers.
- Impose stricter accountability on appraisers and tougher sanctions for those who act improperly (ranging from barring them from doing FHA appraisals to fines to potential prison sentences).

- Allow homebuyers to finance up to $300 in home inspection costs into their mortgage loan.

Q.   *Does FHA have to comply with the Energy Policy Act of 1992 on new construction?*

For both FHA and VA loans, new construction begun after October 24, 1993 must comply with the 1992 Model Energy Code (MEC) of the Council of American Building Officials (CABO). A written certificate must be obtained from the builder stating that minimum energy standards have been met before the loan can be approved.

Q.   *Are there any credits allowed for energy-efficient homes?*

In addition to being able to increase both qualifying ratios by 2 percent, buyers can have the cost of energy efficient improvements financed into the mortgage. The allowable amount is the greater of 5 percent of the property's value (not to exceed $8,000).

LEVERAGE

Q.   *Are coborrowers allowed on FHA loans?*

Coborrowers are allowed on FHA loans. By definition, coborrowers take title to the property and obligate themselves on the mortgage note, but do not live in the property. Loan-to-value ratio on coborrower transactions is limited to 75 percent of the appraised value of the property.

The only exception to this 75 percent loan-to-value rule would be if the coborrowers were related by blood (parent and child, siblings, aunts, uncles, nieces or nephews, etc.) or for unrelated individuals who can document evidence of a family-type long-standing relationship. Individuals proving these relationships can obtain a maximum loan-to-value loan.

Similar to a coborrower, a cosigner with no ownership interest in the property (who does not take title) will be permitted to become jointly liable for repayment of the obligation. The coborrower and cosigner's income, assets, liabilities, and credit history will be used for qualifying.

Second Mortgage Simultaneous to a New First FHA Loan

Q. *Would FHA ever allow a borrower to secure a second mortgage simultaneously with a new FHA first mortgage?*

Remarkably, the answer is yes. Secondary financing simultaneous with a new FHA first mortgage may be allowed if the combined amounts of the first and second mortgages do not exceed the applicable loan-to-value ratio loan. In addition, the second mortgage must not force a balloon payment before ten years, reasonable monthly payments must be made on the second mortgage, and prepayment of the obligation must be allowed at any time.

Borrowers age 60 and older can obtain secondary financing with total loan-to-value ratios of the combined first and second mortgages up to 100 percent of the property's appraised value.

Q. *When might a buyer use an initial second mortgage with a new FHA first?*

This situation would be most likely to occur when interest rates on the first mortgage are high and qualifying for an entire loan at that high rate could be difficult, as in the following example.

FHA interest is at 9 percent. Edith Olson can't qualify for a $90,000 loan at that interest rate, so she secures a $20,000 second mortgage from her credit union at 7 percent interest simultaneous with closing a $70,000 FHA first mortgage, less applicable down payment.

Of course the FHA lender knows of the second mortgage and qualifies Edith for both sets of debt repayments. The two payments are melded together for the purpose of qualifying, and the lower interest rate of the second mortgage is just enough to leverage Edith into qualifying for both loans.

MORTGAGE INSURANCE PREMIUMS

Q. *How is mortgage insurance applied to the loan amount?*

There are two kinds of mortgage insurance premiums with FHA loans: initial premiums and renewal premiums. The rates charged are based on the term of the loan, as well as the amount of down payment. Figure 7.3

contains the rates charged. For example, on a $100,000 loan, minimum down payment, for 30 years, the upfront premium would be 2.25 percent, for a total of $2,250 (paid in cash at closing or financed into the loan. Obviously, most borrowers finance it into the loan!) The monthly or recurring premium would be .50 percent, or $41.67 per month (added to the monthly PITI payment). It's important to note that first-time buyers who take an FHA-approved homeownership class can have the initial premium lowered to 1.75 percent.

Q. *Can a portion of the MIP be refunded to the borrower?*

A borrower may be eligible for a refund of a portion of the insurance premium if the borrower

- originated the loan after September 1, 1983,
- paid an upfront mortgage insurance premium at closing, and
- did not default on the mortgage payments.

Figure 7.3   Up-Front and Annual MIP Rates

Up-Front	LTV Ratio	Premium	Years
	Loan Term More Than 15 Years		
2.25%	89.99 and under	.50%	7
2.25%	90.00 to 95.00	.50%	12
2.25%	95.01 and over	.50%	30
	Loan Term 15 Years or Less		
2.00%	89.99 and under	None	N/A
2.00%	90.00 to 95.00	.25%	4
2.00%	95.01 and over	.25%	8

For mortgages closed on or after September 22, 1997.

Streamline refinances or mortgages closed before July, 1991, are subject to an up-front MIP or 3.8 percent (where the new mortgage will carry a term greater than 15 years) or 2.4 percent (where the new mortgage will carry a term of 15 years or less), but are not subject to the annual premium.

Purchase money mortgages where the first-time homebuyer received housing counseling are subject to an up-front premium of 1.75 percent.

However, there's another category of refunds called *distributive share* that affects mortgages written before September 1, 1983. To be eligible for these excess earnings from the HUD Mutual Mortgage Insurance fund your loan must have

- been originated before September 1, 1983,
- shown at least seven years of payments, and
- been paid off before November 5, 1990.

Because the statute of limitations runs for only six years from the date the payoff notification was sent to the mortgagor, the last deadline for applying for these funds was November 5, 1996.

Note this exception: When an FHA loan is assumed, the seller receives no refund.

Borrowers who want to inquire about possible premium refunds can contact HUD at P.O. Box 23699, Washington, DC 20026-3699, or call 1-800-697-6967 between 8:30AM and 8:30PM (ET).

CONCESSIONS

Q. *What are sales concessions, and why are they limited in an FHA loan?*

A sales concession is a cost paid by someone other than the buyer, such as the seller or another third party. It is viewed as an inducement to purchase and limits the buyer's investment in the property. For that reason, HUD requires that sales concessions paid or offered by the seller or other third party be deducted dollar for dollar from the sale price before the maximum mortgage amount is calculated. Sales concessions include prepaid items, personal property items, decorating allowances, moving costs, buyer-broker fees, condominium or homeowner association fees, excess rent credit, or seller payment of borrower's sales commission on present residence.

Q. *What's the difference between sales concessions and financing concessions?*

Financially, quite a lot. While financing concessions include discount points, interest rate buydowns, mortgage interest payments, or the borrower's up-front mortgage insurance premium paid for the borrower by the seller or other third party, financing concessions are treated differently from sales concessions for qualifying purposes. Financing concessions are not subtracted dollar for dollar from the sale price until they exceed 6 percent of the sale price. Then, they are subtracted dollar-for-dollar before figuring the maximum loan amount.

How does this affect the borrower's position? If possible, it's financially better for a seller or third party to contribute financing concessions rather than sales concessions if the borrower is in need of a maximum-allowable loan. It's best to spell out on the purchase agreement just what the concession is to apply to; otherwise, it would be determined by the lender, possibly not to the buyer's advantage.

ASSUMPTION GUIDELINES

Q.   *What does the term "simply assumable" mean when referring to FHA loans originated before December 15, 1989?*

A simply assumable FHA loan is one that can be assumed by a new borrower without qualifying through the lender. Should the assumptor default on the loan, however, the original borrower could be held responsible for satisfying the debt.

If the initial mortgagor wants to be released of all liability under an FHA loan written prior to December 15, 1989, the assumptor needs to qualify to assume the loan (called a *novation*). This includes providing the lender with information regarding monthly income and debt, as well as credit and employment history, and requesting the novation from the lender. If the borrower meets the lender's criteria, the original borrower may be released from further liability on the loan.

Q.   *What about loans originated after December 15, 1989?*

Borrowers must qualify and meet all FHA guidelines for assumptions. Only owner-occupants, not investors, may assume these loans.

PREPAYMENT PENALTIES

Q.   *Is there a prepayment penalty on FHA mortgages?*

This question has several answers. The guidelines state that if an FHA loan was insured prior to August 2, 1985, the borrower must give a 30-day written notice to HUD stating that the loan will be paid in full. This notice can come from a real estate agent or loan officer and carries 30 days of interest. FHA, however, views this as an interest charge, not as a prepayment penalty.

For loans insured on or after August 2, 1985, FHA will no longer require a 30-day notice to prepay. Under this guideline, however, the lender can refuse to credit full prepayment without requiring interest to the next due date if the payment is not made *on* the monthly due date. The solution? Make sure the loan is repaid on the monthly due date!

DISCOUNT POINTS AND BUYDOWNS

Q. *Who can pay points on FHA loans?*

Anyone can pay points on FHA loans. Because many FHA buyers are short on cash, sellers often assist with points. A third party—such as a relative of the buyer, or someone in another real estate transaction who has an interest in seeing this sale close so that his or her home can be purchased—could also pay points. No matter who pays the points, they are tax deductible for the homebuyer.

Q. *Could a buyer use discount points and then reduce the interest rate using buydowns in the same transaction?*

There's no reason why not. The discount points are charged by the lender to help increase the overall yield and defray the cost of discounting the loan when it's sold to the secondary market. The buydown, on the other hand, uses points (actually prepaid interest) to buy down the note rate either temporarily (like a 3-2-1 buydown) or permanently for the life of the loan (for example, from 8 percent to 7 percent).

REFINANCING

Q. *What are the guidelines for refinancing an FHA loan?*

If the borrower is taking cash out of the property, the loan-to-value ratio cannot exceed 85 percent of the appraised value, and the borrower must occupy the property.

If the borrower takes no cash out of the property, the maximum loan is based on the lower of the FHA purchase formula or costs and liens on the property.

Q. *Is there a streamlined program such as those available with other loan types?*

Yes. The FHA streamlined refinance program is designed to lower the monthly principal and interest payments on a current HUD-insured mortgage and involves no cash back to the borrower.

Streamline refinances can be completed with or without an appraisal but must meet the following guidelines:

- Refinances *without* an appraisal are limited to the unpaid principal balance (but no interest), minus any refund of mortgage insurance premium (MIP), plus the new up-front mortgage insurance premium if it's to be financed in the mortgage. Term of the refinanced mortgage is the lesser of 30 years or the unexpired term of the old mortgage plus 12 years.
- Refinances *with* appraisals allow the closing costs and reasonable discount points to be financed. The lender could also charge a higher interest rate on the loan and pay the closing costs on behalf of the borrower. Loan maximums are subject to FHA loan-to-value limits.

Refinancing is considered a payoff of the old loan and releases the original seller on an assumed loan from all liability.

Borrowers could take advantage of this program to lower a 30-year loan into a 15-year term (provided the new payment does not increase by more than $50), or to convert an FHA adjustable rate mortgage into a fixed rate loan.

OTHER FHA LOAN OPTIONS

The FHA/VA Tandem Loan

Q. *Is there an FHA loan for veterans?*

The loan is called FHA/VA 203(v) and it is used to finance only single-family structures: duplexes and other multifamily units are not permitted. The loan is often used by veterans who have used their VA eligibility or who want to preserve their VA certificate for a later time. In other words, the FHA/VA loan does not involve the veteran's entitlement, and there are no limits restricting the amount of times it can be used.

FHA/VA loans are beneficial because FHA limits some charges typically required with regular 203(b) financing. In addition, some closing costs can be financed into the loan.

The veteran must obtain a Certificate of Veteran Status form from the VA (and a Form DD208 from the commander if the veteran is still in service). Loan ceiling amounts are the same as with the standard 203(b) program.

The FHA Adjustable-Rate Mortgage

Q. *Are FHA ARMs competitive?*

The FHA ARM (FHA loan Section 251) is very competitive, combining the down payment guidelines of the standard (203)b program with the features of an ARM. Here are some of its characteristics:

- Maximum interest rate increase caps are limited to 1 percent per year and 5 percent over the life of the loan. In addition, the FHA ARM allows no negative amortization.
- The loan is assumable (with borrower qualification) at the loan's current interest rate.
- The index is the one-year Treasury Constant Maturities Index, and the margin is determined by supply and demand for GNMA mortgage-backed securities.
- Qualifying guidelines and maximum loan amounts are the same as those found under the 203(b) program.
- The FHA ARM can be used to refinance any existing HUD loan.

The FHA Graduated Payment Mortgage

Q. *What other FHA programs could interest a borrower?*

The graduated payment mortgage (GPM) plan, a variation of the regular HUD mortgage insurance program, can allow a borrower to pay a lower initial monthly payment in the early years of the loan.

With a GPM, mortgage payments rise gradually for a set period, usually five to seven years, then level off and remain fixed for the balance of the mortgage. In other words, a GPM enables borrowers to grow into higher monthly payments as their income increases.

Negative amortization, or payment shortfall, was once a major part of early GPM mortgages. Today, however, most graduated payment programs require larger down payments in order to prevent payment shortfall being added back onto the loan's principal balance.

FHA Growing Equity Mortgage (GEM)

Q. *What is the growing equity mortgage (GEM) and how does it work?*

The GEM program was designed to allow a borrower to grow equity quicker than with the traditional 30-year mortgage, while keeping payments low in the early years of the loan.

In the GEM loan program, payments increase between 2 percent and 7.5 percent per year, depending on the plan chosen, with the annual increase being applied directly to reduce the principal balance. The effect is that the loan retires in a little over 15 years, dramatically reducing the total cost of the mortgage to the borrower.

Unlike a graduated payment mortgage, there is no negative amortization, because the initial interest rate is lowered through up-front interest buydowns.

The GEM loan is easier to qualify for than a shorter-term 15-year loan, because the monthly payments start out lower. By about the tenth year of the loan, however, the payment will be higher than that of the 15-year loan. This is attractive to borrowers who need the benefit of the lower payment qualification upfront, but could manage a higher payment later. Borrowers could include young professionals or buyers in their 50s who are making their last home purchase.

SPECIALIZED FHA MORTGAGE PROGRAMS

Q. *Which other FHA programs might be of interest to borrowers?*

Although many FHA programs are not widely used, here are some that have sparked interest lately:

Disaster Victim Housing Loans

HUD Section (203)h financing is eligible to anyone whose home has been destroyed or severely damaged in a federally declared disaster area. The loan can be used to rebuild a home or purchase a new one, but the borrower's application for mortgage insurance must be filed with HUD within one year of the President's declaration of the disaster.

Benefits of the (203)h loan include:

- 100 percent loans can be obtained (including closing costs). Prepaid expenses like property taxes and insurance can be paid by the

borrower, or the lender can premium price the loan (charge more interest) and pay the prepaids for the borrower.
- Limits on some fees charged including appraisals, inspections, and origination fees.

Borrowers under (203)h must pay FHA mortgage insurance. As with the standard FHA (203)b program, the upfront fee can be paid in cash at closing or financed into the loan. The monthly MIP fee is added onto the PITI payment.

Loans to Rehabilitate Properties

Section 203(k), rehabilitation home mortgage insurance, insures loans used to rehabilitate an existing residential dwelling that will be used for residential purposes, or to refinance an outstanding indebtedness plus rehabilitate such a structure. This program also may be used to convert non-residential buildings to residential use or to change the number of family units in the dwelling.

The 203(k) provides the borrower with interim and permanent financing in one loan. The loan amount, which is based on the property's after-renovation value, can't exceed the current FHA maximum mortgage in the borrower's area.

Even though it's called a rehab program, repairs can include almost anything beyond minor or cosmetic adjustments. Replacing floors, tiles, or carpets is considered rehab work, as is new siding, roofing, gutters, plumbing, heating/cooling, and electrical systems.

- The 203(k) loan can also be used to finance repairs outside the structure such as major landscaping work, patios, or terraces.
- While repairs are underway, borrowers don't have to make mortgage payments. However, tax or insurance payments may be due. The payment moratorium can last up to six months if repairs require and the property is unoccupied.

Manufactured Housing Loans

Q. *Does FHA allow loans on mobile homes?*

FHA calls mobile homes "manufactured homes" and will lend money for their purchase under the FHA Title I program, similar to the residential guidelines under the 203(b) program. In fact, a borrower can receive a loan for purchase of a manufactured home if he or she owns the land on which it will be placed; to fund a combination purchase of home and land; or just for the land, if the borrower already owns the manufactured home.

Because state laws vary regarding manufactured housing as real property, the borrower should check with a local lender to determine program guidelines.

FORECLOSURE ALTERNATIVES WHEN PAYMENTS FALL BEHIND

Q. *Does FHA assist borrowers who fall behind on their mortgage payments?*

Yes. There are five options available from HUD to help borrowers sidestep foreclosure (including various incentives to lenders ranging from $100 to $10,000).

1. Special forbearance: The lender may be able to arrange a repayment plan based on the consumer's current financial situation—including a temporary suspension of payments.
2. Mortgage modification. The lender agrees to add the borrower's back payments, interest, and penalties onto the loan and amortize it over the loan term. HUD requires that the new payment must be lower than the present payment. This is accomplished by lowering the interest rate and/or extending the loan term. The rationale is that while the borrower is paying more over time because the loan principal is higher, the lower payment should be easier to keep current.
3. Partial claim: The lender may be able to obtain an interest-free loan from HUD to bring the borrower's payments current.
4. Preforeclosure sale: Allowing the borrower time to sell the property and pay off the mortgage before foreclosure. This encourages the borrower to keep the property in good repair in order to take equity from the sale.
5. Deed-in-lieu of foreclosure: As a last resort, the buyer may decide to voluntarily "give back" the property to the lender. The lender must agree, which means the value of the property must cover the outstanding loan plus costs to market the property. The mortgagor sidesteps foreclosure and avoids attorney's fees, but gets no equity from a sale.

The bottom line to working out alternatives when a borrower's mortgage payments become delinquent is for the borrower to take a proactive stance, contact the lender as soon as possible, and be prepared to be honest with the lender about his or her current financial situation.

CHAPTER 8

VA LOAN PROGRAMS

This chapter offers an overview of VA single-family housing programs. Information in this chapter comes from standard VA guidelines and therefore may have different applications in your area.

In 1944, Congress passed the Serviceman's Readjustment Act. This legislation, more commonly known as the GI Bill of Rights, was developed to assist veterans in readjusting to civilian life by providing them with medical benefits, bonuses, and low-interest loans. Title III, one of six sections of the bill, guaranteed home loans to eligible veterans. Although loans were to be a type of bonus for those who had served their country, credit standards and underwriting guidelines were strictly enforced so that veterans would not undertake a mortgage obligation they could not fulfill.

A local lender makes a loan for up to 100 percent of the appraised value of the property, with the Department of Veterans Affairs indemnifying the lender against loss on a portion of the loan. Originally, the guarantee was for 50 percent of the mortgage balance, not to exceed $2,000. Today's guarantee is still a maximum of 50 percent of the loan balance, but the dollar amount over the years has increased to a maximum of $50,750.

Unlike FHA loans, with VA loans the veteran does not pay a premium for the loan guarantee (though a funding fee is charged). This factor, plus others discussed in this chapter, helps make VA loans some of the most successful and rate-competitive programs in the mortgage market today.

LEVELS OF VA LOANS

Borrowers who have spoken with someone from a different area about VA loans sometimes find discrepancies in what they thought were firm guidelines or practices. Who was correct? Both probably were. Similar to

FHA, VA national loan underwriting guidelines establish basic guidelines for loan administration. Regional VA offices or local lenders may choose to be more restrictive.

For example, if a military base closing in a local lender's market had foreclosures edging up, that lender might choose to be more cautious about risks in order to help control the problem.

That's why it's important for the borrower to shop not only for the type of VA loan, but for the lender who will make it. Lenders who process a high volume of VA loans will be aware of little-known exceptions and underwriting nuances that can help a veteran qualify for one of these loans.

PROS AND CONS

Q. *What are the advantages of using VA financing?*

- There is no down payment requirement unless the purchase price of the property is greater than the VA appraisal called the Certificate of Reasonable Value (CRV); or if, based on the borrower's qualifications, the lender requires a down payment to make the loan.
- There is no VA limitation on the size of the mortgage. However, the lender or the requirements of the secondary mortgage market may set one.
- Loan rates are typically below market rate when compared to conventional fixed-rate loans.
- A seller can assist a buyer in paying closing costs.
- A veteran can own more than one property secured by VA loans.
- Loans originated prior to March 1, 1988, are simply assumable (assumable without qualification of the new purchaser). All VA loans are assumable (even by nonveterans) at the note rate under which they were originated (with the exception of VA ARMs, which are assumed at their current rate of interest).
- The veteran can pay discount points, making VA loans rate-competitive.
- VA loans have no prepayment penalty.
- Because a new VA loan pays off existing encumbrances, the seller receives all his or her equity, less costs of sale.
- Qualifying guidelines are designed to assist the veteran in financing a home; therefore, some guidelines may be more liberal than found in conventional financing.

- Although the VA doesn't lend money, it acts to guarantee the lender against default on a portion of the loan.
- No mortgage insurance is charged on VA loans (unlike FHA and some conventional mortgages).

Q. *What are the disadvantages in financing with a VA loan?*

- Loans originated on or after March 1, 1988, are no longer assumable under simple assumption guidelines. The VA must approve the new purchase, and an assumption fee must be paid.
- For loans originated prior to March 1, 1988, veterans who sell property with assumptions of the mortgage may not be relieved of liability should the subsequent purchaser default.
- In case of default, the veteran may be held liable for repaying the VA any guaranteed amount paid to the lender.
- Sellers and veterans may object to paying discount points or other closing costs.
- Loan-processing time is typically longer than conventional loans.
- Because the seller's costs of sale are higher than those attributable to conventional loans, the seller may accept only his or her full asking price.
- A funding fee based on the amount financed must be paid at closing.

PROFILE OF A VA BUYER

Q. *Who is the typical person who buys through VA programs?*

Although each buyer's qualification and profile are unique, the following are some typical characteristics. The VA borrower is a veteran who

- has never used his or her entitlement, or has purchased previously with partial entitlement remaining.
- is looking for a zero-down payment loan.
- requests that the seller pay all of the closing costs.
- is looking for a loan that has no mortgage insurance premium.
- wants a loan that can be assumed at the rate originated (with the exception of the VA ARM loan, which would be assumed at the loan's current rate).
- wants a loan that has no prepayment penalty.

ELIGIBILITY

Q. *Who is eligible for a VA loan?*

The following list gives a breakdown of the amount of days of active duty that must have been served in order to be eligible for VA home loan benefits:

	Days of Active Duty
September 16, 1940, to July 25, 1947	90
July 26, 1947, to June 26, 1950	181
June 27, 1950, to January 31, 1955	90
February 1, 1955, to August 4, 1964	181
August 5, 1964, to May 7, 1975	90
May 8, 1975, to September 7, 1980	181
Persian Gulf: August 2, 1990, to present	90

In addition, the following guidelines apply:

- Twenty-four months of continuous active service is required for everyone beginning active duty on or after September 7, 1980 (except Persian Gulf/Desert Storm veterans).
- Persons serving in selective reserve/National Guard are eligible if they have six years' service in the reserves. Service must have been active: that is, one weekend per month and two weeks of annual training each year. Inactive reserve time does not count as qualifying service (Note: The expiration date for reservist eligibility is October 28, 1999, unless otherwise extended by Congress).
- Veterans who were discharged before they served the minimum amounts of time may be eligible if they were discharged for the convenience of the government, for a service-connected disability, or hardship. These exceptions do not apply to persons serving in the Selective Reserves/National Guard.
- Spouses of service personnel missing in action or of prisoners of war may be eligible for one VA home loan if the veteran has been missing in action, captured, or interned in the line of duty for more than 90 days.
- Unmarried surviving spouses (widow or widower of a veteran) may claim VA home loan benefits if the veteran's death was caused by a service-connected injury or ailment. The surviving spouse cannot have eligibility by virtue of his or her own military service.

Any VA eligibility previously used by the veteran will not be subtracted from the full guarantee allowed the surviving spouse.

- Any U.S. citizen who served in the armed forces of a country allied with the United States in World War II is eligible.
- A veteran who meets the qualification guidelines is eligible for VA home loan benefits even if he or she is hospitalized pending final discharge.

Q. *How does one show proof of eligibility?*

The Certificate of Eligibility must be submitted at the time of loan application. This certificate is VA form 26-8320 and contains the following information: veteran's name, Social Security number, service serial number, entitlement code, branch of service, date of birth, date the certificate was issued, signature of an authorized agent, and the issuing office. On the reverse side of the form is the amount of entitlement or guaranty used, as well as the amount of any guaranty available for real estate loans.

Q. *How does one obtain a Certificate of Eligibility?*

The applicant must complete VA form 26-1880, Request for Determination of Eligibility and Available Loan Guaranty Entitlement. This request must be accompanied either by a DD214 (a synopsis of the applicant's military record and the veteran's physical characteristics) issued to service personnel discharged after January 1, 1950; a form WDAGO, Notice of Separation (for veterans discharged before this date); or a computer-generated Certificate of Eligibility, which was issued to veterans who served for one period of service after approximately 1970.

Mortgage lenders who originate VA loans usually will have the necessary filing forms on hand and will assist in procuring the certificate.

Q. *What happens if the applicant has lost his or her form DD214, WDAGO, or other evidence of military service?*

The applicant could substitute GSA Form 6954, Certification of Military Service, available from the applicable service department.

If the veteran has lost the DD214, a duplicate might be obtained from the War Records Department; county records; a civil service agency employing the veteran; the local draft board, if the veteran was drafted; or the branch of service from which the veteran was discharged.

Q. *What does an applicant currently on active duty use for eligibility documents?*

Form DD 13, Statement of Service, is acceptable; or the applicant can submit a statement in letter form on military letterhead from his or her personnel officer or commanding officer. Stated would be the applicant's name, service serial number, active duty dates, previous periods of service (if any), character of service, and notation of any lost time.

Q. *Does the veteran have to be present for loan application or closing?*

No. The veteran's spouse or other member of his or her immediate family can apply on the veteran's behalf. In regard to signing papers, a power of attorney can be used; however, the VA has several guidelines that must be met. If a loan will be closed in the veteran's absence, the borrower should consult the lender for current VA requirements.

Q. *If a veteran served in more than one conflict, would it be possible to apply for and receive two VA loans?*

When the first property is purchased (for example, using World War II eligibility), the dual eligibility would have no impact. However, if the home was later sold and loan payments were not delinquent, the veteran could apply for a second VA loan pertaining to benefits from a second conflict period (for example, the Korean War) regardless of release from the first loan or the amount of the outstanding guaranty. The VA has set specific time limits within which to apply for the second loan.

Q. *How long does a veteran have to use his or her eligibility?*

There are no specific time frames, other than the requirement for dual eligibility just discussed. Eligibility is good until used.

THE GUARANTY

Q. *What are the VA guaranty and veteran's entitlement and eligibility?*

The difference in the terms guaranty, entitlement, and eligibility when referring to VA loans is more semantic than actual. Guaranty in VA loans refers to the amount of the loan the VA will indemnify or guarantee for repayment to the lender should the borrower default. The terms entitlement and eligibility are used more when referring to the VA's relationship with the veteran.

In 1944, the original maximum entitlement available for home loan purposes was $2,000. On December 18, 1989, the VA guaranty became a maximum of $50,750 for homes and condominiums, but the guaranty is based on the size of the loan.

Guaranty Guidelines

The maximum guaranty on a VA loan is the lesser of the veteran's available entitlement or:

1. For loans up to $45,000, 50 percent of the loan.
2. For loans of more than $45,000 and not more than $56,250, the guaranty will not exceed $22,500.
3. For loans of more than $56,250 and not more than $144,000, 40 percent of the loan.
4. For loans of more than $144,000 made for the purchase or construction of a home or to purchase a residential unit in a condominium or to refinance an existing VA guaranteed loan for interest rate reduction, 25 percent of the loan up to a maximum guaranty of $50,750.

Q. *Is there a VA loan maximum?*

No, there isn't. However, most lenders don't make VA loans that exceed the secondary market maximum ($240,000 for 1999) because most VA loans are sold in the secondary market.

Q. *What kind of a home could someone buy for even the maximum guaranty of $50,750?*

Don't confuse the guaranty amount with the loan amount. As a rule of thumb, most lenders will loan four times the amount of the guaranty with no down payment required. In other words, if the VA will guaranty the lender repayment on 25 percent of the loan, the lender making the loan will take the risk.

Q. *So if a veteran has a guaranty of $50,750 available, the lender would make a loan of up to $203,000 without a down payment?*

That's correct, if the veteran qualifies.

Q. *Does the government set the interest rates allowed for VA loans?*

No. Interest rates for VA loans are negotiated between the lender and the borrower. In essence, this means that if more discount points are paid, the borrower can receive a lower interest rate. These points must be paid in cash at the time of closing and cannot be financed into the loan.

Q. *If just a portion of the entire loan is guaranteed, what actually happens if there's a default?*

First, because the lender becomes the owner of the defaulted property after foreclosure, VA could accept the property from the lender by reimbursing the amount of the outstanding loan balance plus foreclosure expenses. Second, the VA could instruct the lender to keep title to the foreclosed property and accept a check equal to the remaining balance times the guaranty percentage originally issued when the loan was originated. Typical risk to the lender in the case of default is minimal. Even with a mere 25 percent guarantee from VA, the lender will generally recoup 100 percent of the outstanding balance.

Q. *When could a veteran have more than one VA loan at a time?*

While the veteran must agree, and sign papers to the effect that he or she will live on the property when purchased, the veteran could have more than one outstanding VA loan at a time. For example, the veteran could purchase another home using VA eligibility and rent the current home. Obviously, he or she would have to have adequate eligibility, and any outstanding loans would need to be paid current.

Q. *If someone can use his or her remaining VA eligibility for subsequent purchases, how does one calculate the amount of the guaranty available?*

It's a little tricky, but let's do an example. Joan Koch previously used $12,500 entitlement not restored (paid off). VA imposes a cap for calculating remaining eligibility at $36,000 (instead of the higher $50,750 maximum). So she has $23,500 additional entitlement available to her.

$$\$36,000 - \$12,500 = \$23,500$$

Q. *So how large a loan could a veteran with a remaining entitlement of $23,500 receive?*

Remember the rule of "four times the amount of the guaranty." If the veteran could qualify, the lender would probably make a loan of $94,000 with no down payment.

Q. *Although the veteran must reside on the property after the initial purchase, does it have to be a single-family residence?*

No, the veteran could purchase up to a four-unit building as his or her residence; however, no additional guaranty is available just because the number of units in the purchase increase.

QUALIFICATION GUIDELINES

Q. *What are the buyer's qualifications for new VA loans?*

The following is an overview of how a veteran qualifies based on income, residuals, and long-term debt.

In 1986, the VA began using a debt-to-income ratio for loan qualification. It is calculated by taking the sum of PITI (principal, interest, property tax, and insurance), any special assessments (such as condo fees or local improvement district levies), and long-term obligations (those with repayment in excess of ten months). Divide that amount by the total income, which includes gross salary and other compensation. The resulting percent or ratio cannot exceed 41 percent. If it does, it is fairly unlikely that the application will be approved.

Residual income remains a secondary VA qualifier along with the ratio. Residual income is determined by subtracting PITI, heat, maintenance, and utilities from the net effective income (income after taxes, long-term monthly debts, child care, child support, or alimony).

Think of residual income as leftover income. For example, according to Figure 8.1, a family of four in the West must have a residual income of $1,117 per month when applying for an $80,000 mortgage.

While each case will be decided on its own merits, these are fairly firm guidelines that most local lenders will use in accepting or rejecting a loan.

Figure 8.1   VA Table of Residual Incomes, by Region

Loan Amounts of $79,999 and Below

Family Size	Northeast	Midwest	South	West
1	$390	$382	$382	$ 425
2	654	641	641	713
3	788	772	772	641
4	888	868	868	967
5	921	902	902	1,004
over 5	Add $75 for each additional member up to 7.			

Loan Amounts of $80,000 and Above

Family Size	Northeast	Midwest	South	West
1	$ 450	$ 441	$ 441	$ 491
2	755	738	738	823
3	909	889	889	990
4	1,025	1,003	1,003	1,117
5	1,062	1,039	1,039	1,158
over 5	Add $80 for each additional member up to 7.			

Geographic Regions

Northeast Connecticut, Maine, Massachusetts, New Hampshire, New Jersey, New York, Pennsylvania, Rhode Island, and Vermont

Midwest Illinois, Indiana, Iowa, Kansas, Michigan, Minnesota, Missouri, Nebraska, North Dakota, Ohio, South Dakota, and Wisconsin

South Alabama, Arkansas, Delaware, District of Columbia, Florida, Georgia, Kentucky, Louisiana, Maryland, Mississippi, North Carolina, Oklahoma, Puerto Rico, South Carolina, Tennessee, Texas, Virginia, and West Virginia

West Alaska, Arizona, California, Colorado, Hawaii, Idaho, Montana, Nevada, New Mexico, Oregon, Utah, Washington, and Wyoming

Q. *Can a borrower exceed the 41 percent ratio rule and still be acceptable?*

The borrower can exceed the 41 percent ratio rule if the residuals are 20 percent (or more) than the residual income amount required based on the number of family members, the veteran's geographical area and the loan amount requested.

Q. *Do in-service veterans and retired service persons get any concessions in qualifying for a VA loan?*

They certainly do. They can qualify with 5 percent less residual income than other applicants. The only criterion is that it must be proven that their military benefits will be continuous.

Q. *Even though the long-term debts are considered those that can't be paid off within ten months, what about substantial short-term payments?*

Good point. The lender must consider the impact of any substantial monthly payment, even though it is scheduled to last less than ten months. It's also the lender's decision to include monthly repayment amount minimums for credit accounts that have no outstanding balance.

A VA qualifying form can be found at Figure 8.2.

Employment History

Q. *Do VA loan applicants need a two-year employment history as required with other loans?*

Yes. Two years of employment history will be verified. In addition, the borrower is asked to supply an original pay stub from his or her current employment.

Q. *What about active duty applicants? What do they have to verify?*

Active duty military must provide the lender with a current (not more than 120 days old) Leave and Earnings Statement.

Service members within 12 months of release from active duty will require additional information. The veteran will need to provide reenlistment documentation, verification of civilian employment following release, or a statement from the service member that he or she intends to reenlist or extend the period of active duty. The latter alternative would need to be supported by a letter from the service member's commanding officer confirming that the veteran is eligible for reenlistment.

Other offsetting factors that would weigh heavily in favor of the veteran getting the loan would be a down payment of at least 10 percent, significant cash reserves at closing, or both.

Figure 8.2   VA Qualifying Form

Loan Amount $_____

Gross Income Per Month (Veteran or Spouse) $_____ (A)
(Including pension compensation or other *net* income)

Less: Federal Income Tax $_____
          State Income Tax   _____

          Social Security Tax _____
          Other   _____

Net Take-Home Pay $_____ (B)

Housing Expense:

          House Payment $_____
          (Principal and Interest)
          Taxes   +_____

          Insurance   +_____
          HOA/Assessments   +_____

               Subtotal $_____ (C)

          Utilities $_____

          Other (pool, air conditioning, etc.) +_____
          Maintenance   +_____

               Total Housing Expense $_____ (D)

Fixed Obligations:
          Total of all monthly debt payments
          which will last six months or longer
          including "job related expenses." $_____ (E)

Balance Remaining for Family Support (B less D and E) $_____

                                   Family Support
          Number of Family Members _____ Balance Required $_____
                                   (refer to table Figure 8.1)

Ratio: (C plus E)   Divided by (A) $_____ = Ratio _____%*
                                                    (round down to two digits)

*A statement that lists all compensating factors that justify approval must be
provided if ratio exceeds 41 percent unless the residual income exceeds the
required amount by at least 20 percent.

Recently Discharged Veterans

Q. *What about recently discharged veterans who are currently employed, but haven't held a civilian job for two years? Would they be able to qualify for a loan?*

Perhaps. Veterans who are recently discharged (including veterans who have retired after 20 years of active military duty) may be able to secure a loan without the two-year employment history. Consideration is made on a case-by-case basis, weighing how similar the current line of work is to the veteran's military duties.

For example, a veteran who was formerly an airplane mechanic in military service, currently successfully employed as a machinist, would give good indication that the work could be performed and the employment steady. But a former airplane mechanic who is now selling insurance may not give the lender a strong indication of employment stability in the early stages of the new job.

OVERTIME AND PART-TIME INCOME

Q. *Could overtime and part-time income count for VA qualifying?*

Again, the guidelines are pretty much the same as with other loans. Unless there is a two-year work history and the income is likely to continue, it might be used as a compensating factor, but not as true qualifying income.

Q. *Can educational loan benefits be included in income qualification for a VA loan?*

No, just on-the-job training benefits and VA retirement or disability income can be included for qualifying.

Q. *If the veteran can't qualify on his or her own, could a coborrower be used?*

Yes, the VA will consider the income and credit of a comortgagor who resides on the property. The VA will only guarantee the portion for which the veteran has qualified. This may pose a problem from the lender's standpoint as a partial guaranty is usually unacceptable to them.

One solution might be to use two veterans as joint mortgagors, thus allowing an extended guaranty amount. Any loan processing in coborrower situations must be done directly by VA, not through automatic approval by direct endorsement lenders. (These are lenders who have met approval guidelines of the VA, and can approve loans in-house, without first submitting them to their respective regional VA offices.)

Borrowers with Bankruptcies

Q. *Would a veteran who had declared bankruptcy ever be able to get a VA loan?*

Obviously, each situation is evaluated on its own merits; and because there are several chapter filings of bankruptcy, each may be handled differently.

In general, the VA will want to see that the bankruptcy has been discharged for at least 24 months, and that credit has been satisfactorily reestablished. However, bankruptcies discharged less than two years may be considered if credit has been reestablished and the bankruptcy was beyond the control of the consumer (such as medical bills, prolonged strikes, etc.).

Compensating Factors

Q. *What compensating factors could a veteran use to get VA loan approval, even with marginal qualifications?*

As with other loans, the VA has its own set of compensating factors:

- Excellent long-term credit
- Conservative use of consumer credit
- Minimal consumer debt
- Long-term employment
- Significant liquid assets
- Down payment or the existence of equity in refinancing loans
- Little or no increase in shelter expense
- Military benefits
- Satisfactory home ownership record
- High residual income
- Low debt-to-income ratio
- Tax credits for child care
- Tax benefits of home ownership

LEVERAGE

Q. *To what extent can a seller financially help a buyer purchase his or her home under VA guidelines?*

Possibly to a great degree. If the buyer has adequate eligibility, the lender can lend 100 percent of the CRV (VA appraisal), and the seller is allowed to pay all closing costs, including prepaid items (such as insurance impounds and property tax impounds). This is sometimes referred to as "zero down, zero closing."

Q. *Could the veteran borrow the down payment for a loan?*

It depends. It would be acceptable if the borrowed funds were used to pay closing costs, or the down payment, provided the total of the down payment and loan do not exceed the CRV. Loan terms would have to be included in the application, and therefore the repayment amounts would be included in the qualifying ratio.

This is one of the areas where a borrower may have to shop for a lender who will take on this type of increased risk.

Q. *Can a borrower have a second mortgage simultaneous with originating a new VA loan?*

It is possible to use secondary financing simultaneous with the origination of a VA first mortgage, within certain boundaries:

- The CRV must exceed the amount of the first mortgage. In this way, the second mortgage could be used to secure the monetary difference between the appraised value and the first mortgage.
- The lender will want to know the repayment terms on the second mortgage and will add the debt service payment into the veteran's debt ratios.
- The lender may ask that the interest rate on the second mortgage not exceed the rate of the first mortgage, and that any second mortgage be assumable. The idea is to avoid putting undue stress on the borrower and to keep both loans from defaulting.

Even though second mortgages initiated simultaneous with first mortgages are approved by the VA, many lenders shun the practice, as they feel it creates too much leverage and possible stress on the veteran, which may strain the loan and cause default. The key here is to shop for local lenders who won't be afraid to take the risk with an otherwise qualified buyer.

Q. *When might someone use an initial second mortgage simultaneous with a new VA first mortgage?*

A veteran might consider initiating a second mortgage simultaneous with a first not only for down payment but for qualifying as well, as in the following example:

> The lender's VA interest rate has just jumped to 9 percent, making it impossible for Joe Smith to financially qualify for a $100,000 loan. However, if his credit union would carry a second mortgage of $20,000 at 7 percent with the balance of $80,000 at the lender's 9 percent first mortgage rate, he could qualify. The melding of the two rates for qualifying was enough to make the difference between no loan and owning his dream home.

CLOSING COSTS

Q. *Could someone other than the seller pay for the veteran's costs of sale?*

Yes. In addition to those charges enumerated before that could be paid by the seller, a third party might pay part of the closing costs—e.g., attorney fees, title company fees, and escrow closing agent fees. In fact, it would not be considered an illegal kickback for a lender to pay any or all of those costs mentioned, particularly if the loan was made to a buyer who was short on closing costs. Remember, if you don't ask, you usually don't get!

Q. *What closing costs can the borrower pay?*

Although allowable charges to the veteran vary by VA regional office, here is a list of some of the more typical allowable costs for the borrower:

- Credit report charge
- Appraisal fee
- Recording and tax fees
- Proration of taxes or assessments
- Survey charges
- Hazard insurance
- Title fees

- Loan origination fee (up to 1 percent of the loan amount)
- Funding fee charged by VA
- Any allowable discount points

Q. *Does each regional office tell the veteran exactly what costs he or she can pay?*

Somewhat; however, they phrase it as "costs the veteran is *not allowed* to pay." Remember that closing costs (except the ones specified for payment by a certain party) are negotiable between the buyer and seller. The VA loan is the most restrictive type of loan when it comes to mandating which party can pay which cost.

Q. *Does the buyer have to pay the funding fee charged by the VA?*

No; in fact anyone can pay the funding fee—the buyer, the seller, or another third party; or the fee can be financed into the loan. Also, the funding fee does not have to be paid by veterans receiving VA compensation for service-connected disabilities, or who but for the receipt of retirement pay would be entitled to receive compensation for service-connected disabilities. The funding fee is also waived for surviving spouses of veterans who died in service or from a service-connected disability.

Q. *Are funding fees different based on whether a veteran was active duty military, reservist, or National Guard status?*

Yes. Figure 8.3 compares funding fees, including a category for veterans who are making a subsequent (repeat) purchase using a VA loan.

DISCOUNT POINTS

Q. *What are discount points, and how do they work with VA loans?*

Lenders use discount points to increase the yield of a loan. Because VA and FHA loans are usually made below conventional-loan market rates, what lender in his or her right mind would be excited about making a guaranteed or insured loan at a lesser rate of interest? They wouldn't. That's why points can help bridge the gap between what they could lend conventional money for compared to what they can receive on government programs.

Figure 8.3   VA Funding Fees Effective October 1, 1993

Served in Active Duty

Down Payment	Fees for First-Time Use	Fees for Subsequent Use
0–5%	2.0 %	3.0 %
5–10	1.5	1.5
10 or more	1.25	1.25

Served in Reservists/National Guards

Down Payment	Fees for First-Time Use	Fees for Subsequent Use
0–5 %	2.75%	3.0 %
5–10	2.25	2.25
10+	2.0	2.00

By definition, a point is equal to 1 percent of the amount financed. Depending on the value of the dollar, it takes between four and six points to increase the interest rate by 1 percent over a ten-year period (which, by the way, is the median time most 30-year loans exist before being paid off). Knowing this, the lender is now ready to evaluate where conventional rates are today, how many discount points need to be charged to equalize the two rates, how much of a discount secondary market investors will charge, and what competing lenders are charging for points.

Therefore, if conventional money is typically going for 8 percent, while VA/FHA funds are at 7.5 percent, the lender would probably be looking at several points to equalize the rates.

Q. *Do lenders ever negotiate points?*

It depends on the lender. Many times, in an effort to be competitive, a lender will negotiate or even waive part or all of the potential points to make the loan. This might occur if someone had been a good customer of a lending institution or had the potential to be a good customer. Lenders will sometimes loosen up on points when there's a glut of money in the marketplace and demand is down, or if they're in an expansion mode, vying for a heftier share of loans in the marketplace.

Q. *Who can pay points on a VA loan?*

Anyone! Points are negotiated between the parties in the purchase agreement. VA loans are getting more competitive; allowing veterans to pay points makes them even more so.

Q. *Are there times when the veteran is most likely to pay VA points?*

Yes, when he or she is building a home on his or her own property, refinancing an existing loan, or purchasing a property from a legal entity that cannot or will not pay points, such as the executor of an estate, a trustee, or a sheriff at a sheriff's sale.

VA APPRAISALS

Q. *Could the veteran ever pay more for the property than the value shown on the Certificate of Reasonable Value?*

Yes, if the difference was paid in cash and did not come from a borrowed source. Note the amendatory language clause (Figure 8.4) which must accompany each VA purchase and sales agreement.

Q. *Would it be wise for a seller who would consider selling a home with VA financing to get a CRV before putting it on the market?*

It depends. Although the CRV does give a reasonable estimate of value, it may sometimes lean towards the more conservative end of the price range. This is particularly true when a VA appraisal is ordered prior to having an offer on the property. It puts more strain on the appraiser to determine valuation when there is no offer setting the stage for what someone is ready, willing, and able to pay for a property. And if the appraisal is low, the damage has been done because it is very difficult to massage the price up to where it should or could be. Unless a particular buyer demands a VA appraisal prior to making an offer, the borrower should use a well-prepared comparative market analysis done by a real estate agent to estimate value.

An appropriate time to secure a CRV prior to placing a property on the market could be in the case of a specialty property, where the approximate market value might be difficult to determine.

Figure 8.4   VA Amendatory Language Clause

The purchase agreement entered into _____ ,
                                                        (date)

between the undersigned seller and purchaser, is hereby amended to include the following statement:

"It is expressly agreed that, notwithstanding any other provision of this contract, the purchaser shall not incur any penalty by forfeiture or earnest
money or otherwise be obligated to complete the purchase of the property
described herein, if the contract purchase price or cost exceeds the reasonable value of the property established by the Department of Veterans
Affairs. The purchaser shall, however, have the privilege and option of proceeding with the consummation of this contract without regard to the amount
of reasonable value established by the Department of Veterans Affairs."

_____   _____
(Date)   (Seller)

                                 _____
                                 (Seller)

                                 _____
                                 (Purchaser)

                                 _____
                                 (Purchaser)

Q. *For what period is a CRV good?*

A CRV is generally good for six months on existing construction and up
to one year on proposed new construction.

Q. *Are there any other points one should know regarding CRVs?*

Here are several additional tips for dealing with VA appraisals:

- The VA accepts FHA appraisals.
- Proposed construction should be preapproved by submission of
  plans and specifications to VA so that it can then make periodic
  inspections. Exceptions to this rule might include any dwelling
  with previous approval by FHA, a new dwelling that has been sub-

stantially completed for more than 12 months, or a house located in a rural area, making routine inspections impossible.

- A veteran cannot be charged for a CRV unless the appraisal is ordered in his or her name.
- VA uses only VA-designated fee appraisers. Some private individuals who have met certain VA criteria are authorized to make VA appraisals.
- A particular VA regional office may change or adjust the value or conditions specified by a particular VA appraiser.

LOAN TYPES

Q. *What types of VA guaranteed loans are there?*

There are far more varieties of VA loans than we tend to think of! Even though VA loans must have a fixed rate of interest, payment amounts can vary according to the needs of the veteran. If, for example, a young couple wants to begin with a moderate payment to suit their budget and then increase the amount paid monthly at the end of five years, they have several VA alternatives from which to choose, as described in this chapter.

VA Graduated Payment Mortgage

Q. *What is the VA GPM?*

The VA GPM is a great loan for using a minimal down payment while "graduating" the payment, typically over the first five years, by approximately 7.5 percent. The starting interest rate for the loan is usually approximately 2 to 3 percent below the standard VA rate.

VA Growing Equity Mortgage

Q. *Does VA have a GEM?*

The VA permits a growing equity mortgage (GEM). Basically, the GEM grows equity more rapidly because, based on a 30-year amortized amount, payments increase 3 percent, 5 percent, or 7.5 percent per year (based on the plan), with the additional monthly payment being applied directly to the principal. Under this program, loan payoffs usually occur in a little less than 17 years.

As mentioned previously, not all lenders may be interested in working with "creative" VA programs, which differ in underwriting guidelines from the regular VA programs. Borrowers may need to shop for the right lender just as fervently as they shop for the right program.

UNDERWRITING GUIDELINES

Q. *Is it possible for a VA loan to have a late charge?*

A late charge may be levied if any installment is more than 15 days late. The amount charged cannot exceed 4 percent of the installment due.

Q. *Does VA insist that all tax and insurance payments be collected monthly along with the regular principal and interest payment?*

Interestingly enough, the VA does not mandate that impounds be held. However, the VA feels that it is a sound practice and therefore allows individual investors to hold escrow accounts if they so desire. In other words, this is a lender request and criterion rather than a VA requirement. The buyer may be able to use this as a bargaining point when applying for a VA loan. For example, the veteran may be willing to hold taxes and insurance fees in escrow monthly with the lender in return for lower points.

Q. *Does the VA require fire insurance as well as title insurance?*

The VA does require fire insurance to protect its collateral; however, the policy coverage could exclude the value of the land.

Q. *Is there a prepayment penalty on a VA loan?*

VA loans can be paid at any time without penalty. Lenders may require that partial payments may not be less than one monthly installment or $100, whichever is less. And, unlike FHA loans that need at least one month's notice before prepaying (otherwise there will be a payment penalty), VA loans can be paid in full without notice.

Q. *What is a Certificate of Commitment?*

That's what this chapter has been about—getting the loan! The Certificate of Commitment, or loan approval, is valid for six months for existing and proposed dwellings. Although it cannot be extended for an existing dwelling, there is an extension period of six months if a proposed dwelling is involved.

ASSUMPTION GUIDELINES

Q. *What about selling a home encumbered by a VA loan? Would the loan have to be assumed by another veteran?*

A veteran or nonveteran can assume an existing VA loan. Loans written prior to March 1, 1988, can be simply assumed, meaning that there is no mandatory qualification process by anyone assuming an existing VA loan unless the veteran wanted either a total release of liability or a substitution of certificate. A total release of liability means that the veteran would not be held liable for any delinquencies or deficiency judgments should the loan default. Substitution of certificate goes one step further and releases the veteran from all liability on the loan, plus reinstates that amount on his or her Certificate of Eligibility. The latter can be accomplished only if the assumptor is a veteran who substitutes his or her Certificate of Eligibility for that of the selling veteran.

Q. *What are the assumption rules governing loans written on or after March 1, 1988?*

All VA loans originated after March 1, 1988 require prior approval by the loan holder (as trustee for the VA) before transfer of the property. Mandated by Public Law 100–198, the mortgage or deed of trust must clearly state the following in large letters on its first page: "This loan is not assumable without the approval of the Veterans Administration or its authorized agent." If the veteran fails to notify the lender before transferring the property or if the property is transferred to a buyer who has failed the creditworthiness test, the lender could accelerate the loan, with the outstanding balance becoming immediately due and payable. The selling veteran has 30 days to appeal to the VA if a lender determines that a buyer is not creditworthy. If the VA overrides the lender's determination, the lender would then approve the assumption.

The assumption clause, which should be placed in all purchase and sales agreements of VA loan properties, is shown in Figure 8.5.

Figure 8.5   VA Assumption Clause

Subject to a mortgage dated _____ , 19_____ , in favor of
_____ , which mortgage grantee hereby
assumes and agrees to pay according to its terms and also hereby assumes the
obligation of _____(Name of Veteran Mortgagor)_____ , under the terms of
the instruments creating the loan to indemnify the VA to the extent of any claim
payment arising from the guaranty or insurance of the indebtedness above mentioned, and consents to his release from his obligations under the loan instruments.

The inclusion of the assumption clause will not, of course, ensure that a release
from the VA can be obtained. This will depend upon the deed being recorded, the
loan being current, and the purchaser's income and credit being acceptable.

Such inclusion will, however, permit releases in many cases that could not otherwise be approved. Also, the inclusion of the assumption clause will afford the
veteran a right of action against the transferee and thus give the veteran some
measure of protection even though VA may decline to release the veteran because
the loan is in default or the transferee's income and credit are not acceptable.

Q. *Will there be a charge for this assumption policy?*

An assumption fee equal to one-half of 1 percent of the loan balance as
of the date of transfer shall be payable to the VA at the time of transfer. If
the assumptor fails to pay this fee, it will constitute an additional debt,
and will be added to the principal amount of the mortgage. In addition,
the loan holder may charge a processing fee to determine the assumer's
creditworthiness.

Q. *If the selling veteran wanted to be free of liability plus have his or her
eligibility reinstated from a particular loan, is it correct that the new
buyer would either have to pay off the loan or be a veteran willing to substitute his or her Certificate of Eligibility?*

That's correct. Although it may seem to be a minor point, it's easy to see
the possible conundrum created after the veteran sells the property and
wants to use his or her entire VA eligibility to buy a new property with a
VA loan, only to find that part of his or her eligibility is still tied up (for
years to come!) on the property just sold.

Q. *If the veteran who initiates a mortgage under the old guidelines sells without obtaining a release of liability, could he or she ever obtain a release?*

Yes, if a subsequent purchaser down the line applied to the VA for the release of liability. The following conditions must be met to qualify:

- The loan must be current.
- Income and credit of the purchaser must be acceptable to VA.
- The purchaser must assume the loan and the indemnity obligation (owner occupancy is not required).

Remember, too, that unless that subsequent purchaser was also a veteran and substituted his or her Certificate of Eligibility, the original purchaser's Certificate of Eligibility (pertaining to that property) would not be released.

Q. *Is there any way the veteran could avoid liability from the VA when the property is sold outside of release of liability?*

No, but the veteran can keep apprised of the condition of the existing loan. The veteran can write the lender using certified mail, with return receipt requested, asking that the veteran be notified of any pending default on the loan. The veteran's address must be kept current with the lender. It also may be a good idea to record this letter at the courthouse. Even though this does not affect the title or the real estate, it does serve as notice should a default arise. It would be quite difficult for the lender to state that he or she was not aware that the veteran desired notification, especially if the buyer were requested to pay a deficiency judgment in the assumptor's behalf.

Q. *But doesn't the lender have to notify the veteran of any possible default?*

There is no VA regulation or law that requires that the initial mortgagor be notified. This has become a misconception by the public due to the fact that sometimes the lender searches out the veteran to step back in and take over payments in lieu of foreclosure (especially given the high cost of foreclosure to the lender). The VA generally attempts to contact the original veteran borrower because courts in some states have ruled that VA may not collect an indebtedness from a veteran who did not receive notice of the foreclosure proceedings.

Nevertheless, should the loan default, the original obligor would still be secondarily liable. And remember, that original veteran was the one who pledged that he or she would repay the obligation, along with his or her VA eligibility entitlement.

The *VA Home Loan Guaranty Informational Issue* looks at foreclosure in this manner:

> Under the governing law, a veteran who obtains a loan from a private lender that is guaranteed or insured by the VA is legally obligated to indemnify the U.S. government for the net amount of any guaranty or insurance claim the VA may hereafter be required to pay to the holder of the loan. This right of indemnity has been upheld by the Supreme Court of the United States, notwithstanding that a deficiency judgment was not obtained or was not obtainable by the mortgage holder under local state law. (*U.S. v. Shimer,* 367 U.S. 374, 1961)

Q. *In a default, could the original veteran purchaser ever be responsible for paying the guaranty amount back to the VA?*

Yes. The VA is entitled to receive indemnification from the veteran, which can be enforced by judicial action within our court system. Through this channel, the VA could attach the veteran's pension or Social Security income, and also withhold any subsequent VA benefits until the defaulted guarantee amount is paid in full.

Q. *Besides obtaining a release of liability, what other precautions should a veteran take when selling a property encumbered by a VA loan originated before March 1, 1988?*

Although there are no guarantees, here are some steps that may help:

- Know as much about the buyer as possible. Is he or she creditworthy? Ask that the buyer provide a credit report (if necessary, ask a credit counselor for help).
- How has the buyer managed his or her rent or mortgage payments in the past? Check with references provided, or ask to see canceled checks to landlords or to mortgage companies. Make these requirements conditions of sale and specify them in the purchase and sale agreement. In other words, if the veteran is not satisfied with the answers provided, there won't be a sale.
- As a condition of sale, require that a performance guaranty be executed by the buyer, secured by a second mortgage on the property or any other real property he or she might have. This is a possible insurance policy in case of default, because the veteran would be notified

of any pending default as a holder of a second mortgage (and therefore could step back into an equity position in the property).

- Ask that the assumptor give you a sizable down payment on your
equity. Foreclosures on VA properties in recent years show that buyers with substantial down payments are far less likely to default.

In addition, if a first or second mortgage was taken on an additional
piece of property owned by the buyer, the veteran could foreclose on it to
recoup any monies lost by the default of her or his own loan. In reality,
most buyers are going to think long and hard before defaulting on a loan
that could potentially take a large sum of money or assets out of their
pockets.

REFINANCING

Q. *Can a veteran refinance an existing loan with a new VA loan?*

Yes. Up to 91 percent loan-to-value of the appraisal amount could be refinanced using a VA loan if equity is being pulled out. (This is 90 percent
loan-to-value plus the 1 percent funding fee.)

The Veterans Administration encourages using an interest rate reduction refinancing loan (IRRRL). The loan must be a VA loan and the new
rate must be lower than the previous rate. No appraisal or credit check is
required and the veteran does not have to currently occupy the property.

The refinanced loan amount may include the outstanding balance on
the existing loan, allowable fees, and closing costs including discount
points and funding fees. In addition, up to $6,000 in energy efficiency
improvements may be financed.

The lender may agree to pay all closing costs for the borrower and set
an interest rate high enough to recover the advance of costs (but the final
rate must be lower than the loan being refinanced).

Q. *Is the Certificate of Eligibility automatically released to the veteran if
the home is refinanced outside of the VA program?*

If one refinances an existing VA loan with a non-VA loan and does not
sell the property, VA eligibility (pertaining to that property) will not be
reinstated until the property is sold. The rationale is that VA housing programs are to benefit the owner/occupant, not to allow someone to amass
income property units. At the time the property was sold or otherwise dis-
posed of, the outstanding eligibility from that property would be reinstated.

Q. *Does an owner have to live in a property in order to refinance it with a VA loan?*

No, the property does not have to be owner occupied. This is good to know if the original VA residence was purchased with the high interest rates of the early 1980s and is currently being used as a rental. Refinancing may be a chance to bring the rate down, lower the monthly payment, and increase rental cash flow.

WORK-OUT PROGRAMS

Q. *It sounds as though the VA really wants to work with veterans to secure home loans. Does it ever help borrowers out if they get behind in their payments, rather than forcing foreclosure?*

The VA understands that base closures, layoffs, and the like not only have adverse affects on borrowers, but can add incredible costs to guaranteeing VA loans in general. That's why they've introduced a VA preforeclosure program to eliminate formal foreclosure and work out loans in trouble.

Here's how it works: A veteran behind in payments contacts the lender. As discussed earlier, any borrower should not hesitate to contact the lender once he or she has trouble making any monthly payment. The lender will evaluate the situation, and if it appears that time, effort, and money can be saved by doing a work-out program, the regional VA office will be contacted. If the regional office agrees and is willing to front any shortfall, the work-out is done.

If the veteran's property has $100,000 worth of liens against it and the fair market value of the property is only $95,000, that's a $5,000 shortfall. The work-out program would allow the real estate agent to bring in (and receive a commission for) a new buyer to step into the $95,000 loan, the $5,000 shortfall would be advanced to the lender from the regional VA office, and the seller (veteran) would be responsible for repaying the shortfall over time. Guidelines require that the veteran start repaying the shortage within 12 months of closing, plus a nominal rate of interest between 7 and 9 percent.

While the veteran's loan eligibility is frozen until the shortfall is repaid in full, at least formal foreclosure has been sidestepped and the veteran may be able to qualify for another loan in the future. In fact, the lien that the veteran pays back is no longer secured by the property, merely by a promissory note to the VA regional office. Should the veteran fail to repay the note, however, the VA would be able to take action to enforce payment, including attachment of the veteran's assets. The VA and lender both win because they have a new, stronger buyer in the property and have not spent the time or expense in a formal foreclosure action. The veteran can then get back on track to use his or her VA eligibility on another home in the future.

It's encouraging to see that the VA and lenders are agreeing that fore-closure is not always the only way to satisfy a potential loan default, and that they are willing to work with borrowers to find alternative remedies.

CHAPTER 9

LOAN PROGRAMS WITH LEVERAGE

As the saying goes, money talks. But for many real estate purchasers today, there is barely enough in their pockets to whisper. That's why many loan programs employ the concept of leverage. By definition, real estate leverage is the use of a small amount of asset to purchase a larger asset (something like robbing Peter to pay Paul). Just like anything else, leverage is an excellent tool when used in moderation. When taken to the extreme, robbing Peter to pay Paul makes Peter a "Paul-bearer."

Lenders offer special programs—usually identified with acronyms such as GEM, RAM, GPM, and PAM—tailor-made to assist a targeted market segment of mortgage buyers. Many of the programs discussed in this chapter are based on leveraging concepts introduced in earlier chapters.

GROWING EQUITY MORTGAGES

Q. *What is the GEM and how does it work?*

The growing equity mortgage, or GEM, is a fixed-rate, 20-year or 30-year amortizing loan, with annual payment increases of 3 percent, 5 percent, or 7.5 percent annually, depending on the lender's individual plan. These characteristics alone may not sound unique; the difference, however, is that the monthly payment increases are applied directly to reduce the principal. This will cause most 30-year loans to be paid in full between years 13 and 15.

Most lenders will qualify GEM borrowers at the initial payment amount and ask for a minimum of 10 percent down. A bonus GEM program even allows the borrower to qualify at a discounted introductory rate, sometimes as low as 2 to 3 percent below the standard rate. This is done by using an up-front temporary buydown of the interest rate.

It's clear to see what type of buyer can benefit from the GEM—one who needs up-front leverage today, but will be able to meet the payment increases of the future: young professionals, M & Ms (married and mortgaged), and first-time buyers who need help in qualifying.

Q. *How about buyers making a final home purchase? Is the GEM good for them?*

It certainly is. As stated earlier, depending on the GEM plan chosen, the loan will be retired between 13 and 15 years. This is great for a final home purchase for people in their early 50s, because they are usually building into their highest income years. Many middle-aged buyers have trimmed their family expenses because their kids are grown, and they want their new loan to retire by the time they do.

Q. *Are there special types of GEM programs?*

Both VA and FHA allow GEM mortgages.

Q. *What are the qualifying guidelines for the FHA GEM?*

The qualifying guidelines for the FHA GEM are the same as those for the standard FHA 203(b) program. Because there is no negative amortization and all payment increases are applied directly to reduce the principal balance, FHA does not see this as a high-risk loan.

Q. *Is it easy to find lenders who do special programs for FHA and VA?*

It may take some looking to find a lender who does enough of them to really know how to do them, and who wants to take them on. It may help to refer back to some of the tips offered in Chapter 7 regarding how to develop a working relationship with a progressive lender.

REVERSE ANNUITY MORTGAGES

Q. *What are reverse annuity mortgages and how do they differ from other types of mortgages?*

As the name denotes, reverse annuity mortgages allow persons over the age of 62 to release equity in their primary residences without having to sell and move from their homes. Instead of making payments immediately after taking out the mortgage, the flow of payments is reversed to the borrower in flat sum amounts, a credit line account, monthly cash advance, or any combination thereof. The RAM was designed to help house-rich and cash-poor seniors tap equity from their homes without having to move or repay mortgages while they lived in their homes.

The mortgagors must occupy the home as a principal residence (where they spend the majority of the year). All programs lend on single-family one-unit dwellings, and some programs also include 2 to 4 unit owner-occupied dwellings, condominiums, and manufactured homes.

Q. *How do RAMs work?*

Because the borrower makes no monthly payment, the loan amount grows larger over time (thus your equity decreases). But federal guidelines on reverse annuity mortgages will not permit the loan value to ever exceed the value of your home at the time the loan is repaid.

Q. *What size loan could a borrower obtain?*

The loan size depends on several factors including the borrower's age, the value of the home, its location, and the cost of the loan (many of the fees can be financed into the loan to limit the out-of-pocket cash required). The maximum-size loan also depends on the loan program chosen. (The most well-known in the marketplace are the FHA-insured program Home Equity Conversion Mortgage and Fannie Mae's HomeKeeper mortgage.)

Additionally, you can obtain a personalized quote as to the size RAM you could qualify for at the Web site of the National Center for Home Equity Conversion at www.reverse.org.

Q. *When does a borrower have to repay the loan?*

The loan doesn't have to be paid back as long as the borrower lives in the home. But it must be repaid in full (including all interest and any other charges) when the last living borrower dies, sells the home, or permanently moves away.

Q. *What kind of interest is charged for a reverse annuity mortgage?*

Most are ARMS that adjust monthly and have maximum lifetime caps (e.g., loans that can't increase more than X percent over their lifetime). The lender is at risk because the total amount of interest accrued would be capped (should the borrower outlive the estimated life of the loan), so rates are considerably higher than standard ARM programs.

Q. *Where can potential borrowers obtain more information?*

From a variety of sources including:

> AARP Home Equity Information Center
> 601 E Street, NW
> Washington, DC 20049
> Phone: 202-434-6042

> Fannie Mae Consumer Resource Center at 1-800-7-FANNIE
> (ask for their HomeKeeper Guide, "Money from Home")

And if you'd like a list of preferred counselors who abide by a code of conduct and ethical principles that provide additional safeguards for consumers, send $1 (for postage and handling) in a self-addressed stamped business size envelope to the nonprofit National Center for Home Equity Conversion:

> NCHEC
> 7373 147th Street West, Suite 115
> Apple Valley, MN 55124

GRADUATED PAYMENT MORTGAGES

Q. *What are graduated payment mortgages?*

A graduated payment mortgage (GPM) is a loan where the payment graduates (increases) annually for a predetermined period (e.g., five or ten years), and then becomes fixed for the duration of the loan. During times of high-rate interest, borrowers used them as leverage to be able to more readily qualify (because the initial payment was less). But the downside is that even though the initial payment is less, the interest owed is not—and the payment shortfall in the early years is added back onto the loan, which can result in negative amortization.

Q. *What kind of borrowers would be well-suited for this type of loan?*

GPMs can be good for borrowers if:

- They have predictable income increases.
- The property value is expected to rise or at least keep pace with the payment increase.

- Ownership of the property is not short-term (requiring that they sell quickly, especially if negative amortization has caused the loan to exceed the home's value).
- And/or they have the ability to refinance eventually into another type of loan.
- Additionally, borrowers requiring jumbo loans (those over the secondary market limit) may benefit using a GPM. For example, initial payments on a $250,000 mortgage would be approximately $500 per month less using a graduated payment mortgage.

Q. *Does FHA insure GPMs?*

Yes; in fact, they have plans that vary in annual payment increases and number of years over which the payments can increase. The greater the rate of increase or the longer the period of increase, the lower the mortgage payments are in the early years. After a period of five or ten years, depending on which plan is selected, the mortgage payments level off and stay at that level for the remainder of the loan.

BIWEEKLY MORTGAGES

Q. *Can a borrower save money by paying one-half of the regular monthly mortgage payment every two weeks?*

Yes. In fact considerable interest can be saved over the life of a 30-year loan with payments via the biweekly mortgage.

Instead of making 12 monthly payments per year, the borrower makes 26 half-payments (52 weeks in the year divided by 2). By attacking the principal balance with a reduction every two weeks, the borrower saves substantially on interest and the loan's payoff period is reduced by approximately 12 or more years, depending on the rate of interest you're paying.

A 30-year $100,000 fixed-rate loan with interest at 8 percent pays off approximately seven years faster with biweekly payments than it does with monthly payments—and costs nearly $55,000 less! When the biweekly payment mortgage is paid off, there would still be more than $47,000 worth of principal remaining on the monthly payment loan!

Q. *What are the drawbacks to having a biweekly mortgage?*

A buyer who misses just one payment in a two-week period would potentially be in default of the mortgage. Also, most lenders require that the payment be automatically withdrawn from the borrower's checking account (and often charge a fee for doing so). That means that the consumer loses the use and the float of the money with less likelihood of it generating interest for him.

Q. *Can borrowers convert their existing loans into biweekly payment plans?*

Yes, depending on the lender. In fact, many mortgage lenders and servicers are blanketing consumers with flyers touting "cut thousands of dollars off your mortgage by converting your monthly payment loan into a biweekly plan." But there's a catch. To do so requires consumers to pay a conversion fee (often hundreds of dollars). Financially this makes no sense. Consumers would be better off structuring their own prepayment program by making additional principal payments monthly or annually and pitching these flyers in the circular file! Be sure to check for any prepayment penalty on the loan before you proceed.

BRIDGE LOANS

Q. *Are bridge loans a good idea, and when might one be used?*

A bridge loan is really an equity loan used for a specific purpose—usually to bridge the cash flow gap from one property into the purchase of another, as shown in the following example.

Nalda Negri has $20,000 worth of equity in her home and wants to purchase and close a loan on another property because it's such a great buy. Small problem: Her first home has not yet sold. A lender might loan a percentage of the current equity in the home to bridge the transactions (usually not more than 75 to 80 percent, which would be between $15,000 and $16,000 in this case).

The bridge loan can be an effective acquisition tool, but the borrower needs to answer the following questions:

- What are the terms of repayment for the bridge loan? (Many lenders may accept "interest only," with balloon payments within six to eight months.)
- What would happen if the first property does not sell within the estimated period of time? Can you afford additional mortgage payments?
- What are the costs of borrowing bridge loan funds? Do they counter any anticipated savings on the second property?
- How will the bridge loan affect the financing possibilities on the sale of the first property? (This is particularly important to consider if there's an underlying assumable first mortgage at a low interest rate.)

CHAPTER 10

LEVERAGE FROM THE SELLER

Very few purchasers of real property today have the financial capability to pay cash for their purchases. In reality, any time someone finances all or part of a property purchase, he or she is using leverage. A 5 percent down payment may be considered a highly leveraged purchase when using seller financing, whereas that amount of down payment may be the norm for a conventional loan from an institutional lender.

This chapter will show the positive and negative effects of leverage and ways it can be used to assist in purchasing real estate. The focus will be on seller financing, including its use along with conventional programs. Two other techniques involving the seller will be discussed—lease purchases and loan assumptions. Seller financing is often an option in a buyer's market. Depending on the circumstances of the seller, it can work well for everyone no matter what the market conditions.

THE POWER OF LEVERAGE

Following is a simple example to show the power of real estate leverage.

The Patels have $50,000 to use as a down payment. They can use it in a variety of ways. They can put the entire sum down on the $100,000 property A; or they can put $10,000 down on each of five separate $100,000 properties, B, C, D, E, and F. If appreciation were estimated at 10 percent per annum, should the Patels decide to sell in one year, they will make $10,000 on property A. But look at the increase in property value with properties B through F—a whopping $50,000! By using leverage, the Patels will be able to double their investment in one year.

The previous example shows how leverage can be positive. When does it become negative? Possibly when any combination of the following are present in extreme amounts: low equity, low appreciation, or low inflation.

The following example shows how these three items may interact to create a leverage nightmare.

The Carpenters have purchased their first home, using a land sales contract/seller finance agreement. They felt that this was the best way to purchase the property because they had less than the typical 10 percent down payment required by local lenders in their area, and were marginally qualified for the $820 per month principal and interest payment. Their offer to the seller contained a provision that they would refinance the property at the end of their fifth year of ownership. This was agreeable to the seller, as she would soon be retiring and would need her equity out of the property at that time to supplement her Social Security.

The Carpenters closed the sale and all appeared fine—until the balloon payment due date neared. A preliminary loan qualification appointment with the lender revealed that not only were the Carpenters not qualified to receive a loan the size of the one needed, but the property would not appraise for anywhere near the amount of the balloon promised to the seller. What could be done? The seller needed her equity to retire and the Carpenters' financial hands were tied, not to mention that they felt that they had purchased a property that might be capable of wagging its tail and barking! The alternative, to not fulfill the balloon payment, could mean foreclosure, with the Carpenters forfeiting their down payment and any potential equity in the property, plus blemishing their credit rating.

But luck was with the Carpenters. The seller was willing to extend the period on the balloon, which not only helped the Carpenters build equity, but gave inflation a chance to bring the appraisal price up.

Q. *Is seller financing negative because it creates too much leverage?*

Absolutely not. Seller financing can serve as one of the most beneficial ways to finance a property, not to mention one of the best sources of higher return on seller investment. To create a win-win situation, however, reality, desires, and financial capabilities of the parties must be addressed.

PROS AND CONS OF SELLER FINANCING

Q. *Who is the typical purchaser who uses seller financing?*

As stated earlier, it is difficult to generalize about types of buyers; however, many purchasers who use seller leverage fall into the following categories:

- He or she is creditworthy but has only a limited amount of funds for down payment and closing costs.
- The buyer has only enough for a down payment, but not heavy closing costs as would be required with lender financing.

Q. *What are the advantages to the buyer in having the seller finance all or part of a real estate purchase?*

Depending on the circumstances, there can be quite a few. Here are some common positive points the buyer should consider:

- Unlike bank financing programs, there are no constraints on what the seller can and cannot pay to assist the buyer.
- The buyer could negotiate the interest rate and the repayment schedule, and might even request that payments be made twice a month in order to save interest during the life of the loan. The buyer could also negotiate a partial amortization of the loan. For example, a $100,000 obligation might have monthly payments on only $50,000 for the first five years. The remaining $50,000 would sit idle, waiting to be amortized at a predetermined date. Balloon payments could also be used to satisfy the balance.
- The buyer could request special conditions of purchase, such as having a portion of the property released free and clear upon the repayment of a certain sum of the principal.
- The buyer could include personal property in the purchase, such as household appliances or vehicles.
- The buyer can save on closing costs because loan processing fees and points are eliminated and can therefore make a larger down payment or buy a more expensive home.
- The buyer would only have to pass the scrutiny of the seller, not a loan committee or loan underwriter as with traditional lender programs. In addition, he or she could stretch to a more expensive property than customarily could be afforded if qualifying through conventional mortgage lenders.

- The buyer could sidestep the cost of PMI by using seller financing.
- The buyer could purchase a property that does not meet appraisal guidelines required by most lenders. The property might vary from the norm in condition, age, amount of land included, or style of architectural structure for the area.
- The buyer can purchase the property without the constraints of an appraisal. Sometimes buyers may want to offer a price at the top of market value to compensate the seller for carrying the financing.
- The buyer could have input as to what type of security document is used to secure the sale, such as mortgage, deed of trust, or land sales contract. For example, if the buyer desired that title not transfer until the obligation was paid in full, an unrecorded land sales contract might be used (depending on the statutes of the state). On the other hand, if the buyer were making a large down payment and desired that title pass at closing, the mortgage or deed of trust might be more appropriate. Obviously, the seller and his or her attorney would have an equal, if not greater amount of input here.

Q. *What are the negative factors of seller financing for the buyer?*

Although the negative factors will vary based on the situation, here are a few of the more common problems. It's interesting to note that the advantages can also become disadvantages, depending on the circumstances.

- Buyer could pay the loan in full and still not receive title to the property. Although uncommon, it could occur when a land sales contract is used and title does not pass until the obligation is paid in full. In rare cases, the seller may not have title vested in his or her name, or there may be liens or other encumbrances against the property about which the buyer or seller did not know. The buyer might have to sue the seller to gain title.
- Purchaser could make payments to the seller, but the seller might not make payments on senior loans that could result in property foreclosure. Placing the documents with, and making the payments through, a third-party escrow holder is advisable for buyer and seller.
- Buyer might be paying too much for the property, because appraisals are not always done in seller-financed transactions.
- Because a technical property inspection or appraisal generally is not part of seller-financed transactions, buyer might buy a property with severe physical deficiencies that go uncovered.

- Buyer may be using only a small down payment and may therefore not be strongly committed to the purchase in case of tough financial times.
- Buyer might get in over his or her head as far as size of monthly payment is concerned. If creative terms such as interest only are used, payments will not be decreasing the principal balance. This could be dangerous, particularly if appreciation is low and the property will be held only for a short period.
- Buyer could finance personal property into the loan, causing depreciated property to cost the buyer many times its value.
- Buyer would have no mortgage insurance to protect any loss he or she might incur. Depending on state statutes, a deficiency judgment could attach to all property owned by the buyer, real and personal, if the property were foreclosed.
- Buyer would not necessarily have the property in his or her name until paid in full (depending on the type of security document used). Therefore, additional loans secured by the equity in the property could not be made to the buyer until the property was paid in full.

Q.   *What are the benefits to the seller in carrying financing for a buyer?*

The following are several of the more common advantages to the seller who carries financing for the buyer:

- The seller could increase his or her yield on investment in the property due to the return of equity plus interest. For example, a $30,000 seller-carried 15-year second mortgage with interest at 9 percent per annum would give the seller $24,774 in additional proceeds on the sale. This is an 83 percent increase over what would have been received without the use of seller financing.
- The seller could possibly negotiate a higher interest rate than could be received on many other types of investments. (Rates are typically on a par with those of commercial real estate funds.)
- The seller could ask for full price because he or she is assisting the buyer with financing.
- The seller could negotiate the terms and conditions of the sale, including remedies for default, maintenance of property conditions, and the repayment schedule (biweekly, etc.).
- The seller could open up the property to a larger field of buyers by offering seller financing.
- The seller could trim closing costs, especially the payment of points and other fees, typical to mortgage lenders.

- The seller could sell the property "as is" without costly repairs required by conventional lending institutions.
- The seller could screen the buyer for creditworthiness, ability to pay, and verification of employment.
- The seller could ask the buyer to provide a PMI policy to protect the The seller against default on the financing.
- The seller could choose (with legal counsel) which security document is best to secure his or her interest until the loan is paid in full.
- The seller could defer payment of tax on gain because tax would only be paid as proceeds are received.

Q. *What is the downside of seller financing for the seller?*

Obviously, many buyer advantages, reversed, could become seller disadvantages. Here's how they stack up:

- Seller could accommodate the buyer by taking a small down payment or paying closing costs, then have the buyer walk away from the property because his or her investment was minimal.
- Seller may not have gotten the true credit picture of the buyer, or the financial strength of the buyer may have changed after the sale was closed. Because there's no loan officer to qualify the buyer based on ratios or debts, the buyer may also have taken on too much of a payment obligation.
- Seller may have to foreclose to regain ownership of the property. Depending on the type of security document used, as well as where the property is located, this could take from 30 days to more than a year to complete.
- Seller may find the foreclosed property in a different condition than when it was sold; repairs may be needed to restore it to proper condition.
- Owner could sell personal property with the real estate, only to find it destroyed or missing should default occur.
- Seller could use creative terms in the loan, such as interest only or balloon payments, then find that there has not been sufficient appreciation to increase the property value, making any subsequent buyer refinancing impossible.
- Seller might use a security document that transfers title to the borrower, such as a mortgage or deed of trust, only to find that the buyer secured a junior lien against the property to pull out equity, and then abandoned the property.

- Judgments or liens may attach to the property, clouding the title and making it impossible to transfer it free and clear to the buyer, even though the loan has been satisfied.
- Tax liens for unpaid taxes may attach to the property, causing it to be sold at tax sale.
- Seller might not use a competent real estate attorney in the preparation of a land sales contract; therefore, seller's interests may be ill protected in a weak, loophole-laden agreement, indefensible in court.

Q. *Although seller financing seems to have many strong points, what are some steps both buyer and seller could take to protect their respective interests?*

A seller-financed sale won't be good for either party unless it's good for both parties. In addition to having a meeting of the minds between buyer and seller, the following questions need to be answered thoroughly and satisfactorily:

- Is the seller aware of the buyer's credit status? Has the buyer's employment been verified? What assets does the buyer have in addition to the property? Remember, the seller is serving the same capacity as a mortgage lender and should ask many of the same qualifying questions.
- Is the payment structure feasible and plausible for the buyer?
- Is the down payment coming from a borrowed source? (Repayment of the down payment may create extra leverage, causing financial strain on the buyer).
- If creative terms or a balloon are part of the transaction, how much stress do they place on the sale? It's amazing how time flies when a balloon payment is due in five years.
- Are both parties' interests addressed in the contract drafted between the parties? Even though one party's attorney may be drawing the document, it's wise for the second party's attorney to review the paperwork before closing.
- Will a third-party escrow holder keep the documents in safekeeping for the parties, as well as receive and disburse payments between the parties?
- Is the remedy feasible for curing a default should it occur? Is the time frame for doing so a standard one based on the security document and applicable legal statutes?

- What are the provisions for insurance coverage? Will the seller continue to carry any coverage? This is particularly important if there are senior lien holders. Will funds be impounded monthly for payment of taxes and insurance, or will the seller merely require that the buyer deposit paid receipts annually with the escrow holder?

As with any type of real estate transaction, emphasis should be placed on making the sale an equitable, positive experience. This is particularly important in seller financing, however, since the business relationship between the parties extends until the loan is paid in full. In this way, the success or demise of the transaction is directly proportionate to the terms and conditions negotiated between the parties.

USING SELLER FINANCING

Q. *In what ways could seller financing be used to put sales together?*

As Second Mortgage

Seller financing typically has been used as a method of bridging the difference for the buyer between an existing loan and the down payment he or she has available, as illustrated in the example below.

> The purchase price of the Carlsons' house is $120,000. The Carlsons have an assumable loan of $95,000. Therefore, it would take $25,000 for the Buxtons to cash out all of the Carlsons' equity. But if the Carlsons would take the Buxtons' $10,000 down payment and agree to carry the remaining $15,000 in seller financing, the sale could be made.

Q. *With so many mortgage loans today containing the due-on-sale clause, isn't it difficult to assume an underlying loan and use a seller-carried second loan without disturbing the terms of the first mortgage?*

Yes. Since the alienation, or due-on-sale, clause began receiving renewed interest in the early 1980s, it has been more difficult to simply assume existing mortgage loans without the lender altering the interest rate, charging assumption fees, and/or qualifying the new buyer. In fact, some lenders will not allow loans with a due-on-sale clause to be assumed at all. It should be stressed here that seller financing is not a method to side-step the due-on-sale clause in loans. The potential downstream effects of trying to hide a sale from a lender are not worth the benefits a seller or buyer might glean from making the sale.

As Wraparound Financing

Q. *I've heard of people trying to sidestep the due-on-sale clause by using wraparound seller financing. Is this a good idea?*

No, it isn't. Wraparound financing, whether financed by a seller or an institution, is exactly what its name implies—it's new financing that wraps around existing financing. The best way to explain it is through an example.

> In the previous example, the Carlsons had an existing $95,000 mortgage, at an interest rate of 7 percent, on their $120,000 house. Because the Buxtons had only a $10,000 down payment ($15,000 short of cashing out all of the seller's equity), the Carlsons agreed to carry the $15,000 on a second mortgage for 15 years including interest at 9 percent per annum. The monthly payment on the second mortgage will be $152.14, plus, of course, the payment on the first mortgage that was assumed by the Buxtons. This situation would be an assumption, with a seller carryback.

The party in control in the earlier example is the lender on the first mortgage. Based on what he or she would require, the new buyer might have to fully qualify to assume the loan, perhaps withstand an interest rate increase on the loan (to current market-rate interest) and pay an assumption fee to the lender. Sometimes the buyer is capable of satisfying the lender's requirements; sometimes not. As mentioned previously, the lender might disallow any assumption of the loan, causing the buyer to find new financing, often at a higher rate of interest.

This is where the wraparound comes in. Prior to test cases in the courts concerning the due-on-sale clause, it was thought that if the first mortgage remained untouched, and a new loan was wrapped around the old loan, the lender wouldn't be the wiser, and ownership of property could transfer without intervention (and fees charged) by the pesky lender.

The configuration of the wraparound is different from that of the assumption and second mortgage. With the wraparound, the sales price minus the down payment gives a new principal balance to amortize, as in the following example.

> Going back to the Carlsons and the Buxtons, if the Buxtons' $10,000 down payment is subtracted from the $120,000 purchase price, it creates a new loan to amortize of $110,000, including interest at 9 percent, payable at $1,116.50 per month for 15 years. These terms could be any-

thing negotiated between the parties, but should at least match the term of years remaining on the first mortgage. This is so title on the underlying loan could be released upon satisfaction of the obligation.

The Buxtons would ideally make their monthly payment to an impartial third-party escrow holder, who would subtract the payment on the underlying first mortgage, mail it to that lender, and send the balance to the seller, or to any other depository the seller designates. This system has some definite benefits for both buyer and seller.

Court cases came hard and fast during the early 1980s, ruling in favor of the lender in virtually all cases (except in California). The lender said that because it had loaned money to one party who was approved of and trusted, and only to that party, any subsequent transfer or assignment of interest in that property could only be accomplished under the lender's approval and scrutiny.

Even though it was presumed that the lender wouldn't discover the wraparound sale, because no documents were recorded at the court house, the lender did know. Most times the sale was discovered when the lender received an insurance rider amendment, showing a new party as the policy holder. The lender could then legally force the first borrower to pay off the initial loan.

Q.   *If a first mortgage didn't have a due-on-sale clause, and could be assumed, why might the buyer and seller choose to use a wraparound mortgage to secure a secondary loan?*

Wraparound financing might be attractive to both buyer and seller for several reasons:

- Higher yield on the seller's investment
- Perhaps a lower interest to the buyer than with financing through a lending institution
- Careful accounting of all payments because they are best made through an escrow holder
- Knowledge that the payment on the underlying mortgage is being made in a timely fashion (best to have the escrow holder disburse it)
- Costs saved by the new buyer in not having to pay new loan fees
- Seller does not have costs customary to lending institution loans
- Loan documents held in safekeeping by the escrow holder

Seller Financing in First Mortgages

Q. *Can seller financing also be used as a first mortgage?*

Absolutely. In fact, in many rural areas in the United States, seller financing has been and continues to be a primary source of real estate financing. This is due in part to qualifying guidelines coupled with the fact that much of the real property contains large parcels of bare land that are not traditionally financed by mortgage lenders.

Seller financing is also considered by many to be the wave of the future. The graying of America finds more than 50 percent of those over the age of 65 owning property that is free and clear of debt. If these citizens have saved well and have funds available for living expenses, it is a golden opportunity for them to sell their real estate through installment sales, thus creating a retirement annuity.

Q. *It sounds as though carrying seller financing could be a good financial move for the seller.*

That's correct. A strong major advantage to the seller in carrying financing is that many times he or she can receive a higher return on investment than with other investment vehicles. It goes without saying, however, that the seller must be doubly sure that several vital points of the sale are covered:

- Sufficient down payment from the buyer
- Creditworthiness of the buyer
- Strong security document written by a competent real estate attorney
- Capacity of the buyer to repay the debt in a timely fashion

Q. *What techniques could be used to negotiate seller financing?*

The following could be major negotiating points between the buyer and seller:

- Interest rate
- Term of the loan
- Balloon payments allowed or disallowed
- Type of security document used (contract for deed, deed of trust, or mortgage)
- Prepayment privileges or penalties
- Time allowed for curing defaults
- Payment of taxes inside or outside of the monthly payment

- Allowing a quitclaim deed (that quits all interest the buyer has or may have in the property) to be placed with the escrow holder to be recorded in case the buyer defaults
- Personal property financed with the real estate
- Collateral in addition to the property secured in the case of default and foreclosure
- The right of the seller to assign or sell the contract to another party (the buyer might be considered a potential purchaser of the contract—maybe even with a discount on the principal balance)

CREATIVE DOWN PAYMENTS

Using Personal Property and Services as Down Payment

Q. *I heard that someone once used a pickup truck as a part of her down payment on a seller-financed property. Could she?*

That's being creative, and there's certainly nothing wrong with that. One of the advantages of using seller financing is that whatever the buyer and seller agree upon (within the law, of course) can create a sale. The buyer might try a combination of cash, personal property, collectibles (such as coins, guns, and antiques), or even services in trade as a down payment. As a real estate broker, I once took three head of cattle as earnest money and down payment on a piece of property. Unfortunately, they were still eating, and nearly broke us in hay costs until the sale closed! We negotiated with the seller (at his request) that the cattle become part of our commission.

The premise is that anything of value can potentially serve as a sale incentive. But one word of caution: Be sure there is a definite value placed on the item being offered. It's best to get an outside opinion or appraisal of value (especially if the buyer and seller can't agree or when the item has fluctuating value). Examples here would include gold, jewelry, coin collections, vehicles, even beef! In the latter case, heaven forbid the collateral should die before closing! For a checklist for exploring financing options between seller and buyer, see Figure 10.1.

Q. *How are services used as a down payment?*

It's really not as difficult as it sounds. Suppose a husband and wife are just shy of having enough down payment to satisfy the seller; but because the wife provides professional child care, buyer and seller strike a bar-

Figure 10.1   Seller Financing Checklist

Exploring Financing Options with the Seller

	YES	NO
1. Carry seller financing?	___	___
If so, at what interest rate?	___%	
For what term? / What LTV?	___yrs. /	___LTV
Are balloons acceptable?	___	___
In how many years?	___yrs.	
2. Participate in seller financing on a partnership basis (low buyer down payment and seller share in equity)?	___	___
3. In lieu of a seller buydown, give the buyer a cash rebate (or seller price discount) that would assist in securing institutional financing?	___	___
4. Consider a lease option?	___	___
5. Consider a lease purchase, with a portion of the monthly lease payment applied to closing costs or to reduce the purchase price?	___	___
6. Purchase a buydown mortgage for buyer (for all or part of the purchase price)?	___	___
7. Consider borrower if strengthened by a coborrower?	___	___
8. Consider liening buyer's other real estate or personal property for collateral? Or take lien positions in same until the property is liquidated?	___	___
9. Have buyer purchase term life insurance with seller as beneficiary?	___	___
10. Seller take out second mortgage, and buyer assume same?	___	___
11. Allow buyer to assume seller's personal debts (using an "assignment of debt" contract)?	___	___
12. Consider a property exchange?	___	___
13. Accept chattel (personal property) as all or part of down payment?	___	___
14. Accept notes held by buyer as partial down payment?	___	___
15. If rental property, take a portion of rents in addition to monthly payments for a period of time?	___	___

gain. The buyers' attorney drafts a personal service contract as part of the down payment, stating that within a specific period the buyers will provide X dollars worth of service in child care to the sellers. Obviously, if the buyers do not fulfill their obligation, the sellers would have no other recourse than to sue them. But in most cases the services are rendered, and all are happy.

A second area of down payment negotiation in seller financing can occur in the area of sweat equity. If the seller agrees to repair certain aspects of the property, but doesn't have the time or money, why not let the buyer do physical labor as part of the down payment? The seller might retain the right to inspect the improvements and it would probably be smart to have a specific time frame for completion of the work. The concept of sweat equity is also acceptable (with guidelines, of course) on conventional loans as well as FHA and VA financing.

Using Seller Debits as Down Payment

Q. *Is it possible to transfer a property with outstanding debts against it when selling with seller financing?*

Yes, it is. Although this method is sometimes overlooked, it can prove to be one of the very best methods of leverage, working positively for both buyer and seller.

The following is a real-life example of a property I purchased in the early 1980s using this technique.

I was the principal broker and owner of a northwestern real estate company. One of my salespeople had listed a six-unit building with a market value at that time of approximately $50,000. (Yes, it's true—it was in pretty sad shape, even for studio apartments.) The agent had decided to follow his wife to the Seattle area because she had "a real job," so I took over the listing. Times were tough, the property had not sold, and one evening the owner called me to say, "I'm two months behind on my contract payments to the seller, one year behind on my taxes, and I want to give the property to you!" At first I thought it was a bad connection, but she assured me that my hearing was not impaired and that she couldn't go on mismanaging the apartment building any longer.

It's easy to see a potential conflict of interest here—I was the broker, the listing agent, and could potentially be the buyer. To separate myself from the negotiations, I had her contact her attorney to bargain for her. In addition, I insisted that an appraisal be secured before we proceeded.

I was buying a new home for myself at the time, so I had very little money to put into a purchase. The only offer I could make to the seller was that I take over her debits (including back payments and delinquent taxes) and use them as my down payment. In real estate, debits are those items that have been used up or are owing; credits, on the other hand, are items that are paid in advance.

As shown in Figure 10.2, debits totaled $8,000 (including a $4,000 charge for a commission since I had, in essence, sold the property); credits totaled $220. The debits minus the credits left a balance of $7,780, which I used as my down payment. Obviously, this down payment was merely on paper since I was assuming the obligation to pay these amounts in the future.

The title insurance, attorney fees, recordation, and water, sewer, and garbage charges totaled $445. This was the only cash I brought to the closing table. So for less than $500 cash, I had leveraged into a $50,000 asset! (Currently worth in excess of $70,000.)

As shown in Figure 10.2, I assumed a land sales contract at 7.5 percent interest and gave the seller a second contract for her equity, including interest at 9 percent.

But what about the delinquent amounts I assumed? I went to the holder of the first contract (with credit report and letters of reference in hand) and asked him if I could pay the delinquent $520 owing him at $100 per month over the next six months. He was most happy to not have to foreclose and signed an agreement to the fact that he would give me the extra time requested to retire the delinquent debt.

In addition, over the next six months I paid the delinquent taxes. (Even though penalty and interest charges were accruing, it made sense to catch the taxes up gradually as the cash flow from the property improved.)

What had been the problem with the property? It appeared to be a classic case of mismanagement. The owner was spending the gross rents as fast as they were paid to her, not enforcing timely payment from the tenants, and ignoring maintenance. An on-site manager remedied most of the problems, and giving the tenants a rent reduction for rents paid for the semester in advance helped, too, because the building is across the street from a college. I even sold my old washer and dryer to the building, converting them to coin-op and therefore creating a new source of revenue (and depreciation).

The moral of this example is that many debits owed by the seller in seller-financed property transactions do not necessarily have to be paid in

Figure 10.2   Example of Using Seller's Debits as Buyer's Credits

Leverage with Expenses, Costs and Prorations

Items	Debit	Credit
	Closing November 1 Purchase Price $50,000	
Seller's Expenses		
Current year's taxes at $100/month	$1,000	
Prior year's delinquent taxes	600	
Utilities		
Water, Sewer, Garbage	50	
(LIDs) Local Improvement Districts		
Current Month's Rent Due		200
Delinquent Rents	500	
Transfer of Rental Deposits	500	
Personal Property (plus coin ops, etc.)		20
Title Insurance Costs	225	
Attorney Fees and Recording	170	
Discount Fees		
Commissions at 8%	4,000	
Interest on Current Loan(s)	175	
Current Month's Loan Payment	260	
Delinquent Loan Payments	520	
Other: _____		
Totals	-8,000	+ 220

Buyer's Costs ("Hard" Costs To Pay)
   Title Insurance, Attorney, Recording (W,S,G) = $445

Debit	Credit		
-8,000	+220	=	$-7,780

Costs Assumed by Buyer (Total Down Payment) $7,780
                                     Cash To Close   445

Payment Calculations

$50,000
- 7,780 Down
$42,220
- 18,000 Assume 7 1/2% Contract
$24,220 at 9% = Second Contract

cash at closing. Letters of debt assumption can be written by attorneys, with negotiations between sellers and buyers setting the stage.

The seller was happy because she protected her credit rating while being able to receive her equity, plus interest, over a period of time. I was pleased because I had been able to turn a negative situation into a positive one.

OPTIONS FOR SELLERS HOLDING FINANCING

Q. *When a seller takes a second mortgage on a property, isn't he or she stuck with it until it is paid off?*

It's true that many times the seller thinks in terms of collecting the principal (and of course, the interest) over the life of the second mortgage. And it's generally thought that should that seller want to convert that second mortgage to cash, he or she will have to deeply discount the face of the mortgage in order to provide a good yield to an investor purchasing it.

Here's a solution to both concerns. I call it "half now, half later." Why not find an investor to purchase all or part of the payment cash flow in lieu of selling the second mortgage outright? Here's how it works. This example is illustrated in Figure 10.3.

Charlene Morgan is willing to sell her home at the $120,000 sale price with the buyer, the Schmidts, assuming the first mortgage of $64,000. In addition, Morgan will take a $44,000 second mortgage at 8 percent ("interest only," with a balloon in seven years). The only problem is that the Schmidts' $12,000 down payment will leave only $2,500 remaining after the costs of sale, which is not enough for Morgan to relocate.

Here's the solution. Simultaneous with closing the sale, an investor is secured to give Morgan one-half of the $44,000 second mortgage, or $22,000. (Investors may be bank officers, relatives, retirees, even the real estate agent.) This, less approximately $2,500 to cover attorney fees and extra title insurance (plus 10 percent for fees if a mortgage broker secures the investor) leaves $19,500—plus $2,500 net from the sale, for a total of $22,000. This is much more palatable to Morgan than merely netting $2,500 from the sale.

What do the Schmidts get for the $22,000? They get the assignment of the interest-only proceeds from the $44,000. And, based on the fact that only $22,000 has been advanced, $3,520 interest per year equals a 16 percent yield!

Figure 10.3   Converting a Second Mortgage to Cash without Discounting

---

Cash for Second Mortgages with No Discount
"Half Now, Half Later" Plan

$120,000	Sales price
– 64,000	First mortgage assumed by buyer
– 12,000	Down payment from buyer
– 44,000	Second mortgage to seller at 8% interest-only with a balloon in 7 years
$ 12,000	Down payment
– 9,500	Less costs of sale
$ 2,500	Net to seller—not enough cash to relocate

SOLUTION:

Investor gives seller half of the second mortgage	$22,000	(Half Now)
Less costs	– 2,500	
	$19,500	
Plus net sale proceeds	+ 2,500	
	$22,000	to Seller

Seller still has $22,000 due at payment of the balloon (Half Later), or can buy the note back at any time for the $22,000 advanced her.

But it's not over yet. Morgan still has $22,000 principal due at the payment of the balloon; or she could buy the note back at any time for the $22,000 advanced her (depending on the minimum amount of time the investor wants to stay in the picture). Thus, the term, "half now, half later."

While the seller is actually sacrificing valuable interest on the principal, the face of the note is not being discounted. This can work well when the seller needs cash for a short period of time and can later step back into the position of receiving interest on the loan.

212   All About Mortgages

Figure 10.4   75/10/15 Flexible Conventional Financing

Sale price	$150,000
75% lender first mortgage	– 112,500
10% down payment	15,000
15% seller financing in 2nd mortgage	$ 22,500

Advantages:

- The seller gets some cash
- Buyer may secure a good rate of interest on the second
- No origination fee on the second mortgage
- No private mortgage insurance required

Note: Lender will count the debt service for both mortgages for the purpose of loan qualifying.

Seller Financing and 75/10/15 Mortgages

Q. *Can seller financing be used in addition to a new conventional loan?*

Yes. The secondary market will allow a buyer to originate a new conventional loan with a loan-to-value ratio not to exceed 75 percent of appraised value to be placed with a seller-carried second mortgage. Of course, if the lender's conventional loan is not going to be sold into the secondary market, the loan-to-value ratio allowed would be determined by the individual lender. This loan is often described as 75/10/15 or piggy-back loan—75 percent conventional loan, 10 percent down payment, 15 percent seller carried second (see Figure 10.4).

In qualifying for this type of financing, the lender will include the repayment of the second mortgage in the qualifying ratios for the first mortgage loan. But the advantages to both parties are great. The seller gets some cash (from the proceeds of the first mortgage, less costs of sale) plus interest on the second mortgage. The buyer sidesteps any origination fee on the second mortgage because it's financed by the seller. In addition, the buyer may negotiate a good interest rate and good terms on the second mortgage, as well as avoid paying PMI, because the first mortgage is less than 80 percent loan-to-value.

What circumstances might be best for using the 75/10/15 approach? Perhaps for a borrower who wants the lower costs and interest rate of a 75 percent loan and has cash coming in several years to pay off the second mortgage.

Or a borrower might use this approach to avoid the higher rates of a jumbo mortgage (a loan amount exceeding the traditional secondary market guidelines). The borrower would secure a first mortgage less than jumbo, make a 10 percent down payment, and the seller would carry the balance.

The 75/10/15 option could also be used by a relocating buyer who only has a 10 percent down payment now, but has the monthly cash flow to qualify for both payments, and could later use proceeds from another home to pay off the second mortgage. The possibilities (and flexibilities) are endless.

One caution: As a condition of making that loan, the lender of the first mortgage may require a copy of the second mortgage's terms and conditions in order to approve them. The rationale is that the lender's first mortgage, although superior to a second mortgage, could be at greater risk if the second mortgage has highly leveraged terms (for example, with a large balloon in two years). Some lenders will require that balloons not occur before five years, that regular monthly payments be made on the second mortgage, and that the terms exceed interest-only payments to the seller.

Q. *Can a second mortgage be used with an existing FHA loan?*

Yes. If the first FHA loan was written prior to December 1, 1986, and the property is being sold on a simple assumption (without qualification), there would be no lender requirement to review and approve (or disapprove) of the terms of the second mortgage. If the first mortgage was originated after December 1, 1986, and is being sold instead under a novation (formal assumption with qualification), the lender approving the assumption will include the debt service on the second mortgage in approving the buyer's new ratios, and may ask to see a copy of the second mortgage to review the terms and make sure it's not too restrictive, putting undue strain on the buyer.

Q. *Can a second mortgage be originated simultaneously with that of an FHA first mortgage?*

Yes, with restrictions. Remember the three levels of the FHA system discussed in Chapter 7? Allowing second mortgages with FHA first mortgages is a prime example of the varying practices and degrees of acceptability between national, regional, and local lenders. The FHA national guidelines state that a buyer can have an initial FHA second mortgage at the time of originating an FHA first mortgage under the following circumstances:

- The standard loan-to-value ratio for the program is not exceeded.
- A copy of the second mortgage is reviewed and approved by the loan officer originating the first.
- Repayment method for the second mortgage is similar to that of the first (meaning that interest-only payments are discouraged).
- No balloon is due prior to ten years after closing.
- The second mortgagee is not a party to the transaction (e.g., seller, real estate agent, etc.).

While these are the national FHA guidelines, regional or local lender guidelines may impose stricter requirements; and, if so, they would take priority over the national underwriting guidelines.

Q. *Is it possible to place a second mortgage behind an existing VA first mortgage?*

The overview given for FHA second mortgages applies here as well. If it's merely a simple assumption, neither it nor the second mortgage will be approved by a lender. If the second mortgage is initiated in tandem to a formal assumption or novation, the lender will include the debt service on the second in the qualifying ratios for the assumption of the first VA loan. In addition, he or she will want to approve of the language on the second mortgage so that the repayment doesn't create a financial hardship for the buyer.

Q. *Can a second mortgage be originated with a new VA first mortgage?*

Yes, under certain guidelines. The tier system as shown in the previous question applies to VA. Again, VA national underwriting guidelines state that second mortgages can originate simultaneous with VA firsts under the following circumstances:

- The loans do not exceed the CRV on the property.
- The mortgagee is not a party to the transaction (e.g., seller or real estate agent).
- The payments of the first and second mortgages are comparable (e.g., no interest-only payments).
- Unlike FHA seconds, there can be a balloon prior to ten years with VA.

Again, if the regional or local lender underwriting guidelines are more restrictive, those guidelines prevail, where the borrower is concerned.

DISCOUNT POINTS AND BUYDOWNS

Q. *Is it true that borrowers who use discount points, interest rate buydowns, and pay extra to lock in an interest rate are using leverage to help them purchase?*

That's correct. All those techniques are a form of leverage; no matter who pays them. (For more information about points, buydowns, and lock-ins, review Chapter 3.)

Discounting the Purchase Price

Q. *Is it better to have the seller discount the purchase price than to pay a buydown?*

It depends. Figure 10.5 shows a comparison of buydown and discount situations, and is based on the following example:

Ed Frye is a builder who prefers to pay $3,600 to a buyer in either a buydown or price discount arrangement than to pay another month's worth of interest on his construction loan.

If Frye pays the $3,600 in increments of $100 per month for three years toward the buyer's payment (temporary buydown), his total cost is a little less than $3,600 because the money is coming from an escrow account that is collecting some additional interest. If, however, the buyers decide they would prefer to have the up-front price of the home discounted by the $3,600, the numbers change. Not only will the buyer's 20 percent down payment be figured on a lesser purchase price, but so will the other costs of borrowing—including origination fees, title insurance, and PMI (if applicable). In fact, should they hold the loan for the entire term, the $3,600 savings will more than double—into more than $7,600 using the discounted sale price.

What about builder Frye? Are there any additional benefits for him in using the price discount? The most obvious drawback is that he may not want to discount the price of the home for fear that it will impact future comparable sales. (Many times not wanting to discount a price is more of a mental roadblock than a financial one.) Nevertheless, if he does discount the price, he also discounts the price of those closing costs based on the sale price, including title insurance, loan origination fees, loan closing fees and real estate commissions.

In comparing buydowns to price discounts, buydowns usually work best with short-term ownership; price discounts work best with long-term

---

Figure 10.5   Buydown Compared with Price Discount

A builder will contribute $3,600 to pay for a buyer's temporary (three-year) interest rate buydown, or will discount the purchase price by the same amount. Here's the comparison:

	Buydown	Discount Sale Price
Sale price	$100,000	$96,400
Loan size (20% down)	80,000	77,120
Monthly buydown	100	
Effective interest rate		
Years 1 to 3	6%	9%
Years 4 to 30	9%	9%
Buyer's monthly payments		
Years 1 to 3	480	620.82
Years 4 to 30	632	620.82
Projected interest cost	142,266	146,268
Projected buyer savings	3,600	7,602
Qualifying income (for PITI)	20,472	26,580

---

ownership. As we've seen with most types of creative financing techniques, unless both parties realize some advantage, the parties may not want to make the concessions it takes to put the sale together.

Q.   *What are blended rates, and how do they work?*

Blended rates are exactly that—two or more rates blended together to yield a more preferential rate to the borrower. They usually make the most sense when the gap between the old and the new interest rate is great, and new mortgage money rates are high. The following example shows how blended rates work.

The Martins have a home worth approximately $120,000, with an outstanding $80,000 mortgage at 7 percent. They want to pull an additional $20,000 out of the property to add on a family room, but are not excited about refinancing with new first mortgage money because rates are at 9 percent. The other option of second mortgage money at 10 percent is also not enticing, so they make a proposal to the holder of their mortgage. Knowing that the lender would like to move the 8 percent loan off the books, the Martins ask that the lender make them a new first mortgage, based on a blended rate of the 8 percent old money and the 9 percent new money. The new loan will be $100,000 for 30 years, at a rate of 9 percent. This moves the 8 percent loan off the books, while giving the Martins a much more attractive overall rate of interest.

Obviously the lender has to win, too, so it may require some new origination and processing fees.

Also, as with most types of lending, if the borrower has other borrowing options, the pressure on the lender to make these concessions will be greater. In other words, the borrower who doesn't need the money can probably get it! For example, if the existing loan can be assumed, that's in the borrower's negotiating favor. If the interest rate on the underlying loan is at a rate much lower than current market interest, that's a plus for the borrower, too. And if the borrower has cash on hand, letters of credit from other banks, or second mortgage alternatives with competing lenders, it all contributes to the borrower's favor.

Q. *Could a new purchaser use a blended rate loan rather than using a second mortgage or a wraparound?*

As seen with the prior question, the answer here is yes, by working with the right mix of circumstances. It's a little more difficult to convince a lender to use a blended rate with a new purchaser, however, because the recycling of funds is a primary base of profit for the lender, through charging origination fees, exercising the due-on-sale clause, and so on. But remember, if you don't ask, you don't get!

Q. *When a buyer uses a second mortgage simultaneous with a first, isn't that similar to blending the rates?*

Effectively, yes. Even though the rates may differ on the two separate loans, overall one could say that the rates are blended. The effect of this blended rate could be seen if a lender were qualifying the buyer on ratios from the standpoint of the two interest rates and the loans' repayments. The lender would use the debt service on both loans in determining whether the buyer could qualify to pay both obligations.

LEASE-PURCHASE

Q. Is there a difference between lease-option and lease-purchase?

Most definitely, yes. A lease-option is a lease with an option to buy, which the optionee is not obligated to exercise. Only if he or she exercises the option to purchase is a sales contract created.

A lease-purchase is already a purchase. It is drafted on a purchase and sales agreement and is merely awaiting the fulfillment of a term or condition before it culminates in a closing (the date of which is predetermined).

Joan Cohn, who is short of the total down payment to purchase, might ask that the seller, Walter Jones, enter into a lease-purchase arrangement. The terms of the contract would set a future closing date, as well as spell out the balance of the terms, such as financial arrangements and payment of closing costs. The buyer usually takes possession of the property, and terms and conditions as to the occupancy are spelled out.

In addition, Joan might ask that a portion of her monthly lease payment apply to reducing either the purchase price or closing costs. Note the difference here: If on a $1,000 per month lease payment $100 per month will be attributed to her closing costs when the sale closes in six months, someone should be impounding the $100 monthly for a total of $600 actual cash available to her at closing. On the other hand, it would not be quite so important to impound the $100 monthly if the total amount were merely to be subtracted from the sale price (unless Walter had virtually no net proceeds coming from the sale).

It's important to note that most lenders will only allow a credit to the buyer if it exceeds the fair market rent paid. With our previous example of $1,000 per month lease payment, monthly credit would have to exceed the fair market rent to be counted. So if $1,000 was truly fair market rent, usually as determined by an appraiser or other market expert, the buyer would have to pay $1,100 in order to receive a $100 per month credit toward the purchase price or closing costs.

The Seller's Advantage

Q. When could a lease-purchase be an advantage for a seller?

A lease-purchase could make sense for a seller if the real estate market is slow and the property hasn't sold, or if the seller needed to move quickly. In addition, the seller might feel that a prospective buyer of the property would take better care of it than a renter would, and might add improvements.

The Buyer's Advantage

Q. *When could a lease-purchase be an advantage for a buyer?*

A lease-purchase could allow a buyer time to accumulate the balance of a down payment, establish a two-year work history, or meet some other lending requirement, such as paying off debts.

Q. *It sounds as though a lease-purchase could be quite tricky to put together. What questions can be asked to make it a positive choice?*

It's true that lease-purchases, particularly if engineered incorrectly, can result in a nightmare situation. That's why they should be utilized only for the right reasons.

First, the buyer needs to be a strong buyer, merely needing extra time to fulfill his or her obligation because of special circumstances. For example, the buyer's prior home may be in the final closing process, the balance of the down payment may be coming from a verifiable estate, or the buyer may be waiting until his or her CDs mature to avoid penalty for early withdrawal. It's sometimes difficult to tell how legitimate the lease-purchase buyer is, but there are some questions to pose:

- Is the down payment source valid, timely, and logical?
- Is there sufficient safe earnest money? Depending on the area and property price, minimums may range from $1,000 to 5 percent of the sale price. Also, what happens to the earnest money should the sale fail? Is it returned to the buyer or defaulted pursuant to the language in the purchase and sales agreement? Most contracts go with the latter.
- Has the buyer had a preliminary financing prequalification for the type of loan he or she is seeking? Also, what will be the seller's costs, if any, for the buyer to secure this financing?

Q. *What are the lease-purchase guidelines?*

Either in the purchase and sales agreement, or as a lease-purchase addendum to the sales agreement, the following questions should be answered:

- Who pays what and when in regard to the lease? (For example, when are utilities prorated? When are deposits transferred?)

- Are improvements allowed on the property prior to closing? (This is one area the seller should consider carefully because mechanics' liens for unpaid materials or labor could attach to the property and become the seller's debt.)
- Who has insurance coverage? (It's usually a good idea if the seller keeps his or her existing coverage until closing, with the buyer adding any additional liability insurance deemed necessary.)
- What are the provisions and the remedies for default? (Usually they are the same provisions for default as under the purchase and sales agreement.)
- What monthly lease amount credit will apply (if applicable) to closing costs or to reducing the purchase price?

Additionally, it may be wise to have a preliminary title report drawn prior to the buyer taking occupancy. This will list any possible defects on the title, liens against the property, and judgments against the seller.

By using these guidelines, there should be less havoc should the buyer and seller choose to take this course of sale.

ASSUMPTIONS

Q. *Is loan assumption a form of leverage?*

Yes it is, because it means less loan that the borrower has to arrange, or less cash that the borrower needs to bring to closing. When the borrower assumes a seller's debt, that amount is subtracted from the purchase price. For example, a buyer assuming a $40,000 loan as part of a $90,000 purchase price would only have to make up a $50,000 difference, either in cash or in another type of financing.

Q. *Why don't borrowers hear more about loan assumption if it's a form of leverage?*

It's because many of the previously assumable types of loans have gone the way of the dinosaur! Lenders realized that buyers assuming loans were not always as good a risk as the first borrower, not to mention that the lender wanted the ability to make new loans with new fees and possibly higher interest rates.

While some loan types (such as FHA, VA, and ARMs) originated today are assumable with a qualified borrower, most others are not. And a majority of the simply assumable (without qualifying) loans are those originated before the mid 1980s, many of which bore high interest rates and were either refinanced or paid off.

Q. *If a borrower did get a loan that allows an assumption, would he or she automatically be off the hook for the loan if someone assumed it?*

Not necessarily. There are three different types (or levels) of assumptions, each with different sets of obligations and liabilities attached to them. They are assignment, "subject to," and novation.

Q. *What is an assignment of mortgage?*

An assignment of mortgage is the first level of loan assumption. Assignment transfers the responsibility to pay an obligation from one party to the other. In essence, the assumptor actually steps into the shoes of the first mortgagor, assuming the repayment of the debt. Should the second party default, however, the first party is secondarily liable for paying the remaining balance on the note. (In other words, a co-stuckee!) Note that the first borrower is responsible only for repaying the note balance should the assumptor default—for example, there could be no deficiency judgments against the first borrower for other liens if the property did not sell for enough to satisfy the debts.

This is a less common type of assumption than the "subject to," assumption.

Q. *What is assuming a "subject to" mortgage?*

A "subject to" mortgage assumption is one that is subject to the terms and conditions of the existing loan. This rather dangerous type of assumability is very much like the assignment in that it transfers the obligation to pay the debt from one party to another. But the "subject to" assumption goes one step further. In addition to being secondarily liable for repayment of the debt should the second borrower default, the original borrower is also responsible for any deficiency (shortfall at foreclosure sale) against the property. This excess of debt can attach to the first mortgagor in the form of a judgment against him or her, depending on the state and the type of security document used, e.g., mortgage or deed of trust.

In other words, on a sale subject to the loan, the assumptor of the loan is liable only for the loss of his or her equity in the property should default occur. Following is an example.

An assumptor of a "subject to" loan hires a contractor to build a carport on the property. The owner does not pay for the improvements, and mechanics' liens subsequently attach to the property. Simultaneously, the property falls into default, causing the lender to foreclose. Should the property not bring enough at sale to satisfy both the outstanding mortgage plus the mechanics' liens, the original obligor could be held responsible for satisfying the deficiency to the lender! Not only would the original borrower be stuck with the mortgage obligation, but he or she could be faced with other debts secured by the property as well.

Because each state's statutes vary regarding deficiency judgments, the consumer could check with local lenders, title company representatives, or legal counsel before taking on this kind of assumption.

If a loan written today is assumable, it typically contains either assignment or "subject to" language.

Q. *What is it called when a seller is relieved of both the mortgage payment and the liability when he or she sells on an assumption?*

That's called a novation, coming from the root word *nova,* meaning new. A novation is an entirely new obligation, releasing the original obligor from all further liability on the loan. The buyer steps into the loan and the seller steps out.

One of the reasons that many erroneously believe that they are receiving a novation when they sell is that the lender asks the new buyer "to qualify to assume" the existing mortgage. This process includes employment verification, a credit check, and research to ensure that the qualifying ratios are within standard guidelines. The seller, however, may not be receiving a novation, but is merely transferring ownership; lenders go through nearly the same qualifying process for all types of assumptions.

Depending on the loan type, additional paperwork and assumption charges may be involved with the novation, but in most cases the biggest difference comes in asking. Many lenders will not grant or process a novation unless one is requested. The rationale here is that the lender has made the loan to one borrower based on that party's qualifying strength, and until the second borrower can provide the information needed to prove that he or she is equally strong, the lender will not relieve the original mortgagor of secondary liability.

Q. *What can happen when a lender is asked for a novation?*

Responses can vary. First, it will depend on the type of loan being assumed. With FHA and VA loans (see Chapters 7 and 8), some cannot be assumed without qualification (depending on the date of origination).

With adjustable rate mortgages, it depends on the plan used and what the individual mortgage documents allow. A payoff notice is used to request loan payoff information from the lender, including whether the loan is assumable and under what conditions.

Q. *When is the best time to ask the lender about assumption options?*

The time to inquire about assumption policies regarding a specific loan is before the loan is originated, not when the property is put up for resale. If the initial borrower asks questions concerning the assumption guidelines of a particular loan prior to loan closing, he or she may be able to negotiate to change the loan language and assumption guidelines (depending on the lender and the loan type). The borrower may even ask the lender to hold the loan in portfolio to allow a novation later.

It may not always be possible to get a definite answer from the lender. The lender may state that it depends on how well the borrower repays and to whom the loan is sold, as well as policies of the institution's board of directors at the time of the assumption. What the borrower can do, however, is to ask what the current assumption procedures are for that specific loan. Assumption policies rarely get easier, so if the borrower can live with the current guidelines, chances are they will set the stage for future policies. The downstream effect of this action may more than compensate for the time and effort it takes the borrower to clarify the situation.

Q. *If a seller has liability under an assignment and "subject-to" sale, would that show up on his or her credit report?*

Because an original obligor is not totally released from liability on the loan in an assignment or "subject-to" situation, a lender may report the contingent liability in his or her name for credit reporting purposes. While this is not a widespread practice, it's easy to see the potential conundrum created when the seller attempts to qualify for a second loan, only to find that his or her credit report shows an outstanding mortgage. This is why a seller may want to request a novation on an outstanding loan.

If this occurs, the original obligor should request that the lender remove this posting from the credit report, citing the strengths of the second borrower and his or her positive loan repayment history. The original obligor should then check back with the credit bureau in approximately 30 days to make sure it has been removed from the record. The best protection against this is to obtain a novation when the property is sold.

Q. *If the seller can't get a novation, doesn't the lender have to notify the seller in case of any pending default by the assumptor?*

No. Realistically, most lenders notify the original obligor so that a financial arrangement might be worked out prior to foreclosure proceedings, but the lender is not required by law to do so. It's typically done in times of low appreciation, when property values have actually decreased, and where selling the property at a loss only compounds the situation. Because foreclosure is expensive for the lender, avoiding it saves time and money.

If the original mortgagor had carried back seller financing, and notice of it was recorded, he or she would be formally notified prior to sale of the property.

The prudent thing for the original mortgagor to do, however, is to send a written request by certified mail to the lender, asking that he or she be notified of any potential default on the outstanding loan. In addition, this notice could be recorded at the county courthouse. Even though it creates no lien or other encumbrance on the property, it is on record. If these steps are taken when the sale to the assumptor occurs, a lender would later find it difficult to claim that he or she was not aware that the original mortgagor wanted notification in advance of any pending default.

In addition, some sellers even request that the buyer purchasing with an assumption give the seller a small second mortgage (say $100), payable at some time in the future (say the year 2030) with no payment due until that time. Once this mortgage is recorded, it makes the seller a lienholder of record and he or she would be notified in the case of any default by the second owner. The seller would have to release the lien before the second buyer could sell with a clean title.

CHAPTER 11

AFTER THE CLOSE: MANAGING THE MORTGAGE

The buyers and sellers have made it through the closing, albeit with some sweaty palms. The buyers don't need to be reminded that the mortgage is a significant financial obligation. But it's also a financial opportunity, and buyers should give it attention as they plan their families' financial futures.

This chapter answers some common questions borrowers have after the mortgage is closed. The focus is on two significant choices to make in equity management: to prepay the mortgage (thus building equity faster), or to refinance with a new mortgage (to lower the interest rate, lower the payback period, or both). Equity management is a critical issue today, especially because it represents many a family's largest asset.

Contrary to popular belief, it doesn't always pay to prepay nor to refinance. We'll give you real-world examples, plus formulas to help you decide if it makes sense for your financial situation.

Last, we'll tackle tough issues, like what to do when your mortgage payments fall behind and you're considering giving the house back to the lender. There are alternatives, especially when it comes to parting with something you've worked hard for—your equity.

ESCROW/IMPOUND ACCOUNTS

Q. *Is there a limit as to how many months of cushion the lender may require in our escrow account for taxes and insurance?*

Federal law allows the lender to impound no more than one-sixth of the anticipated annual charges as a cushion. The rule of thumb used by lenders is that at least once each year, the balance should fall to a level no greater than the two-month cushion immediately after paying taxes and insurance. Any overage must be automatically returned to the mortgagor/consumer.

WHEN THE MORTGAGE IS SOLD

Q. *Sometimes people get a loan through one lender but are advised after closing to send their payments to a different company in a different state. Why?*

Because the loans or their servicing (payment collection) have been purchased by another company. The terms and conditions of the original loan stay the same; just the company and the location to which payments are sent change.

By law, the original lender must send the borrower a "good-bye letter" at least 15 days before the date of the next payment. This letter should state the name of the new company, its location, and the name and phone number of a contact person or department in case the borrower has questions.

Under the same time guidelines, the new company is also required to send the borrower a "welcome letter" outlining the same information.

It is very important that the borrower receive both letters, and that they are on both companies' letterheads. If a letter is received only from the supposed new servicer, the borrower should call the original lender to verify that the loan was sold. Several bogus operations have recently attempted to intercept mortgage checks by claiming to be the new servicing company.

If the borrower's monthly payment is made each month through automatic checking withdrawal or electronic transfers, the borrower will need to cancel the present arrangement and fill out new forms. Often there is a time lag, so the borrower may need to send a check directly to the new company before the new servicer receives the withdrawal. The welcome letter (or a call to the new company) can help determine this.

If during the loan transition, you send a payment on time but to the wrong company, late fees will be waived for up to 60 days after the loan transfer.

A free booklet entitled "When Your Loan Is Transferred to Another Lender" is available from the Mortgage Bankers Association of America. It can be requested by writing to them at 1125 Fifteenth Street, NW, Washington, DC 20005.

PREPAYING A MORTGAGE

Benefits of Prepaying

Q. *What benefits does a borrower get for prepaying a mortgage?*

Prepaying a loan offers a borrower many advantages:

- Saving thousands of dollars in interest. For example, a $100,000 30-year loan with interest at 8 percent would cost the borrower $264,240 in interest if the loan ran to maturity. But the same loan amount paid in just 15 years would cost the borrower only $172,080, or $92,160 less. Even though mortgage interest is tax deductible, the savings to you are real!
- Owning a home free and clear can be a liberating feeling. If monthly cash flow were to shrink, owners would not be plagued with worry over making monthly mortgage payments and potentially losing their homes. And their equity could always be a potential source of cash through refinancing or equity lines of credit.

Detriments to Prepaying a Mortgage

Q. *Are there any detriments to prepaying a mortgage?*

Every positive can have a negative. You need to weigh that:

- You'll be parting with cash that could deplete your financial liquidity.
- You'll be using funds that could otherwise be used to make other financial investments (with perhaps higher yields).
- Paying less interest may impact your tax picture (although paying more interest is never a valid reason for carrying a mortgage).
- It doesn't make financial sense to prepay a mortgage before you retire high-interest, nondeductible interest consumer debts.
- The lower the interest rate, the less you'll save when prepaying. Prepayments you made when your loan was at 10 percent won't have the same impact now that you've refinanced into a 7 percent loan.
- Make sure you monitor your mortgage to guarantee that prepayments are being properly applied to reduce the principal balance. (You did negotiate this choice into your mortgage, right?)

Questions to Ask before Prepaying a Mortgage

Q. *What questions should a borrower ask before choosing a mortgage pre-payment plan?*

Here are a few potential questions a borrower should explore:

- Is the current mortgage payment a burden? Have some payments been late or even missed? If you receive a windfall of cash, paying off the mortgage may make sense, because erratic payments may put the loan in jeopardy and damage your credit.
- What impact will the lack of interest deductibility have on your overall tax picture? Consulting a tax adviser for preplanning is always a wise move.
- What are your long-term cash needs? Are your current savings sufficient to meet them? If savings are minimal or nonexistent (a six-month minimum of living expenses is suggested), it may be financially premature to use extra funds to prepay a mortgage.
- Is a change pending in the borrower's financial future that would make it prudent to save more money instead of using cash to pay off the loan? Financing a child through college or aiding an elderly parent might be better paid in cash, rather than borrowing through a nondeductible consumer interest loan.
- How long does the borrower plan on keeping the property and the loan? Retiring the loan may not be a wise financial move if the borrower is going to sell quickly or replace the loan with another one soon.

The Best Time to Start Prepaying a Mortgage

Q. *Should a loan be prepaid when it has just a few more years to run?*

While there's never a bad time in a loan's history to make prepayments, a look at a loan amortization schedule (Figure 11.1) can help answer this question. Considering how much of the monthly payment goes to principal and interest, it's easy to see that a larger portion goes to interest in the early years of the loan. The best time to make extra principal reductions, then, is in the early stages of the loan where prepaying has a bigger impact.

A Structured Prepayment System

Q. *What logical, systematic plan might a borrower follow to reduce the loan balance without going bankrupt?*

Before the borrower begins any prepayment program, structured or not, it's advisable to make sure the loan has no prepayment penalties, even if it means contacting the lender or loan servicer to find out. This is important as some newer loans are going back to prepayment penalties in order to offer lower interest rates to consumers.

If you receive prepayment information from the lender over the phone, ask the lender to put the information in writing and send it to the borrower. At the very least, the borrower should document on the mortgage payment book the date called and the name of the person who gave the prepayment information. Putting the lender on notice of the intention to make loan prepayments also alerts him or her to make sure advance payments are posted correctly.

The following program is a favorite of many savvy real estate purchasers because it's simple to calculate, methodical, and won't financially break the borrower. Additionally, be sure to mark on both your check and your loan payment coupon to apply the prepayment to principal.

1. The borrower should obtain an amortization schedule of the loan, showing each payment's principal and interest distribution for the life of the loan. A computer printout can be secured from the lender (or any financial institution), real estate professional, or financial adviser. Additionally, you can access many online sites like www.ourbroker.com to calculate principal and interest for you.
2. The borrower should look at the next payment, say January. When the January payment is made, the borrower should make an additional payment to include February's principal reduction (Figure 11.1).

The borrower, in essence, eliminates one full payment from the 30-year loan schedule because the loan balance after that payment would correspond to the loan balance shown at the end of February.

In February, the borrower should send in March's principal reduction payment in addition to the February payment, and so on, every month thereafter.

If this procedure is followed religiously every month, a 30-year loan will be paid off in a little more than 17 years. How's that for savings?

Figure 11.1   Loan Amortization Chart and Prepayment Schedule
($100,000 loan, 30-year term, 8 percent interest)

Month of Loan	Payment	Interest Portion	Principal Portion	Balance
1. January	733.77	666.67	67.10	99,932.90
2. February	733.77	666.22	67.55	99,865.36
3. March	733.77	665.77	68.00	99,797.36
4. April	733.77	665.32	68.45	99,728.91
5. May	733.77	664.86	68.91	99,660.00
6. June	733.77	664.40	69.37	99,590.63
7. July	733.77	663.93	69.84	99,520.79
8. August	733.77	663.47	70.30	99,450.49

Note how the portion of your monthly payment that is interest payment goes down as the principal is reduced. By making extra payments applied to principal only, the interest portion will reduce even faster.

Remember that just because a principal prepayment has been made, it doesn't allow the borrower to skip a payment! Missing payments would put the loan in default because prepayments have no bearing on scheduled payments.

Documenting Prepayments Is Vital

Imagine the myriad terror stories from borrowers who thought they had made prepayments, only to later discover that the amounts had been erroneously applied to late fees, advanced interest, insurance premiums, or taxes.

Following are some precautions borrowers can take:

- If using payment coupons, be sure to mark "principal prepayment" and the amount on the face of the coupon.
- Make the prepayment in a separate check so it can be tracked and shown as evidence if prepayments are later disputed.
- If making prepayments on a separate check, borrowers should be sure to mark the loan number and the words "principal prepayment" on the face of the check.
- If possible, the borrower should request an annual accounting of payments. While many lenders don't do this as normal procedure, many will accommodate a borrower who requests it. The borrower can compare the lender's balance with canceled checks to make sure the prepayments were applied correctly.

Having prepayment options with a loan can add incredible payment and financial flexibility to the borrower's situation, while not saddling him or her with the higher payments of shorter-term loans.

COMMUNICATING WITH THE LENDER

Q. *Is there a law that requires the lender to respond to inquiries about our mortgage loan?*

Yes. The Real Estate Settlement Procedures Act (RESPA) requires that the lender respond to you within 20 business days after receiving your "qualified written request." This is any written correspondence other than a note on your premium notice or payment coupon. Within 60 days after receiving your request, the lender must have corrected any errors found on your account and/or notified you of written clarification regarding the dispute.

REFINANCING

Q. *How can I tell if it makes financial sense to refinance my mortgage?*

In most cases, it pays to refinance your mortgage if you can lower your interest rate and/or lessen your loan amortization period and you'll keep the property (and the loan) long enough to recoup the costs of refinancing. There's a refinancing formula at Figure 11.2 that can help you be more exact, or you can use an online calculator like the one found at www.homefair.com.

Basically, borrowers tally up the total amount of payments they would make for the remaining time they would own the property, subtract the lower payments they would make under the lesser interest rate, then add back the costs of refinancing, plus any additional income taxes they would pay because of the reduced interest deductions. Take what is saved in payments and deduct what is paid in refinancing and taxes to figure your net gain or loss.

When Not to Refinance

Q. *Could refinancing cost more money than it saves?*

Yes. The following example shows how refinancing can be an imprudent choice.

■■■■■■

Figure 11.2   Refinancing Worksheet

A general rule of thumb is that if a borrower can cut the interest rate and/or trim the loan term and will hold the property (and loan) long enough to recoup the cost of refinancing, it may pay to refinance. Following is a worksheet to use in analyzing each individual situation:

Refinance Worksheet

Present monthly payments	$ _____	
*Number of months to pay	× _____	
Total payments	$ _____	A
Payments at the lower rate	$ _____	
*Number of months to pay	× _____	
Total payments	$ _____	B
Difference in total payments (A − B)	$ _____	C
Refinancing costs:		
Prepayment penalty (if applicable)	$ _____	D
Closing costs for new mortgage,		
including points	$ _____	E
Added income taxes over loan term due		
to reduced deduction from lower interest	$ _____	F
Total (D + E + F)	$ _____	G
Net savings over life of mortgage (C − G)	$ _____	

*Be sure that the number of months to pay is for the period the borrower expects to own the property, not the number of months remaining on the loan.

The Johnsons own a home worth approximately $100,000. They wish to refinance to reduce their 10 percent interest rate to 7 percent, and won't be taking any cash out.

The lender informs them that it will loan up to a maximum of $85,000 (including points and closing costs). With out-of-pocket expenses (such as title work, etc.) plus two discount points to obtain the lowest possible rate, the Johnsons finance $3,926 in costs into their loan. At the time of closing, the Johnsons' new loan total is $84,926.

It's now one year since refinancing, and the Johnsons decide they need a larger home. The market has shown little appreciation in real estate values, so the Johnsons list their home for $100,000 (the previous appraisal figure). After four months of marketing the property, a buyer, Jim Judge, offers them $94,000 contingent on his obtaining a 100 percent VA loan.

Judge asks the Johnsons to pay the two discount points needed to get the loan ($1,880). With the other costs the Johnsons need to pay— $5,640 for the real estate commission and miscellaneous closing costs of $840 (plus paying off the remaining loan, reduced now to $84,331), guess how much the Johnsons will net from the sale? A whopping $1,309. That's not even enough to pay first and last month's rent, let alone to make another purchase.

If they accept the sale, they will have used $12,286 worth of their equity in one year's time on refinancing and sales costs, and still will be unable to achieve their goal of a larger home.

What should the Johnsons have done? They should have thought ahead to their future housing needs and purchased a new home instead of refinancing their old one. Their mistake was using precious equity to buy a lower interest rate while forgetting how long it would take to recoup the cost of refinancing (29 months, based on their $137 per month payment savings). Come April 15th, they may find that they actually owe income tax because they now have less mortgage interest to deduct.

As with the Johnsons, refinancing could cause a low-equity or no-equity position should the homeowner sell in a short period of time. In fact, good lenders counsel and caution homeowners to carefully evaluate refinancing if they do not plan to own the property for a minimum of three to five additional years. (Lenders will be glad to do break-even projections based on a homeowner's individual circumstances.)

One way the Johnsons could have radically improved their equity position was to shop for lower refinancing costs in the first place. Fees and points can vary widely from lender to lender. Taking the time to check out what's available from several lenders may make the difference between preserving equity or losing money.

Cautions when Refinancing

Q. Are there any other cautions to consider when refinancing?

Because lenders estimate that between 20 and 30 percent of borrowers take cash out of the property when they refinance, it goes without saying that prudent use of this cash is important. If the cash is used to add a hot tub, pool, or other improvement to the real estate that may not add dollar-for-dollar resale value to the property, is that a prudent decision? Paying off nondeductible high interest consumer loans is good. Using equity to pay cash for a lessening value asset such as a car or new refrigerator may not be prudent, based on the individual's financial circumstances.

It's also wise to consider the type of loan being retired. A simply assumable, no-qualifying low interest rate loan may be more enticing when the borrower sells than one that is not assumable. And remember, too, that if the borrower obtains a new loan of greater than 80 percent of the appraised value, he or she may be faced with PMI. This could add approximately $35 more per month to an $80,000 loan.

Should a Borrower Pay Points when Refinancing?

Q. Is it a good idea to pay higher points to get a lower interest rate?

Paying higher points to secure a lower rate of interest depends on several things. First, how long will the borrower keep the loan on the property? Obviously, paying hefty points up front to secure a lower-than-market interest rate loan won't be as valuable if the loan and the property will be held for only a short time. This is illustrated in the example below.

A lender gives Gus Wellington a choice of an $85,000 loan at 7 percent with two points ($1,700 paid at closing) or at 8 percent with no points. Which is better?

It depends on what Gus wants to accomplish. While the difference between the rates is just $58.19 per month principal and interest, it would take more than 29 months to retrieve the $1,700 ($1,700 divided by the monthly payment savings of $58.19). So paying points only makes sense if Gus is planning to hold the property for at least 30 months.

Paying points at settlement also means the borrower has lost the use of that money, plus any possible interest or investment potential.

Refinancing into Shorter-Term Loans

Q. *What are the pros and cons of going to a shorter-term loan when refinancing?*

It may be helpful to review the basic differences of payment terms in Chapter 3.

The following example shows some of the benefits and problems of short-term loans.

> Mr. and Mrs. Russell are in their late forties and are thinking of refinancing their 8 percent 15-year mortgage, which is paid down to $51,000 after five years. Their choice is between a 7 percent loan for another 15 years or to go with higher payments for a 10-year term.
>
> After crunching the numbers, they find that it would be a financial misstep to take another 15-year loan. While their monthly payments on the 10-year loan would be $592 per month compared to the 15-year loan payments of $458 (a difference of $134 per month), the 15-year loan would add another five years of payments for a net increase in cost of $11,400.
>
> Because the Russells have paid five years on their existing loan, they've whittled down a fair amount of interest. That's why the new 10-year loan makes the most economic sense.

Remember, when making this decision, the borrower should consider the time he or she wishes to keep the home and the amount of monthly payment he or she can afford to make.

Closing Costs

Q. *When would the borrower find out exactly what the closing costs would be if he or she were refinancing?*

Lenders do the same up-front disclosure of costs for a refinance as they would do for a new purchase loan. Therefore, lenders should make certain disclosures to a borrower at application or within three days after application. The disclosures describe the settlement costs of the loan, the effective interest rate, and the possibility that the lender will transfer the servicing rights.

But, as many lenders take refinance applications over the phone, disclosure may be verbally minimized. Broad quotes on costs and discount points may change drastically by the time closing rolls around.

If the refinanced loan were for an ARM, the lender should disclose a worst-case scenario on the loan. This should be disclosed at time of application or before any nonrefundable loan fees are paid.

If a borrower feels he or she can't go through with closing on a loan that was misrepresented, there is an escape through the three-day right of rescission law that applies to refinances. This federal law allows a borrower to cancel a loan if he or she does so in writing within three business days of loan settlement, provided the lender is different from the one holding the old loan.

Because there are no maximum ceilings on costs of refinancing, the term "standard costs," used by some lenders, means little. A lender not willing to update cost estimates for the borrower may have something to hide and may not be worth the borrower's time and effort. Avoiding these lenders is the consumer's best protection.

Q.   *Can I deduct the points I pay in refinancing?*

Yes, but not in the same way as those paid when you purchased. Discount points paid in refinancing must be amortized over the years of the loan for the purpose of tax deductions. For example, $2,000 paid to refinance a 20-year loan would give you an annual deduction of $100.

When Refinancing Makes Sense

Q.   *When does it make sense to refinance?*

The answer lies in what it can achieve for the borrower. Depending on the borrower's circumstances, good reasons could include lowering the interest rate, lowering the monthly payments, reducing the term of the loan (e.g., from 30 to 15 years), and pulling out cash to pay off high, nondeductible consumer debt such as credit cards.

The bottom line is to look at the total picture of refinancing. How can this be done? The borrower can ask the lender to prepare an analysis in order to evaluate the options. The homeowner should also answer the following eight questions before refinancing:

1. How long will the homeowner keep the property? (If this period is not long enough to recoup the costs of refinancing, the homeowner should not refinance.)
2. What types of situations are anticipated in the homeowner's personal and economic future? (Will equity be needed in three years to send a child to college or pay possible expenses for personal health care or nursing home care for an elderly relative?)
3. Will cash pulled out now be used for a sound reason that makes economic sense (such as adding a second bath in lieu of moving to a more expensive home)?
4. What are the benefits in keeping the existing loan on the property (such as easy loan assumability or flexibility by adding seller financing if the property is sold)? Do they outweigh the tradeoffs?
5. Would a new loan require additional costs of PMI or impound accounts for taxes and insurance that weren't previously required?
6. How does the proposed loan compare to others based on interest rate, points, closing costs and fluff fees (unregulated extra fees for services like tax checking, courier service, and so on)? In the previous refinancing example, the Russells' high loan fees were a big part of their problem.
7. How would a lower interest rate affect the homeowner's tax picture?
8. If the homeowner wants cash out, which is better for his or her situation: a new refinanced loan or an equity line of credit?

The reality is that a home (and its equity) are, for most people, their largest personal asset and savings account. The homeowner should make changes with the right loan, the right lender, and for the right reasons.

REFINANCING VIA THE INTERNET

Q. *Can you really save time and money refinancing via the Internet?*

Done carefully and prudently, online refinancing can save you time and money. In fact, many lenders offer interest rate and closing cost discounts because online applications limit the amount of personal contact (and therefore lender overhead) required to make mortgages.

There are various ways you can use online resources for refinancing. You can shop online for competitive rates and closing costs, submit your application via the Internet, or merely request that an employee contact you to take your application over the phone, then fax documents to the lender. The possibilities are endless.

While there is concern that a borrower's personal information will fall into the wrong hands, that can be equally true when dealing in person with a lender who's less than scrupulous. No matter how you initially contact a lender, it's wise to take the time to check it out using resources like business references and the better business bureau. Don't let the ease and convenience of online refinancing take the place of your good common sense when it comes to security.

EQUITY LOANS

Q. *How do equity loans differ from refinancing?*

Equity loans (also called equity lines of credit) don't disturb the existing first mortgage and do not require the strongest of personal financial profiles because they are underwritten primarily based on the value of the property. These loans don't have to be sold to the secondary market so lenders may be likely to accept higher-risk borrowers. They do have some negatives, however:

- Some lenders may make equity line of credit loans (up to 125 percent loan-to-value for conventional loans) solely on a "drive-by" appraisal. This could result in overleveraging, especially if the owner needs to sell in a short period of time.
- Equity lines of credit can bear higher-than-market interest rates, and/or adjustable rates and can overleverage borrowers who make "interest only" repayments. Beware that deeply discounted initial interest rates may be used to lure you into a financially unfavorable loan.
- While borrowers access only the amount needed (up to a predetermined ceiling) and interest accrues only on the amount borrowed, the loan may include balloon payments or other negatives. If not met, the borrower could risk losing the property.
- If the borrower tries to refinance a first mortgage and not disturb the equity line, the equity line holder probably won't allow it. This means that a new refinance would have to pay off both loans, causing a higher payment on the combined loans.

125 PERCENT MORTGAGES

Q. *What are 125 percent mortgages?*

They are first and second mortgages (equity lines of credit) that total up to 125 percent of your property's market value. Lenders are making them in the hopes that strong property appreciation will last and that the homeowner won't need to sell until the debt is paid down. Lenders typically require that borrowers have great credit, which also helps to limit the lender's risk.

While not for everyone, 125 percent mortgages do make sense if the borrower:

- owns a home with above-average appreciation in a stable neighborhood.
- is realistic about what the future holds for the local economy (a single-employer town could convert to a ghost town, with no real estate selling, virtually overnight).
- anticipates keeping the house long enough to whittle down the debt.
- is willing to shop diligently to obtain the lowest interest rates and costs for the loan as this type of financing can easily run 2 to 3 percent over first-mortgage rates.

Be cautioned that the IRS only allows homeowners to deduct interest up to 100 percent of the market value of their property—and yes, they will be watching for 125 percent mortgages!

Q. *Is it a good financial idea to keep pulling equity out of your house, keeping it highly mortgaged, so the money can work in other ways?*

Some financial planners would like to have you believe so. But just as there's no one stock market investment panacea, handling your home equity is a very individual decision.

Having a large mortgage is a better alternative than paying loads of nondeductible consumer debt. And it's great to have equity to use for financial events like sending a child to college. But it's up to each homeowner to decide how much mortgage debt is enough, based on levels of both financial and psychological risk.

WHEN THE BORROWER FALLS BEHIND IN PAYMENTS

Q. *If a borrower's financial position changes after getting the loan, and he or she falls behind in the payments, what can be done?*

Contrary to popular belief, lenders really do want to work with delinquent and potentially defaulting borrowers. The cost of foreclosure for the lender can be as high as 20 percent of the remaining principal balance. And a delinquent loan on the books as a nonperforming asset continues to cost the lender money. That's why most lenders see foreclosure as a last, and many times unattractive, resort.

It's important that the borrower who is behind on payments does not take a wait-and-see approach. Being proactive and immediately contacting the lender to discuss the situation is imperative: some of the most attractive alternatives are those exercised in the early stages of default.

The lender will want to know what caused payments to fall behind, whether that cause has been remedied, and how the situation can be reversed. For example, a borrower with delinquent payments caused by temporary job loss, who is once again employed, may need just a few additional months to catch up payments. Conversely, a borrower with a severe long-term illness might need other options.

Lenders could assist the borrower by accepting "interest only" payments, partial payments, or deferring payments entirely for several months (these amounts would be added to the end of the loan).

The borrower should ask the lender under what circumstances someone else could assume the loan. This solution could bypass formal foreclosure, get the current owner out of the picture, and supply the lender with a stronger loanholder.

Q. *Do homeowners have any protection against mortgage lenders who harass them for late payments?*

Yes. Though lenders have the right to contact consumers to request payments, consumers are protected under the Fair Debt Collection Act against calls that exceed the type and/or frequency specified by law.

Two free booklets are available to inform the consumer:

1. "Fair Debt Collection" published by the Federal Trade Commission, Pennsylvania Avenue and 6th Street, NW, Washington, DC 20580 or obtain information online at www.ftc.gov. The publication outlines what a debt collector can and can't do.

2. "Fair Debt Collection Practices Act," published by the Federal Reserve Bank, P. O. Box 66, Philadelphia, PA 19105-0066, outlines violations under the law and describes how and where to report violations.

Because reporting violations must be backed by proof, it's best if the consumer keeps an annotated log of all contacts with the lender and respective outcomes.

Q. *Does a delinquent borrower have any other recourse if the lender is not willing to work with him or her?*

If the loan has PMI, or is an FHA or VA loan, there may be other options.

Private mortgage insurance companies insure the conventional lenders' loans against loss. So when the borrower can no longer make the mortgage payments, the PMI company stands to lose as well.

Many PMI companies are focusing their efforts on preforeclosure work-out programs, designed to intercept the defaulting loan and work it out before formal foreclosure occurs. Their rationale is that if they can find a way to help a new, stronger buyer get into the property by merely paying the lender some of the defaulting owner's back payments, they stand to lose less than if they paid an entire claim for loss. (For a breakdown of these costs, see Chapter 5.) A work-out program might create a more equitable solution than foreclosure for all parties.

Q. *If it's a conventional loan, how does the borrower find out which PMI company insures the loan?*

Lenders are usually willing to contact the PMI company to see if a work-out program can be done (especially if the property owner requests this). If not, however, the borrower might check his or her loan settlement papers from the purchase to see which company the initial PMI premiums were paid to. (All of the PMI companies are listed in Chapter 5 and have toll-free numbers.)

FHA and VA Work-Out Programs

Foreclosure can be expensive, not only in terms of payments lost, but also in preforeclosure property maintenance fees until foreclosure, and other costs of property repair. Understanding this, FHA and VA have initiated preforeclosure work-out programs for their loans. You can find these explained in Chapters 7 and 8.

Deed-in-Lieu of Foreclosure

Q. *What is the worst that could happen if a borrower gives the property back to the lender?*

I don't know about worst, but something adverse could certainly happen.

This situation is called a deed in lieu of foreclosure, also called a friendly foreclosure. This means that the lender agrees to take the property back and the borrower forgoes any equity in the property. But that may not be all that happens.

While the borrower could negotiate with the lender to waive negative information from being posted to the borrower's credit report (and may even put this agreement in writing), other parties to the default, such as the PMI company, might make a negative posting to the borrower's credit.

Because a deed in lieu of foreclosure can carry major impact for the borrower, giving the property back to the lender or agreeing to a work-out program should only be done after consulting with a real estate or tax attorney.

Q. *Are there any tax consequences if a borrower gives the property back to the lender?*

Potentially, yes. Because the IRS may consider deeding the property back to the lender to be debt relief or a taxable sale, an accountant or tax adviser should be consulted before the borrower agrees to transfer the property.

BEST WISHES FOR GROWING YOUR EQUITY

I hope that *All About Mortgages,* 2nd edition, has helped you secure an affordable loan, provided you with tips for sound equity management, and will continue to be your bible for home affordability issues. Visit my Web site at frugalhomeowner.com and let me know what information helped you most.

Then sit back and watch that equity grow!

APPENDIX

AMORTIZATION FACTORS

To determine the monthly P and I (principal and interest) payment:

1. Locate the factor for the desired interest rate and term.
2. Multiply this rate/term factor by the loan amount.

To determine the principal amount of the loan:

1. Locate the factor for the desired interest rate and term.
2. Divide the monthly P and I payment by this rate/term factor.

Term in Years	4%	4¼%	4½%	4¾%	5%	5¼%
			INTEREST RATE			
5	.0184165	.0185296	.0186430	.0187569	.0188712	.0189860
8	.0121893	.0123059	.0124232	.0125412	.0126599	.0127793
10	.0101245	.0102438	.0103638	.0104848	.0106066	.0107292
12	.0087553	.0088772	.0090001	.0091240	.0092489	.0093748
15	.0073969	.0075228	.0076499	.0077783	.0079079	.0080388
18	.0065020	.0066319	.0067632	.0068961	.0070303	.0071660
20	.0060598	.0061923	.0063265	.0064622	.0065996	.0067384
25	.0052784	.0054174	.0055583	.0057012	.0058459	.0059925
30	.0047742	.0049194	.0050669	.0052165	.0053682	.0055220
35	.0044277	.0045789	.0047326	.0048886	.0050469	.0052074
40	.0041794	.0043362	.0044956	.0046576	.0048220	.0049887

Term in Years	5½%	5¾%	6%	6¼%	6½%	6¾%
			INTEREST RATE			
5	.0191012	.0192168	.0193328	.0194490	.0195661	.0196835
8	.0128993	.0130200	.0131414	.0132640	.0133862	.0135096
10	.0108526	.0109769	.0111021	.0112280	.0113548	.0114824
12	.0095017	.0096296	.0097585	.0098880	.0100192	.0101510
15	.0081708	.0083041	.0084386	.0085740	.0087111	.0088491
18	.0073032	.0074417	.0075816	.0077230	.0078656	.0080096
20	.0068789	.0070208	.0071643	.0073093	.0074557	.0076036
25	.0061409	.0062911	.0064430	.0065970	.0067521	.0069091
30	.0056779	.0058357	.0059955	.0061570	.0063207	.0064860
35	.0053702	.0055350	.0057019	.0058710	.0060415	.0062142
40	.0051577	.0053289	.0055021	.0056770	.0058546	.0060336

Term in Years	INTEREST RATE					
	7%	7¼%	7½%	7¾%	8%	8¼%
5	.0198012	.0199193	.0200379	.0201570	.0202764	.0203963
8	.0136337	.0137585	.0138838	.0140099	.0141367	.0142640
10	.0116108	.0117401	.0118702	.0120010	.0121328	.0122653
12	.0102838	.0104176	.0105523	.0106879	.0108245	.0109620
15	.0089883	.0091286	.0092701	.0094128	.0095565	.0097014
18	.0081550	.0083017	.0084497	.0085990	.0087496	.0089015
20	.0077530	.0079038	.0080593	.0082095	.0083644	.0085207
25	.0070680	.0072281	.0073899	.0075533	.0077182	.0078845
30	.0066530	.0068218	.0069921	.0071641	.0073376	.0075127
35	.0063886	.0065647	.0067424	.0069218	.0071026	.0072849
40	.0062143	.0063967	.0065807	.0067662	.0069531	.0071414
50	.0060169	.0062089	.0064023	.0065970	.0067927	.0069896

Term in Years	INTEREST RATE					
	8½%	8¾%	9%	9¼%	9½%	9¾%
5	.0205165	.0206372	.0207584	.0208799	.0210019	.0211243
8	.0143921	.0145208	.0146502	.0147802	.0149109	.0150423
10	.0123986	.0125327	.0126676	.0128033	.0129398	.0130771
12	.0111006	.0112400	.0113803	.0115216	.0116637	.0118069
15	.0098479	.0099949	.0101427	.0102919	.0104422	.0105937
18	.0090546	.0092089	.0093644	.0095212	.0096791	.0098382
20	.0086782	.0088371	.0089972	.0091587	.0093213	.0094852
25	.0080523	.0082214	.0083920	.0085638	.0087370	.0089114
30	.0076891	.0078670	.0080462	.0082268	.0084085	.0085916
35	.0074686	.0076536	.0078399	.0080274	.0082161	.0084059
40	.0073309	.0075217	.0077136	.0079066	.0081006	.0082956
50	.0071874	.0073861	.0075857	.0077860	.0079871	.0081888

Term in Years	INTEREST RATE					
	10%	10¼%	10½%	10¾%	11%	11¼%
5	.0212471	.0213703	.0214940	.0216180	.0217425	.0218674
8	.0151742	.0153068	.0154401	.0155740	.0157085	.0158436
10	.0132151	.0133540	.0134935	.0136339	.0137751	.0139169
12	.0119508	.0120957	.0122415	.0123881	.0125356	.0126840
15	.0107461	.0108996	.0110540	.0112095	.0113660	.0115235
18	.0099984	.0101598	.0103223	.0104859	.0106505	.0108162
20	.0096503	.0098165	.0099838	.0101523	.0103219	.0104926
25	.0090871	.0092639	.0094419	.0096210	.0098012	.0099824
30	.0087758	.0089611	.0091474	.0093349	.0095233	.0097127
35	.0085967	.0087886	.0089813	.0091750	.0093696	.0095649
40	.0084916	.0086882	.0088857	.0090840	.0092829	.0094826
50	.0083911	.0085939	.0087972	.0090010	.0092052	.0094098

Term in Years	INTEREST RATE					
	11½%	**11¾%**	**12%**	**12¼%**	**12½%**	**12¾%**
5	.0219927	.0221184	.0222445	.0223710	.0224980	.0226254
8	.0159794	.0161158	.0162529	.0163906	.0165289	.0166678
10	.0140596	.0142030	.0143471	.0144920	.0146377	.0147840
12	.0128332	.0129833	.0131342	.0132860	.0134386	.0135921
15	.0116819	.0118414	.0120017	.0121630	.0123253	.0124884
18	.0109830	.0111507	.0113195	.0114892	.0116600	.0118317
20	.0106643	.0108371	.0110109	.0111857	.0113615	.0115382
25	.0101647	.0103480	.0105323	.0107175	.0109036	.0110906
30	.0099030	.0100941	.0102862	.0104790	.0106726	.0108670
35	.0097611	.0099579	.0101555	.0103537	.0105525	.0107519
40	.0096828	.0098836	.0100850	.0102869	.0104892	.0106919
50	.0096148	.0098200	.0100256	.0102314	.0104375	.0106438

Term in Years	INTEREST RATE					
	13%	**13¼%**	**13½%**	**13¾%**	**14%**	**14¼%**
5	.0227531	.0228813	.0230099	.0231389	.0232683	.0233981
8	.0168073	.0169475	.0170882	.0172296	.0173716	.0175141
10	.0149311	.0150789	.0152275	.0153767	.0155267	.0156774
12	.0137463	.0139014	.0140572	.0142139	.0143713	.0145295
15	.0126525	.0128174	.0129832	.0131499	.0133175	.0134858
18	.0120043	.0121779	.0123523	.0125276	.0127038	.0128809
20	.0117158	.0118944	.0120738	.0122541	.0124353	.0126172
25	.0112784	.0114671	.0116565	.0118467	.0120377	.0122293
30	.0110620	.0112578	.0114542	.0116512	.0118486	.0120469
35	.0109520	.0111524	.0113534	.0115548	.0117567	.0119590
40	.0108951	.0110987	.0113026	.0115069	.0117114	.0119162
50	.0108502	.0110569	.0112637	.0114707	.0116778	.0118850

Term in Years	INTEREST RATE					
	14½%	**14¾%**	**15%**	**15¼%**	**15½%**	**15¾%**
5	.0235283	.0236590	.0237900	.0239241	.0240532	.0241855
8	.0176573	.0178011	.0179455	.0180904	.0182360	.0183821
10	.0158287	.0159808	.0161335	.0162870	.0164411	.0165959
12	.0146885	.0148483	.0150088	.0151701	.0153321	.0154948
15	.0136551	.0138251	.0139959	.0141675	.0143400	.0145131
18	.0130587	.0132374	.0134169	.0135972	.0137782	.0139600
20	.0128000	.0129836	.0131679	.0133530	.0135389	.0137254
25	.0124217	.0126147	.0128084	.0130026	.0131975	.0133929
30	.0122456	.0124448	.0126445	.0128446	.0130452	.0132462
35	.0121617	.0123647	.0125681	.0127718	.0129758	.0131801
40	.0121213	.0123267	.0125322	.0127380	.0129440	.0131502
50	.0120930	.0122973	.0125072	.0127148	.0129225	.0131303

Term in Years	INTEREST RATE					
	16%	16¼%	16½%	16¾%	17%	17¼%
5	.0243181	.0244511	.0245846	.0247184	.0248526	.0249872
8	.0185288	.0186761	.0188240	.0189725	.0191215	.0192710
10	.0167514	.0169075	.0170643	.0172217	.0173798	.0175385
12	.0156583	.0158225	.0159874	.0161530	.0163193	.0164862
15	.0146871	.0148617	.0150371	.0152133	.0153901	.0155676
18	.0141425	.0143257	.0145096	.0146942	.0148795	.0150654
20	.0139126	.0141005	.0142891	.0144782	.0146681	.0148584
25	.0135889	.0137855	.0139825	.0141800	.0143780	.0145764
30	.0134476	.0136494	.0138515	.0140540	.0142568	.0144599
35	.0133847	.0135895	.0137945	.0139998	.0142053	.0144109
40	.0133565	.0135630	.0137696	.0139764	.0141832	.0143902
50	.0133381	.0135459	.0137538	.0139617	.0141697	.0143777

Term in Years	INTEREST RATE					
	17½%	17¾%	18%	18¼%	18½%	18¾%
5	.0251222	.0252576	.0253935	.0255296	.0256662	.0258032
8	.0194212	.0195719	.0197233	.0198751	.0200274	.0201804
10	.0176979	.0178579	.0180186	.0181798	.0183417	.0185041
12	.0166539	.0168222	.0169912	.0171608	.0173311	.0175021
15	.0157458	.0159247	.0161043	.0162844	.0164652	.0166467
18	.0152519	.0154391	.0156269	.0158153	.0160042	.0161938
20	.0150494	.0152410	.0154332	.0156258	.0158190	.0160127
25	.0147753	.0149746	.0151743	.0153744	.0155748	.0157757
30	.0146633	.0148669	.0150709	.0152750	.0154794	.0156841
35	.0146168	.0148228	.0150289	.0152352	.0154417	.0156483
40	.0145973	.0148045	.0150118	.0152192	.0154266	.0156342
50	.0145858	.0147939	.0150020	.0152101	.0154183	.0156264

RESOURCE GUIDE

PRINT RESOURCES

The following booklets are available (free of charge) from:

The Mortgage Bankers' Association
1125 15th Street, NW
Washington, DC 20005

"A Consumer's Glossary of Mortgage Terms"
* Great for the first-time buyer who needs to know the language, players, and the plays.

"Self Test"
* Ideal to use prior to qualifying with a lender. Will help you determine how much house you can afford and what documentation the lender may require.

"What Happens after You Apply for a Mortgage"
* Walks you through the process and explains the mysteries of underwriting the mortgage loan.

Choosing the Best Loan and Lender

The following booklets are available from:

Federal National Mortgage Association
Drawer MM
3900 Wisconsin Avenue, NW
Washington, DC 20006

"Unraveling the Mortgage Loan Mystery"
* Great for information on who makes loans, types of loans available, and how to choose the best loan and lender.

"When Your Home is On the Line":
* A comprehensive booklet describing how to evaluate equity lines of credit.
    When writing, ask FNMA for a list of other publications available, or request information on a certain topic. Available from:

Federal Trade Commission Bureau of Consumer Protection
Pennsylvania Ave and 6th St., NW
Washington, DC 20580

"The Mortgage Money Guide"
- Gives detailed comparisons of costs borrowers can expect to pay for various types of loans. Good for loan comparison shopping.

General Real Estate and Homebuying Information
Write for a free catalog from this federal government source:

Consumer Information Center
P.O. Box 100
Pueblo, CO 81002

A selection of booklets on homebuying, insurance, radon, and home hazards are available. Costs range from free to $1.50.

Home Safety

"Home Modifications for the Elderly"
- A preplanning home safety audit. For a free copy, write to:

NAHB Research Center
Attn: L. Rickman
400 Prince George's Boulevard
Upper Marlboro, MD 20772

"The Doable, Renewable Home"
- A home safety booklet for the elderly. Write for free booklet D12470 to:

AARP Fulfillment, EE094
1909 K Street, NW
Washington, DC 20049

Environmental Safety

"A Home Buyer's Guide to Environmental Hazards"
- To obtain a copy of this free brochure, write to:

The Federal National Mortgage Association
Department E
P.O. Box 23867
Baltimore, MD 21201-9998

Accessibility

"Easy Access Housing"
- For a free booklet, write to:

National Easter Seal Society
230 West Monroe, Suite 1800
Chicago, IL 60606

Discriminatory Practices in Housing

"Fair Housing: It's Your Right"
- To order a free booklet (ask for publication HUD-1260-FHEO/July 1990) or to speak to a HUD representative, call the HUD hotline at 1-800-669-9777.

ONLINE RESOURCES

Sorted alphabetically by topic. Unless otherwise stated, all are preceded by *http://www.*

City Comparisons
cityguide.com

Credit Agencies
experian.com
equifax.com
tuc.com

Crime Information
crimewatch.com

Environmental Information
epa.gov

FHA (Federal Housing Administration)
hud.gov

Flood Insurance
fema.gov

Foreclosure
fanniemae.com
freddiemac.com
ginniemae.gov
hud.gov

For-Sale-By-Owners
fizbo.com
fisbo.com
fsbo.com
ired.com
open-house-online.com
owners.com

Governmental Sites
hud.gov
hudclips.gov
epa.gov
ftc.gov

Homebuilding
bobvila.com
nahb.com

Homebuyer/Seller Information
countrywide.com
fanniemaefoundation.com
frugalhomeowner.com
homeadvisor.com
inman.com
ired.com
loanshop.com
ourbroker.com
quickenmortgage.com
realtimes.com
realtor.com

Home Inspections
ashi.com

Home Repair
askbuild.com
buildnet.com
misterfixit.com

Interest Rates
hsh.com
interest.com

Insurance

homefair.com
homeshark.com
prudential.com
safeco.com

Listings Online

cyberhomes.com
homeadvisor.com
homes.com
homescout.com
homeseeker.com
listinglink.com
matchpoint.com
realtor.com

Manufactured Housing

mfdhousing.com

Mortgages

bankofamerica.com
countrywide.com
e-loan.com
homefair.com
homeshark.com
loanshop.com
loanworks.com
mortgage-mart.com
quickenmortgage.com
realtor.com
wellsfargo.com
1stmtg.com

Payment Calculators

countrywide.com
homefair.com
loanguide.com
quickenmortgage.com

Pricing Property

cswonline.com

experian.com

Private Mortgage Insurance

mgic.com
pmirescue.com

Real Estate Education

reea.org

Refinancing

countrywide.com
homeshark.com
loanshop.com

Relocation

homefair.com
relo.com

Rentals

rentnet.com

Rent versus Buy

homefair.com

School Information

schoolreport.com

Tax Rates

irs.gov

Unbundled Real Estate Services

frugalhomeowner.com
owners.com
realestatecafe.com

VA (Department of Veterans Affairs)

va.gov

GLOSSARY

acquisition cost Cost of acquiring a property, in addition to purchase price, such as title insurance and lenders' fees (e.g., with FHA, acquisition is a set amount based on the appraised value of the property).

addendum rider An addition to the standard contract (e.g., the lender attaches the due-on-sale clause to the loan via an addendum rider).

adjustable-rate mortgage (ARM) A mortgage tied to an index that adjusts based on changes in the economy.

adjustment period The period during which an ARM adjusts (e.g., six months, one year, or three years).

alienation clause (due-on-sale clause) A type of acceleration clause in a loan, calling for payment of the entire principal balance in full, triggered by the transfer or sale of a property.

amendatory language Language usually added to FHA and VA sales contracts when the contract is written prior to the completion of the appraisal. (This specifies what the options are if the appraisal amount varies from the offering price.)

amortization Retiring a debt through predetermined periodic payments, including principal and interest.

appraisal An estimate of value.

ARM See *Adjustable rate mortgage.*

assignment The transfer of rights to pay an obligation from one party to another, with the original party remaining secondarily liable for the debt, should the second party default.

assumption To take over one's obligation under an existing agreement. (Note: This can be done with varying degrees of release—see *assignment, novation,* and *subject-to*).

automatic approval The processing of a VA loan, done solely by the lender, without prior submission of the documents to the regional office.

balloon payment A principal sum coming due at a predetermined time (may also contain payment of accrued interest).

biweekly mortgage A mortgage under which one-half of the regular amortized monthly payment is payable every two weeks, giving the benefit of 13 full payments per year; this allows a 30-year loan to retire in approximately 18 years.

blended rate The melding together of two rates to create a lower overall rate of interest. For example, blending the rate of an 8 percent first mortgage, and a 10 percent second mortgage, allows the buyer to more readily qualify.

buydown Permanent: Prepaid interest that brings the note rate on the loan down to a lower, permanent rate. Temporary: prepaid interest that lowers the note rate temporarily on the loan, allowing the buyer to more readily qualify and to increase payments as income grows. (A common example of a temporary buydown is the 3-2-1 plan—3 percent lower interest the first year, 2 percent the second, and 1 percent the third.)

cap A ceiling, usually found on ARM loans; can be expressed as per period (e.g., annual, or lifetime, meaning for the entire loan term).

carryover An interest rate that is too great to add to the ARM adjustments because of the predetermined caps, so the interest amount is carried over until it can be applied. Note, however, that this amount is *not* added onto the principal balance, such as in negative amortization. (Because of the 2 percent annual cap on a loan, an additional 1 percent interest adjustment cannot be applied—so it is held until the annual adjustments fall short of their cap, and then applied.)

cash reserves The amount of buyer's liquid cash remaining after making the down payment and paying all closing costs.

Certificate of Commitment The lender's approval of a VA loan, which is usually good for up to six months.

Certificate of Eligibility VA certification, showing the amount of entitlement used and the remaining guaranty available.

Certificate of Reasonable Value (CRV) The formal name for a VA appraisal.

chattel Personal property.

collateral/collateral agreement Means "additional," but is generally termed to mean security for a debt.

commitment period The period during which a loan approval is valid.

contract for deed (installment sales and land sales contract) A document used to secure real property when it is seller-financed; contains the full agreement between the parties, including purchase price, terms of payment, and any additional agreements.

convertible ARM An adjustable-rate mortgage containing a clause allowing for the rate to become fixed during a certain period (e.g., between months 13 and 60 of the loan term).

convertibility option The clause that allows the ARM loan to convert to a fixed rate during a certain period.

credit scoring Electronically giving a numerical weighting to various financial factors in the borrower's credit in order to determine the risk of lending to that borrower.

CRV See *Certificate of Reasonable Value.*

debt assumption letter/assignment of debt The formal transfer of debt from one person to another, backed by a formal contract of assumption, signed by the parties. This is done to reduce the amount of a person's long-term debt.

debt ratios The comparison of a buyer's housing costs to his or her gross or net effective income (based on the loan program); and the comparison of a buyer's total long-term debt to his or her gross or net effective income (based on the loan program used). The first ratio is termed *housing ratio;* the second ratio is *total debt ratio.* (See particular programs for applicable ratios.)

deed of trust (trust deed) A document used to secure the collateral in financing the property; title is transferred to the trustee, with payments made to the beneficiary by the trustor (grantor in some states).

desktop underwriting Using software programs to underwrite and otherwise evaluate the repayment capacity of the borrower; and to reference programs underwritten using FNMA's Desktop Underwriter® loan processing system.

direct endorsement lender Lenders approved by FHA to make loans without having loans first approved by the regional FHA office.

direct loan, VA A loan made to the veteran borrower by the VA, without using a lender (done infrequently, and then only in remote outlying areas).

discount points (points) A point is equal to 1 percent of the amount financed. Points are used to increase the lender's yield on the loan, so as to bridge the gap between what the lender could get with conventional monies, and the lower rates of VA and FHA.

discounting, seller Reducing the sales price in lieu of paying points or other fees from the seller's gross price.

distributive share MIP The FHA mortgage insurance plan in effect prior to 1983.

dual contracts Double contracts on the same property by the same buyer. Usually refers to an illegal second contract requesting a higher loan amount from a lender, even though the first contract bears the agreed-upon price between the seller and buyer.

due-on-sale clause (alienation clause) See *alienation clause.*

entitlement Also known as VA guaranty; the amount of the veteran's eligibility in qualifying for a VA loan.

equity The difference between what is owed and what the property could be sold for.

equity loans Tapping into an owner's equity, with the property used as the collateral.

escrow An impartial holding of documents pertinent to the sale and transfer of real estate; also the term used to describe the long-term holding of documents, such as with seller financing. Called a long-term escrow or escrow collection.

escrow holder An impartial third party who holds the documents pertinent to the transfer and sale of real estate.

FannieMae Foundation A nonprofit foundation affiliated with FNMA, designed to educate consumers on home affordability and home buying options.

Federal Home Loan Mortgage Corporation (FHLMC) Called Freddie Mac; a part of the secondary market, particularly used to purchase loans from savings and loan lenders within the Federal Home Loan Bank Board.

Federal Housing Administration (FHA) The FHA is part of the federal government's Department of Housing and Urban Development. It exists to underwrite insured loans made by lenders to provide economical housing for moderate-income persons.

Federal National Mortgage Association (FNMA) Also called Fannie Mae, a privately owned part of the secondary mortgage market used to recycle mortgages made in the primary market; purchases conventional, FHA, and VA loans.

FHLMC See *Federal Home Loan Mortgage Corporation.*

fixed-rate mortgage (FRM) A fixed-rate mortgage is a conventional loan with a single interest rate for the life of the loan.

FICO The Fair, Isaac, & Company credit scoring system used by many leaders to determine a borrower's ability to repay a mortgage; uses a scoring range of 450 to 850—the lower the score, the higher the risk.

FNMA See *Federal National Mortgage Association.*

foreclosure A proceeding, in or out of court, to extinguish one's rights in a property, and pay off all outstanding debts via a sale of the property.

fully indexed rate The maximum interest rate on an ARM that can be reached at the first adjustment.

funding fee An origination fee on VA loans, usually equal to 1 percent of the amount financed.

GEM See *Growing equity mortgage.*

gift letter A letter from a relative (or party with whom a strong relationship has been established—for some loans) stating that an amount will be gifted to the buyer, and that said amount is not to be repaid.

GNMA See *Government National Mortgage Association.*

Government National Mortgage Association (GNMA) Ginnie Mae is a governmental part of the secondary market that deals primarily in recycling VA and FHA mortgages, particularly those which are highly leveraged (e.g., no or low down payment).

graduated payment mortgage (GPM) A type of conventional loan containing a fixed rate for the life of the loan, but graduates, or increases the payment during a certain period of the loan. (Example: 7.5 percent payment increase for the first seven years of the loan, then the payment remains fixed at that level.)

growing equity mortgage (GEM) The GEM has a fixed interest rate for the life of the loan; but payments increase 3 percent, 5 percent, or 7.5 percent (depending on the program) for a period during the loan (usually not to exceed ten years), with all payment increases applied directly to reduce the principal. Thirty-year amortized GEM loans typically pay off between 13 and 15 years.

guaranty, VA The amount which the Veterans Administration will indemnify the lender against loss on a VA loan.

housing expense ratio The amount of either gross income or net effective income (depending on the loan program) that can be allocated for borrower's housing expense. This percentage will also vary based on the loan-to-value ratio of the loan.

income qualifications The amount of either gross income or net effective income (depending on the loan program) required by the lender for loan qualifying.

index An indicator used to measure inflation, which is a basis for the ARM loan. There are various sources of indexes, including treasury securities, treasury bills, 11th district cost of funds and the index of the Federal Home Loan Bank Board. The index, plus the margin, becomes the interest rate in the ARM.

inflation An increase in value; most often used as an indicator of the economy. When inflation is high, real estate performs well, because it appreciates in times of inflation.

initial interest rate The introductory interest rate on a loan; signals that there may be rate adjustments later in the loan.

in-service eligibility Qualifying a veteran buyer for a VA loan while still in active duty.

installment sales contract See *contract for deed.*

interest only Payments received are only applied to accrued interest on the loan; therefore, there is no principal reduction.

interest rate The note rate charged on the loan.

interest rate cap The maximum amount of interest that can be charged on an ARM loan. Can be expressed in terms of annual or lifetime figures.

jumbo loans Mortgage loans that exceed the loan amounts acceptable for sale in the secondary market; these jumbos must be packaged and sold differently to investors and therefore have separate underwriting guidelines.

kickback The illegal payment of a fee or other compensation for the privilege of securing business referrals from a source. (Example: a lender illegally receives $50 per referral sent to the title company.)

lease option A lease with an option to buy; said option can either be exercised to culminate in a purchase or forfeited by the optionee.

lease purchase A type of delayed closing. A lease purchase is drafted on a purchase and sales contract, stating the terms of the purchase, as well as a date for closing the sale. Should the buyer default, the seller has all of the remedies available under the sales contract.

leverage Using a small asset to purchase a larger asset. Leverage allows a buyer's down payment to go further. (Example: Instead of using $50,000 down on a $100,000 property, the buyer could use $10,000 down on five properties of $100,000.)

liability, release of The type of liability release for the original borrower, found under a novation.

LID (local improvement district) A legal entity (district) established under state law to benefit a certain geographic area. Districts issue bonds to finance real property improvements such as water distribution systems, sidewalks and sewer systems. To repay funds, districts then levy assessments on real estate located in the geographic area affected.

lifetime cap The maximum amount of interest an ARM loan can reach during the life of the loan.

loan qualifying Meeting the criteria for a loan as required by a mortgage lender; varies greatly from program to program.

loan-to-value ratio The amount of the loan as compared to the appraised value of the property.

lock-in The fixing of an interest rate or points at a certain level, usually during the loan application process. It is usually done for a certain period of time, such as 60 days, and may require a fee or premium in the form of a higher interest rate.

long-term debt For qualifying purposes, debts that cannot be paid off within a certain amount of time, which varies depending on the loan type. (Example: conventional long-term debts are considered to be those in excess of ten months, six months for FHA, and 12 months for VA. Note, however, that individual lenders could choose to be more restrictive than these national guidelines.)

margin An amount added by the lender to an ARM index in order to compute the interest rate. The margin is set by the lender at the time of loan inception and remains constant for the life of the loan. The margin is considered to be the lender's cost of doing business plus profit.

maximum entitlement The maximum amount of VA guaranty available to a veteran.

mortgage insurance premium (MIP) The mortgage insurance required on FHA loans for the life of said loans; MIP can either be paid in cash at closing or financed in its entirety in the loan. The premium varies depending on the method of payment.

negative amortization An interest payment shortfall which is added back *onto* the principal balance.

nonsupervised lender An FHA lender that operates outside of strict governmental control (such as mortgage companies), and is able to be an automatic approval lender upon application to the FHA regional office.

note rate The rate of interest shown on the face of the promissory note, or in the contract of sale language; the rate of interest charged on an obligation.

notice of separation The VA form received when the veteran is discharged from the service.

novation From the root word *nova*, meaning new. A novation is a total release of liability to the first borrower under a loan, and the substitution of a subsequent borrower; usually not automatic, requiring a lender's approval (see *assignment, assumption,* and *subject-to*).

online lending Accessing mortgage programs and lenders via the World Wide Web.

on-the-job benefits Noncash compensation to an employee, such as car or day care provided or extra guaranteed per diem. Lenders may consider this for loan qualification if a trackable history can be shown.

owner occupancy Occupied by the buyer of the property; a requirement in VA loans; many times a requirement in conventional and FHA programs as well.

package mortgage A mortgage loan that includes the financing of personal property.

PAM See *pledged account mortgage.*

payment cap The maximum amount the payment can adjust at any one time (e.g., 7.5 percent per period).

payment shock The shock of the payment change affecting the buyer's ability to repay the loan.

PITI Principal, interest, taxes (property) and insurance.

pledged account mortgage (PAM) Instead of using all of the down payment at closing, part of the funds are placed in an interest-bearing account, and drawn from over time to help pay the mortgage payment. These impounded funds are said to be pledged to the lender.

PMI See *private mortgage insurance.*

POC (paid outside of closing) Funds disbursed on behalf of the borrower outside the formal closing with that borrower.

portfolio lending Instead of selling the mortgage into the secondary market, the lender keeps it "in portfolio" (in the in-house file) for the life of the loan.

power of attorney Also termed *attorney in fact.* A legal power given to a person to act on behalf of another. This right can either be specific (for special circumstances), or general (in all activities).

premium yield adjustment Denotes that a lender is receiving compensation from the party funding the real estate mortgage.

prepaids Property expenses that are paid in advance and are usually prorated at the time of closing (e.g., insurance).

prepayment privilege The right of the borrower to prepay the entire principal sum remaining on the loan without penalty.

private mortgage insurance (PMI) Insurance that indemnifies the lender from the borrower's default, usually on the top 20 percent of the loan. Premiums are paid as an initial fee at time of closing, and as a recurring annual fee based on the principal balance, but paid monthly with the PITI payment. Both the initial and recurring fees are customarily paid by the buyer.

prohibited costs Certain costs that cannot be paid by a particular party to the transaction, as determined by a certain type of loan. (Example: buyers cannot pay discount fees under VA loan guidelines.)

planned unit development (PUD) A type of housing development based on high density (cluster buildings) and maximum use of open space generally resulting in lower-cost housing requiring less maintenance.

The common areas of ground are owned by a nonprofit community association, not by individuals. Developers will often mix residential with light commercial zoning to maximize land use. PUDs can also be used for resort housing and shopping center projects.

qualifying ratio Percentages used by lenders to compare the amount of housing expense and total debt to that of the buyers' gross income or net effective income (depending on the loan program).

RAM See *reverse annuity mortgage.*

rate cap The maximum amount of interest that can be charged on an ARM loan; expressed as either per period or lifetime, or both.

rate ceiling The maximum to which the rate can go in an ARM loan, specified in an interest amount, e.g., 14 percent.

rate gap The difference between where the rate is now and where it could adjust to on an ARM. Also used to compare the difference between a current conventional rate and that of an ARM.

ratio A percentage; used as a qualifying guideline in mortgage lending.

Regulation Z A federal regulation requiring disclosure of the overall cost of borrowing (truth in lending); states that if you disclose one piece of financial information, you must disclose it in its entirety (including the total of all payments and the number of payments). The only exception to this rule is the use of the annual percentage rate. If this is used, no other piece of financial information is necessary.

release clause A clause allowing a portion of the real estate to be released as security from the loan; usually occurs upon a payment of a substantial portion of the principal.

renegotiable rate mortgage (RRM) The forerunner of today's ARM; RRMs got a black eye in the late 1970s in that lenders required the borrower to renegotiate and requalify at specified intervals during the loan.

reservist A person who has served in a reserve branch of the armed forces.

residual income Monthly leftover income after deducting housing costs and fixed obligations from the net effective income in qualifying for a VA loan.

RESPA The Real Estate Settlement Procedures Act is the up-front view of the costs of borrowing in a mortgage loan, including the APR (annual percentage rate), which is the note rate plus the up-front costs of borrowing.

restoration of eligibility/entitlement When a VA loan is paid in full or otherwise satisfied, or when a veteran assumes another veteran's VA loan, reinstating the first veteran's eligibility.

reverse annuity mortgage (RAM) A loan developed for senior citizens to unlock a portion of their equity in their home without selling the property.

sales concession A cost paid by the seller or other third party, even though the cost is customarily paid by the buyer. Some loan programs have limits as to the amount of sales concessions that can occur before overage would decrease the amount of loan available.

secondary market Comprised of FNMA, GNMA, and FHLMC, which recycle lent funds from the primary market.

Section 203 FHA programs, divided as follows:
203(b): the standard single-family FHA program
203(h): disaster-victim financing
203(i): loans to outlying areas
203(k): rehabilitation loan program
203(n): co-op financing
203(v): (FHA/VA) for veteran borrowers
220: urban renewal
220(h): urban renewal repair
221: low-cost housing
222: in-service military FHA plan
245: graduated payment mortgage
251: adjustable rate mortgage

security document A legal document that creates a lien against a property as security for repayment of a debt (such as mortgages or deeds of trust).

seller financing The seller allows the borrower to finance the property, using a portion of the seller's equity in the property.

shared appreciation mortgage (SAM) A mortgage under which a co-borrower investor gives; facetiously called the CYD (call your dad) loan.

shared equity mortgage (SEM) A coborrower mortgage wherein the equity of the property is shared when the property is sold.

simple assumption A type of loan assumption that is actually a no-qualifying assignment with the lender. The original obligor remains secondarily liable should the assumptor default.

subject-to The transfer of rights to pay an obligation from one party to another, with the first party remaining secondarily liable should the second party default. In addition, the first obligor could be responsible for any deficiency judgment caused by the second borrower. (See *assignment, assumption,* and *novation.*)

supervised lender An FHA lender that is generally supervised by a governmental regulating body, such as a commercial bank that is a member of FDIC.

surviving spouse The widow or widower of a deceased veteran.

sweat equity Materials or labor used by a buyer in addition to, or in lieu of, cash.

supervised lender An FHA lender that is generally supervised by a governmental regulating body, such as a commercial bank that is a member of the FDIC.

surviving spouse The widow or widower of a deceased veteran.

teaser rate An unusually low introductory rate for an ARM, used to entice borrowers into a loan and allow them to more readily qualify.

transfer charge The cost of transferring or assuming an existing mortgage.

Veterans Affairs, Department of (VA) A branch of the federal government that guarantees lenders against borrowers' default in order to assist veterans in the purchase of single-family dwellings.

WDAGO A veteran's notice of separation.

wraparound An original loan obligation remains stationary, while a new amortizing obligation wraps around the other loan. One payment is made (many times to an escrow holder), out of which the underlying payment is made, with the remainder going to the seller.

yield Return on investment.

zero-net When the seller is receiving little or no net proceeds from selling the property.

INDEX